Women

Around the World
and Through the Ages

to Carmen
to Carl

First published in the United States 1990 by

Atomium Books Inc.
Suite 300
1013 Centre Road
Wilmington, DE 19805.

First edition published in French, by Editions Hermé, Paris, 1987 under the title
"Femmes, Les Grands Myths Féminins à Travers le Monde".
Revised edition text and pictures copyright © Editions Hérme
and © Atomium Books 1990.
English translation copyright © Atomium Books 1990.

Printed and bound in France.
First U.S. Edition
ISBN 1-56182-016-4
2 4 6 8 10 9 7 5 3 1

Women

Around the World
and Through the Ages

Sabrina Mervin
Carol Prunhuber

atomium books

TABLE OF CONTENTS

TABLE OF CONTENTS

ACKNOWLEDGMENTS

Many people contributed their heartfelt efforts to create our first English edition of this book, which has expanded upon the original French edition. In particular we would like to thank

Sabrina Mervin and Carol Prunhuber, the authors, for their work in revising and extending the book;

Goele de Bruyn for her cover design and artwork;

Betty Jackson, Alison Mouthan, and Missy Schmelzer-Chenu for their translation of the original French texts;

Carolyn Griffith and Missy Schmelzer-Chenu for their adaptation of the English text;

Catherine Desaive and Catherine Blackman for their research;

Roswitha Gans and Catherine Desaive for their photo research;

Jeannine Führring for her secretarial help;

Carolyn Griffith for her copyediting and proofreading; and

Rebbecca Brite for her superb help in managing the editorial project and making sure the details were right.

We know their contributions were not only a tribute to Women, but also the expression of their desire to share with you, the readers, all that this book contains.

Ralph Abadir   Helen Bloom
Publisher   Editor

PREFACE

People often talk about "great men" but less often about great women. Yet such women certainly have existed, do exist, and will exist all over the world. In addition, the heroines of myths, legends, folktales, and literature exist in our hearts and minds even though they never lived. These are the women who stand out in a culture or a period; who evoke images and archetypes, who feed the collective imagination. They are mythic women. In a sense, they *are* myths.

Mothers and mistresses, madwomen and wise women, angels and demons, martyrs and betrayers, warriors and patient wives, women of shadow and of light . . . Here are more than a hundred of them, among hundreds.

Humans have always felt the need to explain the world: this is the function of myth. In Greek, *mythos* meant a tale or fable, and these fabulous tales allowed humanity to live firmly anchored in reality while feeling a link with something beyond reality. Myth encompasses a people's past, its history, the roots of its cults, the rules of its social relationships. It is a way of making sense of the world.

Probably the first phenomenon that puzzled man was procreation. Overwhelmed by the event, he could not help noticing what it revealed about the powers of his mate, woman. He ascribed supernatural, magical qualities to her, for out of her round belly came children as if by miracle. Woman, at once precious, awesome, charming, and venerable, inspired fear but also needed to be protected. Rich, fecund, life-giving woman was associated with Earth, the mother goddess whom the Greeks would name Gaia. But one fine day, man, with dawning perspicacity, got the idea that there was a cause-and-effect relationship between copulation and birth. We do not know what led to this revelation; the only sure thing is that man took advantage of his discovery. The knowledge that he shared the power of parenthood without having to put up with the inconveniences of motherhood must have seemed a godsend to him. Man became father, and he probably grew full of his own importance at once, and the reign of the mother goddess came to an end. She began a long process of decline, and finally hid herself in the deepest part of human memory, ready to spring out now and then like a jack-in-the-box.

Still, the mother goddess left traces in the myths of creation. She is no longer considered the origin of the world, for she is generally given a father, but she remains the mother of humanity or, like the Eskimo goddess Sedna, the mother of part of creation. She often represents daughter, wife, and mother at once, which allows a role in many societies for the most forbidden of forbidden acts: incest. Whether divine or semi-divine, woman inspires fear: associated with death, she descends into hell like the great Ishtar, like Hine-Nui-Te-Po of the Maoris, like Lilith of Jewish tradition, who was replaced by docile Eve, symbol of the total downfall of woman. "The cosmogonic myth is the exemplary myth in the highest sense of the word: it is used as a model for human behavior," writes Mircea Eliade. Through the myth of creation, each society sets the tone for all the offspring of the divinity or of the first woman. And each society in the process establishes the rituals, the belief systems, that will allow it to renew its ties with the higher powers.

After the mythical comes the historical, but first myth mingles with history in the epic. Celebrating a hero or a major event, the epic mixes the real with the supernatural, and although founded in history, it derives its strength, depth, and truth from myth. Women are not absent from epics, but we cannot help but note that they often play negative roles. To justify wars, defeats, invasions, or other inglorious events, all one needs is someone to blame them on — and by a curious chance it is usually a woman. The Trojan War? Helen. She was too beautiful to be quite true, too attractive not to be a tempter, too frivolous and thoughtles, and so she "caused" the Trojan War. Much later, in the Iberian peninsula, the Arab invasion was blamed on another woman, La Cava Florinda.

Fortunately, epics and early histories do not always convey negative images of women. Legendary founders of nations have been glorified, made transcendent, connected with goddesses. Even if Semiramis did not build the hanging gardens of Babylon, she may have given them the dimensions that made them one of the seven wonders of the ancient world. Whether the founders begin by making history or by being superimposed on it, they become part of it and eventually surmount it. "Myth is a word chosen by history: it could not come out of the 'nature' of things," said Roland Barthes. In West Africa, Queen Pokou gives a common past to tribes that have a common present. In France, Marianne, though purely imaginary, symbolizes her country just as surely as the semi-historical founders do theirs.

Some women serve as transition between the human and the sacred: we have called them the intercessors. They may have their roots in reality, even in history; the Pythia at Delphi — or the Virgin Mary, at once woman and mother of Jesus — may act as a bridge from humans to their gods and intercede in people's favor. Other intercessors are divine entities who play the same role, such as Maria Lionza of Venezuela or Ezili in voodoo.

Sirens, too, are halfway between the human and the supernatural, but they remain imaginary, and most of the time they fail in their desperate attempts to form ties with men. They are usually born in water and remain in close contact with their element even if they live outside of it. Connected with fate, sirens bring ill fortune because they live in misfortune; though they can be beneficent or maleficent, they will always be perceived as negative. Seeking the love of men, they seduce, tempt, betray, bewitch, and infatuate. Being of popular origin, their stories are spread by oral tradition until literature and art take hold of them: this is the case of the Lorelei, the girl of the Rhine.

Many legends become crystalized at a given moment through writing. Folktales change in the telling, depicting situations and characters that are found as archetypes all over the planet. And then one day somebody writes them down and they are frozen. Their heroines, such as Cinderella, become models, and the stories initiate children to adulthood. We might wonder what kind of societies we would have if we were bereft of folktales and their wisdom.

Women of flesh and blood who have stood out because of their actions, their influence, their beauty, or other qualities, have been mythified in one way or another throughout history. From Cleopatra to Joan of Arc to Marilyn Monroe, there are historical women who became legends and sources of legends.

"Beside every great man," said the German poet Friedrich Schiller, "we find a beloved woman. Love is the sun of genius." Phryne, a beautiful Greek courtesan, inspired the sculptor Praxiteles and gained immortality. Other courtesans and favorites have haunted the corridors of power and played such important roles that they entered the realm of legend, like Wallis Warfield; still other women, whether insignificant or remarkable, became myths because artists took them as their inspirations. Without Dante, who would know Beatrice? Without Leonardo da Vinci, nobody would have heard of Mona Lisa. But what would Dante and Leonardo have done if there had been no Beatrice and Mona Lisa to serve as their muses?

If art makes myths, so even more so does religion, with women who rise above their own humanity: powerful women like Aisha, wife of the Prophet Mohammed, mystical women like Saint Teresa of Avila — these are examples to follow indeed. Still, though capable of such heights, woman is also fatal, being human, and one has to distrust her sometimes. Those who carry the seeds of destruction can hardly help but become myths: Salome, mentioned but not named in a few lines of the Bible, gave rise to numerous tales, for she symbolizes female perversity. Among the femmes fatales we also find the spy Mata Hari and a Hungarian countess, Erzsébet Báthory, who literally wallowed in the misfortune of her victims.

The outlaws could be as dangerous as these women but are seen in a better light. Whether pirates or beloved bandits, they break through the barriers imposed by society, escape everyday life, and give us something to dream about. They are beautiful, brave, rebellious, and insolent, and they bear witness to another life, one that is almost possible. As for the warriors and other fighting women, they are always braver than brave men. The popular imagination seizes upon them; it prefers them to be virgins, since they are dedicated to everyone. They are admired, even worshiped, and the objects of many fantasies. Even after their deaths they can easily be resurrected when a symbol is sought for a movement,.or a champion for some school of thought: this is how Joan of Arc was rediscovered, thanks to the 19th century historian Jules Michelet.

The healers, women who devote themselves to the good of others, in saving lives transform their own lives into objects of worship. Thus Florence Nightingale and Mother Teresa have become incarnations of love.

Sappho was probably the first woman writer to acquire the status of myth. Although the church destroyed a great part of the Greek poetess' work, it did not succeed in consigning her to oblivion and its efforts may even have encouraged the growth of her mythical dimensions. Always admired by intellectuals, Sappho of Lesbos passed into common speech in the words "sapphic" and "lesbian," referring to female homosexuality. Her poems, even in the truncated forms that survive, are continually being rediscovered. The women writers of the past whose works have stood the test of time easily became myths, for they were few. But in the late 20th century, when women take up a great deal more space on the library shelves, we must wait for time to sort out the geniuses. We can only guess which modern writers will be deemed myths in centuries to come — perhaps Virginia Woolf, who transformed the face of fiction? Readers in the future will know.

For the women we have called the artists, the process of becoming a myth was faster, for artists are perpetually "on stage," displaying their talents and their lives. Many of the artists here represent or even personify their particular art forms: Maria Callas, the diva (or "goddess," in the first sense of the word), is the epitome of opera; Sarah Bernhardt is theater eternal; Coco Chanel embodies fashion and style; Georgia O'Keeffe personifies a vision of the world . . .

Nowadays the artists' offspring, the stars, are shaped by the media into phenomena that surpass time and frontiers. We risk mistaking a fad for a myth if we do not wait for the image of the star to crystalize. We do not yet know in which category the singer Madonna fits, for example. Marilyn Monroe, on the other hand, was a living myth, and paid the price: she was out of her depth, her life did not belong to her anymore, and she was suffocated by her own image. Death crystalized her myth. Greta Garbo, the opposite extreme, understood quite well, perhaps even unconsciously, how to remain eternally faithful to the image created of her: by vanishing from public life, she preserved her myth, hiding her real face so that our only memory of her is the face in the movies. As for Grace Kelly, she surpassed myth in becoming a princess. The myths made by Hollywood are reproduced ad infinitum on posters, postcards, T-shirts, and pins. So are the images of popular singers, who, like movie stars, can become cult figures, especially through fan clubs. Buoyed up by enormous audiences, they cross frontiers and come to represent a culture, a soul, a style that is typical of their origins: Billie Holiday is the voice of jazz, Edith Piaf is the voice of French chanson, Amalia Rodrigues is the voice of fado.

The politically powerful also thrive on the worship of crowds — and so do their myths. Cleopatra has experienced a kind of resurrection in the 20th century through the cinema and through advertisements. Eva Peron, a former actress, knew that in the field of politics one had to

appear before the public and play well, just as on the stage or screen. Power may give its holders wings, as the French say, but its ephemeral quality must be overcome before one can reach immortality. Eva wanted to be a goddess; she encouraged her own cult, and her premature death helped her become a myth. Some people view her as a saint. One wonders how Margaret Thatcher — who has entered into legend by using the strength, tenacity, and weapons of men — will be recorded in the Book of Judgment.

There are generally no cults of scholars, scientists, explorers; those who seek wisdom and knowledge are perhaps more honored when they are alive. Yet they, especially, leave indelible traces in history. Women provide another face of history in this area, for their values are different from those of men. Symbols of life, they play a humanist role.

If myths have become profane, still when people encounter them they behave as they did when myths were sacred. Humanity, which never ceases to look at itself, sometimes offers the mirror to remarkable women. The world will always need goddesses.

Sabrina Mervin   Carol Prunhuber

LUCY
PREHISTORIC ETHIOPIA

It was in Ethiopia, in a desert looking much like this, that researchers awoke Lucy from her deep sleep.

The first woman . . . dreams dreamed, stories recounted, decades of research carried out, volumes written speculating on her origins. Woman may have lived in Africa two hundred thousand years ago, that much may be surmised. But what about her grandmother?

After Mary Leakey discovered an important skeleton in Tanzania in 1959, East Africa became the promised land for paleontologists searching for man's — and woman's — beginnings. Certainly it proved to be so for Donald Johanson and Timothy White, part of a team from the Natural History Museum of Cleveland, who were digging in the Afar desert near Hadar in November 1974. What they unearthed proved to be one of the most important finds in the history of the quest for the origins of humankind.

She was a little woman, no more than three feet tall, and she walked upright. "Woman" is a big word for her; "woman-ape" is more accurate, with "hominid" the preferred term. She died between twenty-five and thirty years of age, and for three and a half million years her skeleton remained under layers of the sand and mud of the Afar desert in Ethiopia. On November 30, 1974, Donald Johanson brought her to life again and gave her a name: Lucy.

Following established procedure, she was classified as *Australopithecus afarensis*, after the region where she was found. But the name we know her by was chosen much more whimsically. The night of her discovery, the research team was inspired by a Beatles song they were listening to at their campsite: "Lucy in the Sky with Diamonds."

Lucy seems to have died peacefully, for her remains were discovered intact. This fact, plus the age of the skeleton, made it the oldest, most complete, best preserved skeleton ever found among the human race's upright ancestors.

Research into the origins of humans, through the competitive and often conflicting work of paleontologists, biologists, biochemists, and geneticists, is perplexing. The search for the famous "missing link," begun more than a century ago, has taken on the aura of a treasure hunt, yet we

Lucy was not quite woman, as shown by this portrait created by Michel Garcia under the scientific direction of Yves Coppens.

still do not know how or when the australopithecine "woman-ape" became woman.

During the last few years, biology has taken the lead in providing clues. Allan Wilson, a controversial biochemist, theorized that if human descended from ape, there are certain apes — such as the gorilla and the chimpanzee — that must have descended from humans. It was a revolution in scientific thought, inevitably contradicted.

Later, after studying women in different regions of the world, Wilson asserted that the first true woman came from Africa, where she lived two hundred thousand years ago. Once again, this thesis upset accepted theories. The future will undoubtedly teach us more.

In the meantime, we can hold on to the heritage of the ancients, who did not wait for science but imagined their own beginnings . . .

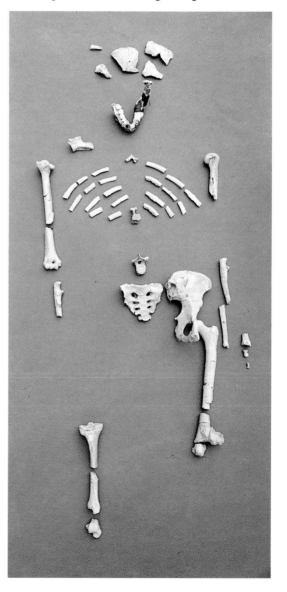

A skeleton, three and a half million years old: the oldest, most complete, best preserved of its kind.

Gaia — one of the most ancient Greek divinities — is today the goddess of environmentalists.
This sculpture of her, by David Wynne, stands amid tropical gardens on Tresco, in Britain's Isles of Scilly.

GAIA

GREEK CIVILIZATION

Gaia or Gea, Mother Earth, primordial force risen from Chaos, the goddess of life, death, and fertility, is one of the most ancient Greek divinities, a mother who must save her children from being devoured by the father she herself created.

In his *Theogony*, the lineage of the gods, the poet Hesiod reveals a dark story of primal excess. First there was Chaos, and from Chaos arose Gaia, the Earth, then Eros, or Love. "Eternal and safe abode of living beings," Gaia brought forth Uranus, the star-filled Sky, to cover and protect her. In the same way, Gaia gave birth to the mountains and to Pontos, the ocean. Mating with Uranus and Pontos in turn, Gaia then bore the next generation of deities, who had evolved one step away from their primordial parents. Pontos fathered the marine divinities, while from Uranus' seed came the Titans. Cronus was the last-born of these huge beings. After him came the Cyclops, giants with a single eye, and the Hecatonchires, with their one hundred gigantic arms.

Uranus loathed his offspring, for he feared they would challenge his disordered rule. "As soon as they were born, instead of allowing them to emerge into the light, the Sky imprisoned them in the bosom of the Earth, rejoicing in his wicked action," Hesiod tells us. But Gaia had no intention of abandoning them to this fate. She tried to incite her children to violence against their father. Only Cronus heeded her. Gaia forged a metal sickle — which would become the symbol of death — and gave it to her son so he could kill his father.

Night fell as Uranus approached Gaia to spread over her and impregnate her. But before the sky could envelope her, Cronus seized his father's testicles in his left hand, cut them off with the sickle, and threw them into the sea. Since then, the left hand has signified bad luck.

The drops of Uranus' blood that spattered the Earth were enough to fertilize her again; thus the Furies, giants, and nymphs were born. According to Hesiod, from the testicles floating on the surface of the ocean emerged the celestial Aphrodite, goddess of beauty and love. But Homer attributed the birth of Aphrodite to the union of Gaia with Zeus.

Now free, the Titans and Cyclops yielded to the rule of their liberator, Cronus, who soon proved as hard a tyrant as his father. His union with his sister Rhea engendered the next generation of gods, who would inhabit Olympus: Hestia, Demeter, Hera, Hades, Poseidon, Zeus. Cronus

Gaia incited her children to attack their father, Uranus, and forged the metal sickle that has become the symbol of death.

Voluptuous Gaia symbolizes Mother Earth — the nurturer of humankind.

feared that he would be overthrown by one of his offspring. To prevent this he devoured each one at birth. Horrified, Rhea sought Gaia's help in outwitting Cronus. On the advice of the Earth Mother, Rhea hid her last child, Zeus, and wrapped a stone in swaddling clothes to present to Cronus, who immediately swallowed it.

Zeus grew up hidden in a cave and reached adulthood determined to overthrow Cronus. First,

with Rhea's help, he caused Cronus to drink a potion that made him spit out Zeus' sisters and

The vital force of Gaia springs out from this massive, modern marble sculpture by David Wynne, entitled "Awakening Earth", that stands in a square in Geneva, Switzerland.

brothers. Then he joined forces with his siblings to battle Cronus and the Titans. The fight dragged on for ten years, and Gaia prophesied that only an alliance with the Cyclops and the Hecatonchires, imprisoned in the underworld by Cronus, would bring Zeus victory. Zeus freed them and received their weapons of thunder and lightning, which turned the tide. The vanquished Cronus was emasculated and chained to a stone for eternity. Atlas, head of the Titans, was condemned to carry the weight of the heavens on his shoulders.

Gaia and Uranus represent opposing forces of equal strength. Together they brought forth the first generation of gods in a chaotic, ever-changing universe. But over the centuries, the reign of Gaia's primal energy was gradually reduced to make way for a patriarchal hierarchy in which Zeus was credited with paternity of humans and gods. As the "masculine" virtues of reason and the mind gained ascendancy, Gaia was relegated to the underworld. There she continued to rule over the birth, death, and rebirth of nature. To modern-day environmentalists she still symbolizes the Earth that, in a less destructive age, was believed capable of infinite self-healing.

ISHTAR

SUMERO-BABYLONIAN CIVILIZATION

Goddess of love and fertility, Ishtar was also the goddess of war. She assumed many aspects under differing names and was worshiped for centuries by many civilizations.

As the personification of the feminine reproductive forces of nature, Ishtar overshadowed and even absorbed all the other goddesses of Assyrian and Babylonian mythology. She particularly assumed the attributes of Inanna, the most complex goddess in the Sumerian pantheon. According to Sumerian legend, the chief god, Enki, overlooked Inanna when he distributed specific tasks to each god and goddess. Consequently, Inanna exercised her power in all areas of human life. The Mesopotamian heroic tale, *The Epic of Gilgamesh*, tells of Inanna's descent to the netherworld, the result of her desire to reign over the lower regions — the realm of her elder sister — as well as the upper regions.

The myths tell that when first there was light, there was An, the first of the gods. An desired Ishtar, and from their union was born the Evening Star, or Ishtar herself. Ishtar was thus both the first wife and the daughter of the first god. She took new form and life and became identified with the moon, from which her name Sin, goddess of the moon, was derived.

As the Evening Star, Ishtar was the goddess of love. But she also radiated in the morning through her synthesis with Venus, the Earth Mother. Ishtar was believed to be the source of fertility both of women and of crops, and her followers begged for her intercession when they were ill.

In her role as goddess of war, Ishtar is depicted as a lion or as a woman armed from head to toe. She exercised her power from the beginning of the first Babylonian dynasty and attained her zenith during the Assyrian era. The Assyrian kings prayed to her on the eve of battle.

As the goddess of love and of sex, Ishtar was reputed to have had many amorous adventures.

Goddess of war who promised victory to the faithful, Ishtar could take the form of a lion. On this stele, now in the Louvre, Ishtar is portrayed astride her favorite animal.

14

The epic hero, Gilgamesh, whom she attempted to seduce, rebuked her for the number of her lovers and was the only man to reject her. Naturally, Ishtar wanted revenge for this affront, and asked the god of the moon to send the Bull of the Sky to kill Gilgamesh. But the bull was vanquished, and Enkidu, the hero's servant and friend, threw its thigh at Ishtar's face. This insult cost Enkidu his life. The goddess grieved over the beast, and it became a part of the fertility cult.

The Epic of Gilgamesh recounts Ishtar's descent to the lower regions to seek her consort, Tammuz, whose death she could not accept. She made her way "towards that place where the inhabitants have dust for sustenance, mud for nourishment." A porter greeted her.

Ishtar was also the goddess of fertility. She brought prosperity to those who knew how to worship her. In this mural, Zimri-Lim, king of Mari, begs for her divine favors. Mari Palace, Syria.

Goddess of love, Ishtar attempted to charm the hero Gilgamesh, who rejected her advances. Sargon Palace, Khorsabad, Iraq, 8th century.

The first gate was thrown wide open, and he made her step through, and from her head removed the high crown. At each of the seven gates through which she passed, Ishtar had to take off a jewel or an article of clothing. When she arrived in the realm of her elder sister she was naked. Her laments and her tears softened the hearts of the seven great judges, who interceded to free Tammuz. When Ishtar returned to the Earth, grass began to grow again in the pastures, animals once again started to breed, and the monsters of the lower regions returned to their subterranean dwelling places.

The cult of Ishtar symbolically re-enacted this event. The high priestess retired for seven days within the temple while Ishtar's young handmaidens surrendered themselves to sacred prostitution. They were obligated to lose their virginity — the symbol of their power — just as Ishtar had lost her clothes at the gates of hell.

Having offered their hymens to the goddess, they became forever free because they never became attached to any one man in particular. If they had children, they gave them away. This rite was a form of collective liberation.

Called Astarte by the Phoenicians, Mytilla by the Chaldeans and sometimes Dilbat or Belit in Babylonia, the great goddess shone throughout the Mediterranean basin. The Greeks associated her with Aphrodite. The Arabs called her Alat, and in Carthage, she merged with the Berber mother goddess and became Tanit.

I am Ishtar, goddess of the evening. I am Ishtar, goddess of dawn.
I am Ishtar who opens the bolt of the shining heavens. I glory in my power.
The heavens I pacify, the earth I appease; I glory in my power.
I am she who pacifies the heavens, I am she who appeases the earth. I glory in my power.

LILITH
JUDEO-CHRISTIAN CIVILIZATION

Lilith is all but absent from the Old Testament as we know it today, yet she, not Eve, was the first woman created, Adam's first wife. She was cast out of Eden for her misdeeds and banished to the shadowy world of the subconscious.

"So God created man in his own image, in the image of God created he him; male and female created he them." In Genesis 1:27 the human race is born. But the woman created here is not Eve. She comes later, in Genesis 2:21-22, where Yahweh removes a rib from the sleeping Adam and from it fashions a new mate for him. So who was this mysterious woman who preceded the mother of humanity as Adam's wife? The Bible does not name her, but she is Lilith.

While she has been nearly eliminated from the Old Testament, Lilith can be found in Jewish mystical tradition. In the Zohar, a 13th century commentary on the mystical bases of the Torah and other scriptures, we find part of her story:

At the same time Jehovah created Adam, he created a woman, Lilith, who like Adam was taken from the earth. She was given to Adam as his wife. But there was a dispute between them about a matter that when it came before the judges had to be discussed behind closed doors. She spoke the unspeakable name of Jehovah and vanished.

This leaves us to wonder what could have required such secrecy. An 11th century cabalistic work is more explicit: the conflict arose from Adam's insistence that Lilith lie beneath him during the sexual act. This was his way of asserting his authority as head of the family. Lilith, who considered herself Adam's equal, refused. The dispute escalated, ending in Lilith's flight.

After her exile from paradise, Lilith was condemned to wander in the shadows, and the Bible avoided mentioning her name. But she played her own part in the story of Eden. In this vision of paradise, is she the serpent, come to tempt Eve? *The Earthly Paradise*, by M. Wohlgemuth, 1491.

At the entrance to Notre Dame Cathedral in Paris,
between Adam and Eve, Lilith watches.

*pestilence that walketh in darkness, nor for the
destruction that wasteth at noonday. (Psalm
91:5-6)*

Lilith is far older than Christianity or Judaism.
She is found in various guises throughout ancient
mythology. In Sumero-Babylonian tradition,
dating from around 3500 BC, she appeared as the
demon Lamashtu, banished from heaven for her
wickedness. In later Sumerian myth she was named
Ardat Lili, or Lilitu, goddess-consort of the male

Released from her shadows, a shining Lilith symbolizes
the reign of woman, free and powerful. Engraving by
Fidus, Berlin, 1895.

Here we return to the Zohar's version, which
tells how a weak-willed Adam begged for his mate's
return. God sent three angels to pursue Lilith, but
she resisted their pleas. In the end the angels let
her live, on condition that she never harm a
newborn bearing her name. Jehovah then "gave
Lilith over to Sammael (Satan); and she was the
first of the Devil's four wives."

Other versions of this legend vary in recounting how Lilith came to marry the devil; they say
Satan met and fell in love with her during her
wanderings, instead of receiving her as a gift from
God. In this union, Lilith got the sexual bargain
she wanted: each would have his (or her) turn,
first on top, then beneath. This reversal of traditional sexual roles can be interpreted as an allu-
sion to androgyny, a theme present in one version
of the Lilith legend: it describes her as the first
human created by Yahweh, a duo-sexual being
who gives birth to Adam and then marries him.

The name Lilith occurs only once in the
modern Old Testament, in Isaiah 34:14:

*The wild beasts of the desert shall also meet with
the wild beasts of the island, and the satyr shall
cry to his fellow; Lilith also shall rest there, and
shall find for herself a place of rest.*

The translators of the Jerusalem Bible include
her name in Job 18:14-15:

*The wicked man shall be snatched from the
shelter of his tent and dragged before the King of
Terror. Lilith shall dwell there and her breath
shall cover the fold.*

Rabbinical tradition disputes this translation,
claiming that the word Lilith does not indicate a
particular woman but is a metaphor for undesir-
ables and outlaws. In Christian tradition Lilith's
name is not used, but she is the temptation personified by the demon of noonday:

*Thou shalt not be afraid for the terror by night,
nor for the arrow that flieth by day, nor for the*

demon Lilu. Here she personified licentiousness
and lust, a nocturnal ravisher who seduced men
in their sleep and devoured children.

Lilith is always portrayed as a demon, and
sometimes as a creature with the head of a woman
and the body of a winged serpent. In all her incarnations she symbolizes feminine power, thwarted
by the established order and exiled to the darkness — yet still dangerous.

"The daughter of Satan, the woman of the
shadows, that Lilith who is called Isis at the end of
the Nile," wrote Victor Hugo, who associated her
with the goddess-mother and great sorceress of
ancient Egypt. Lilith, forever doomed to the
shadows of hell and of the mind, suffers from her
fate. Perhaps she is not so terrible after all . . .

And the Lord God caused a deep sleep to fall upon Adam, and he slept: and He took one of his ribs, and closed up the flesh thereof; and of the rib, which the Lord God had taken from man, made He a woman, and brought her unto the man. (Genesis 2:21-22)

The second Biblical version of the creation of the first woman exiles Lilith to obscurity forever and promotes the concept of woman as a by-product of man. In Hebrew, the word for woman is *ishshah*, from *ish*, or man. Genesis recounts that Adam said:

This is now bone of my bones
and flesh of my flesh:
She shall be called Woman,
because she was taken out of Man.

Adam named his wife Eve, "mother of all the living," alluding to the pagan idea of woman's sacredness. Within Eve is concealed the omnipotent mother goddess, worshiped in the ancient Middle Eastern religions from which Genesis draws its sources. This mother goddess was overthrown by a masculine warrior god who established order and civilization.

The Haggadah, which forms part of ancient Hebraic lore, explains why Yahweh chose Adam's rib to create Eve: he could not use Adam's head, for fear Eve would be filled with pride; nor his eyes, or she would be coquettish; nor his ears, for she might be inquisitive; nor his mouth, lest she want to gossip; nor his heart, which would predispose her to jealousy; nor his hand, for so she might steal; nor his feet, which might lead to her gadding about. Little else was left!

One Jewish legend holds that Eve was created not from Adam's rib but from his tail, and humans still retain the useless coccyx as a souvenir. A second legend, this one Islamic, claims she was created from the serpent's feet, explaining both woman's craftiness and snakes' lack of feet.

Adam and Eve were content in Eden until a

Eve, idealized in a 1917 painting by Gustav Klimt, symbolizes femininity and makes the perfect mate for Adam . . . but beware of Satan, who will upset this delicate balance.

EVE
JUDEO-CHRISTIAN CIVILIZATION

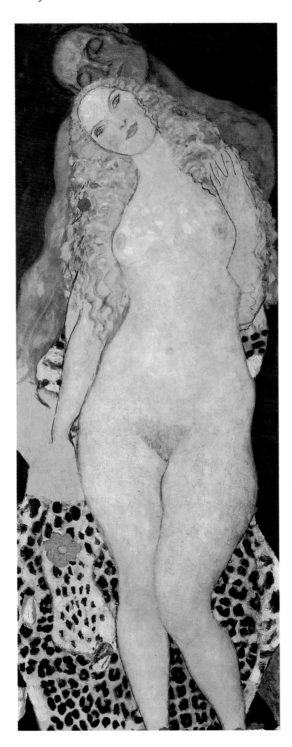

jealous Satan decided to meddle. He sent the snake, an evil creature if ever there was one, to convince Eve to taste the forbidden fruit. This fruit grew on the tree of the knowledge of good and evil, but Yahweh had strictly forbidden the two humans to touch it.

Eve was tempted. Perhaps she touched the tree first, and then, when nothing happened, agreed to bite into the apple, the source of so much misfortune. Was it through fear of her own death, fear that Adam would take another wife, that she persuaded her husband to taste the fruit as well? Through Eve's transgression, she and Adam lost their innocence and found original sin.

Guilty of having introduced carnal desire into the ascetic order of a god who required no companion goddess, Eve was condemned. Yahweh told her,

I will greatly multiply thy sorrow and thy conception; in sorrow thou shalt bring forth children; and thy desire shall be to thy husband, and he shall rule over thee. (Genesis 3:16)

As for Adam, he was doomed to know the sweat of toil. Having been made aware of the differences between man and woman, Adam and Eve were separated forever from Yahweh and exiled from Eden.

Eve bore Cain and Abel, then, according to one tradition, lived apart from Adam for one hundred and thirty years before being reunited with him and giving birth to Seth. It is said that when she died, she was buried at Adam's side.

The myth of the fall from grace has given men justification to hold women responsible for all their misfortunes and all their weaknesses. The embodiment of sin, sexuality, and death, Eve can be redeemed only by the coming of the Virgin Mary, who represents obedience and purity. The Virgin is chosen to bring the world eternal life because she, unlike Eve, accepts and obeys the law of God.

Eve's sin, however, is not merely disobedience. She has opposed the established order by acting independently of Adam and making a decision that jeopardized that order. By challenging the

inequality of woman, by reaching to satisfy her desire for knowledge, Eve forfeits the right to both knowledge and authority:

> *Let the woman learn in silence with all subjection. I suffer not a woman to teach, nor to usurp authority over the man, but to be silent. For Adam was first formed, then Eve. And Adam was not deceived, but the woman being deceived was in the transgression. Notwithstanding she shall be saved in childbearing, if they continue in faith and charity and holiness with sobriety.* (First Timothy 2:11-15)

Who has not dreamed of "paradise regained?" Here it is envisioned by Hieronymus Bosch in *The Thousand-year-old Kingdom*.

The myth of Eve and its interpretation by the church hierarchy have defined the image of woman in Western civilization. For if there sleeps inside each woman a Lilith wanting only to be awakened, it is still Eve, forced into submission for her transgressions, who dominates.

From the belly of man emerged . . . a woman filled with gratitude. Flanders, 15th century, *Mirror of Human Salvation*.

HINE-NUI-TE-PO

PACIFIC ISLAND CIVILIZATIONS

Assuming the name Hine-Nui-Te-Po, Hine-Titama took possession
of the kingdom of the dead, where she hid her shame over having
married her own father. Watercolor of a Polynesian funeral rite by Maximilien Radiguet.

What a shock it was to Hine-Titama, ancestress of the Maori, to realize that her husband was none other than her own father. Overcome with shame, she fled to the underworld, where she changed her name to Hine-Nui-Te-Po. She has lured humans ever since to her kingdom of death.

Here is how her story begins:

In their lovemaking, Papa, the Earth goddess, and Rangi, the sky god, brought forth Life. But Life remained confined, for as long as Papa and Rangi remained locked in embrace there was neither light nor darkness. The first gods the couple engendered consulted among themselves, seeking a way to liberate imprisoned Life. Tu, god of war, proposed the destruction of Papa and Rangi, expressing his desire for Life with neither beginning nor end. Tawhiri, lord of winds and storms, wanted to keep things just as they were. Tane, master of forests and birds, suggested separating Papa and Rangi gently. His idea was approved by all his brothers save Tawhiri, who adamantly opposed any change.

Tane carried out his plan, stationing himself like a pillar between Earth and sky to separate them. At once the world was engulfed in light. Furious, Tawhiri launched his army of winds in pursuit of his brothers. Only Tu, the war god, held his ground and fought; the others fled. After battling Tawhiri's tempests for a long time, Tu undertook to punish his brothers for abandoning him, and he overwhelmed them. But the master of forests and birds, Tane, succeeded in conquering the war god, chased him from the sky, and exiled him to the physical Earth.

Tane took sand and clay and fashioned the first woman, called Hine-Titama. Then the god married his earthly daughter and they begat the Maori tribe. But when she learned of the incestuous nature of their union, she turned to hide her shame in the bowels of the Earth, where she became queen, calling herself Hine-Nui-Te-Po, "Daughter of the Night."

Well-known throughout the Pacific islands, this myth has many variations. One tradition maintains that the first female created by the gods was Hine-Ahu-One, "Daughter of the Earth," who bore Hine-Ata-Vira, the first woman, mother of humanity. Hine-Ata-Vira married Tane, whom she discovered to be her father, and then fled in shame to the underworld. In many versions, Hine, who is nicknamed "the man-eater," represents the moon.

In all her forms, Hine reappears throughout Maori mythology. One episode describes her defeat of the hero Maui:

Maui rebelled against death; he wanted it to be temporary — like the moon, which is renewed

Woman plays an important role
in Polynesian primitive art.

each evening after bathing, or the sun, which wakes up each morning strengthened by its passage through darkness. The only solution was to conquer Hine-Nui-Te-Po.

Maui went to his father to ask advice. "What does she look like?" Maui asked.

"Her eyes, which you see blazing, are as dark as jade; her teeth are as sharp as the stone of Obsius; her mouth is like a barracuda; the hair on her head is like seaweed; only her body has a human

Henceforth, Hine ruled over the underworld and tried to lure human beings there.
Funeral and Mourning in Otaiti, engraving ca. 1811.

form," his father replied. He encouraged Maui to seek Hine, and the hero decided to leave at once. A flock of birds of all breeds and colors joined him. Night had fallen when they arrived at Hine's house.

"I am going to enter this old woman's stomach," Maui explained to his companions. "Don't laugh until I have crawled through her; when I emerge from her mouth, you can make fun of me." Maui knew that if he succeeded in coming out of Hine alive, she would die but humans would live forever.

Hine-Nui-Te-Po was asleep. Maui undressed and entered her bowels, head first. His shoulders and chest had hardly disappeared when one of the birds burst into laughter at the grotesque sight. The noise woke the old woman just as Maui reached her throat. Hine opened her mouth and

cut him in two at the waist. Thus Maui perished in his attempt to achieve immortality. But his descendants survived him.

In another version, Maui says to Hine, "Let's make death very brief." She replies, "Let's make death very long so that man can sigh and grieve." Maui tries again: "Let's make man die and be reborn, like you, the moon — you die and live again." But Hine, imperturbable, answers, "No, let's make man die, become like the Earth, and never be reborn."

Through Hine, the Maori believed, humans had lost immortality forever. The first incest introduced humanity to the throes of death. Maui's journey into the bowels of his ancestress — a second incest, in a way — ironically reinforced the effects of the first. The order of the world — birth, life, death — became irreversible.

AMATERASU

JAPANESE CIVILIZATION

The Japanese people's veneration of their emperor is largely due to the fact that according to Shinto theology he is a direct descendant of Amaterasu, the sun goddess, who reigned over the realm of the High Celestial Plain.

Shinto cohabits in Japan with Taoism, Buddhism, and Confucianism, but it is the only religion native to the islands. At the end of the 7th century the Emperor Temmu ordered that all the legends concerning the gods and their descendants, the emperors, be written in the *Kojiki*, or Record of Ancient Matters, the sacred book of Shinto, and the *Nihongi*, or Chronicle of Japan. In these two books we learn how the world was formed with Japan at its center.

The Earth was still seawater when Izanagi and his sister, Izanami, descended via a rainbow and formed the island of Onokoro, where they married. From this union the gods of the winds, of the mountains, and many others were born. The god of fire scorched his mother during his birth. She died of her burns and departed for the underworld. Her husband attempted to follow her, but she repulsed him. In purifying himself, Izanagi engendered a daughter, Amaterasu, born from his left eye, and a son, Susanoo, who sprang from his nose. Amaterasu's beauty was astonishing. Izanagi gave her the chain from around his neck and said: "May Your Highness reign over the Realm of the Celestial Heavens." He then declared to Susanoo, whose nature was depraved and violent: "May Your Highness reign over the Realm of the Oceanic Plain."

Susanoo was an exceedingly bad ruler and spent most of his time complaining because he wanted to join his mother in the underworld.

To enduce the sun goddess to emerge from her cave, the Kamis employed ruses and a divine mirror. The mirror has since become one of the symbols of imperial power.

22

Thoroughly exasperated, his father ejected him from the Oceanic Plain but consented to let Susanoo visit his sister before disappearing. Amaterasu, convinced that her brother harbored some evil intention, prepared for war before she received him. He proposed a pact to prove his intentions were honest. "We will both engender children," he said. "Should the children I bring forth be female, you will know that my heart is impure. But should the children be male, then you must admit that my heart is true."

Amaterasu bit on her brother's sword, puffed, and from her breath three goddesses were born. Susanoo bit on his sister's chain, puffed, and five male Kamis* came into being. The eight children were given the task of escorting the Celestial Powers down to the Earth.

Pleased with himself, Susanowo acted as if he were lord and master. Amaterasu put up with his boorish behavior until the day he threw a flayed pony into the middle of the weaving workshop where she was supervising her companions' work. Terrified, the sun goddess took refuge in a celestial cave and bolted the door. She refused to stir, and eternal night descended upon the Earth.

All the Kamis, in a state of utter confusion, joined forces in an effort to make Amaterasu reappear. Omoîkane-no-kami, "He who embraces thought," devised a plan. First he gathered the birds "and made them trill a prolonged song." Then the Kamis manufactured an "ideally beautiful mirror" and a chain with five hundred gems, which they placed under a tree along with offerings of white and blue fabrics. They piously recited the great liturgies and the dancer Uzume approached the cave's door. "She lighted the fires of sacred joy and pronounced divinely inspired words." Then she danced. Her dance provoked the mirth of the eight hundred myriads of Kamis. Hearing their laughter, Amaterasu emerged from the cave. The world was illuminated once more and the Kamis begged the sun goddess never again to hide her face.

From that time forth, Amaterasu ruled over both the sky and the earth, while Susanoo was

Women play an important role in the Shinto religion. These women are assistants to the priests at the Mikosan Shrine.

ejected from the Celestial Plain for having caused all the trouble. He descended to the land of Izumo, in Japan, and from there sent his sister a gift of a sharp-edged sword.

Amaterasu decided that her grandson, Ninigi, should govern the islands formed by Izanami and Izanagi. She gave him a treasure to solemnly invest him with this office, commanding him to respect the treasure as the symbol of her divine spirit. The treasure consisted of what are now the imperial regalia: the chain with five hundred gems, the divine mirror, and the sword given to her by Susanoo.

Ninigi's grandson brought his clan to Yamato, where he became Japan's first emperor. Today the divine mirror is believed to be kept in the Grand Shrine of Ise and the sword in the Shrine of Atsuta. Copies of them, along with what is reputed to be the original jeweled chain, are conserved at the Imperial Palace. The emperor may be sure of his power, secure in his divine origins and his divine right to rule as holder of the treasure and the "living presence" of the sun goddess.

* * *

* A vague term covering everything that is of a divine nature. The Kamis are said to number eight million.

IXQUIC
MAYAN CIVILIZATION

Tlazoltéole, a counterpart of the goddess Ixquic, giving birth.
The drawing to the right illustrates a very early version of the legend
in which the virgin Ixquic is impregnated by the god of
the fields, a counterpart of the Ahpu.

In bearing the descendants of the seven lords of wisdom, Ixquic held out hope for a new world order. According to Mayan mythology, she is both the earth and the moon, the mother of humankind.

Very little is known of the origins of the *Popul Vuh*, the sacred book that reconstructs the history of Mayan civilization. The legends, originally transmitted orally, were not written down until the 16th century. A copy of the book was found in the 18th century by a monk, who translated the narrative into Spanish. It is in the *Popul Vuh* that we find Ixquic's legend.

Many years ago, before time was recorded, in the highlands where dwelt the Quiché Mayas, there lived seven lords called the Ahpu who were endowed with wisdom, gifted at magic, and versed in the arts and poetry. One day while the Ahpu were playing ball, the noise of their laughter and joy reached the ears of the lords of the underworld, which was called Xibalba. Jealous, these evil beings sent four messengers, the Owls, to the earth's surface to summon the Aphu. After taking leave of their mother, they followed the Owls to Xibalba. There they were killed and their heads were hung on a barren tree. After a dark and sinister night, the heads disappeared and in their place hung seven calabash.

Ixquic, daughter of one of Xibalba's lords, was overcome by an irresistible desire to gaze on the forbidden, miraculous tree. When she reached the foot of the tree, she wondered what kind of fruit the tree bore and whether these fruits were edible. One of the skulls said to her: "There is nothing but bones on these branches. Do you want us?" Ixquic replied: "I do." The skull said: "That is good. Stretch out your hand." And the skulls spat into her palm, but when she looked at her hand, her palm was empty. "In our saliva, we have given you our descendants," said the heads of the dead. In this way the Ahpu transmitted their collective knowledge, suffering, and heritage to Ixquic. They then commanded her to climb to the Earth, promising that she would not die.

The maiden instead returned home, having conceived two children by virtue of the saliva. Six months later, her father noticed that she was pregnant. He considered his daughter dishonored and informed the high council of Xibalba. The council insisted that she reveal the name of her lover. Ixquic confined herself to stating the truth: "I have never known a man's countenance." The Mayan custom of forbidding single women to look at men's faces was derived from this legend.

The intolerant lords of Xibalba refused to believe Ixquic and ordered the four Owls to sacrifice her, and bring back her heart in a bowl.

For the Maya, the goddess Ixquic was the mother of humankind. Maya statuette.

The Owls went to fetch the sacrificial flint knife and the bowl. They then led the young maiden to the sacrificial stake. On the way, she begged them to spare her. "My heart does not belong to them. You must not obey them, nor remain in that house, for it is dishonorable to kill people needlessly." With these words, Ixquic renounced the underworld people and their religion. She who had received the word of the Ahpu would soon establish a doctrine that would be the foundation of Mayan religion.

The Owls were loath to sacrifice an innocent but they were obliged to take her heart back to the lords of the underworld. Ixquic suggested that they gather the sap of the tree of sacrifice. Red

Ixquic was impregnated by the skulls of the seven Ahpu lords of wisdom, who spat into her hand.
She gave birth to twins. The wall of skulls at Chichen Itza in Mexico.

liquid immediately flowed into the bowl and coagulated like blood. The Owls presented this to the lords as the proof of sacrifice. It was placed over a glowing fire. Everyone came near to see and to sniff the pleasing scent that the burning "heart" exuded. This incense plunged the lords of Xibalba into a deep torpor and they were vanquished.

Ixquic had mounted to the earth in the meantime and the Owls hastened to join her. She made her way to the home of the mother of the Aphu and introduced herself as the lady's daughter-in-law. The mother of the Aphu refused to believe Ixquic and declared that her sons' only descendants were Hun Batz and Han Chouen, who lived with her. But she agreed to put Ixquic's words to the test by giving her an impossible task: filling a huge sack with corn even though there was only one ear of corn in the field.

Ixquic placed herself in the hands of her supernatural protectors. "I am guilty of many sins," she cried. The gods, hearing this confession, rewarded her. She gathered enough from the ear of corn to fill her sack. Her mother-in-law observed the miracle, welcomed the pregnant Ixquic to the

family and promised to take care of her children.

One day Ixquic went off alone to the forest and gave birth to twins, a son called Hunahpé and a daughter named Ixbalamqué. Hun Batz and Han Chouen were jealous and complained about the noise the twins made. They threw the children out of the house, to grow up in the wild.

To the Mayas, Ixquic triumphed over oppression and established the new order of civilization and harmony recommended by the Ahpu. She was the mother goddess who gave birth to humankind, as well as the earth goddess — the goddess of fruitfulness and fertility. In addition, she was the goddess of repentance, to whom one submitted in hopes of receiving rain from the sky to water the crops.

Ixquic was also the full moon, as represented by her swollen belly, while her mother-in-law symbolized the waning moon and her daughter personified the waxing moon. These three together represented the female role in Mayan mythology. And as the mother who passed on to humans the wisdom of the Ahpu and renounced the beliefs of the underworld, Ixquic held out hope for a just and harmonious social order.

SEDNA

ESKIMO CIVILIZATIONS

In the land of ice, in the sea depths, there is a large mansion. It is the home of Sedna, the hairy one-eyed goddess, sensitive and temperamental, mistress of seals and whales, to whom she gave birth.

For the Eskimos, the earth is a tent resting on poles, topped with the canopy of heaven. The slashes at its four corners allow the four winds to escape. Human in origin, the gods took possession of the moon, the sun, the sea.

The story of the goddess of the sea depths has many forms, her name changing according to the region. In Greenland she is called "the old woman" or "the majestic woman," while elsewhere she is "the one who didn't want to marry." But most often she is known as "the one who is below, in the depths of the sea": Sedna.

Sedna did not want to marry — unacceptable behavior in Eskimo society, which has no place for single people. Finally, she married a man who turned out to be her father's dog. From this union, she bore many children, some human, some canine. But one day, her husband was killed by his father-in-law, and sank to the bottom of the sea. Sedna, who could no longer support her children, sent them out into the world. Some say that her canine children fathered the Caucasian race while her human offspring were the forebears of the Chipewyan Indians.

After this unfortunate marriage, Sedna had a second unhappy experience. She was kidnapped by a petrel and the bird married her. Sedna's determined father followed them and carried his daughter away in a kayak. The bird, unwilling to release her, pursued the fleeing pair and called up a violent storm.

For the Eskimos, the gods were originally humans who took possession of the earth, sun, and sea. 19th century Italian depiction of a Greenland family

From Sedna's fingers were born seals, whales, and all other sea animals.
Contemporary Eskimo art from the Soviet Union.

To keep his boat afloat, the father unhesitatingly threw his daughter overboard. As she clung desperately to the kayak, he cut off her fingers to make her let go. From these fingers were born the sea mammals, such as the seals and whales. Finally, Sedna's father put out her right eye and she sank into the depths of the sea, where she reigns still as its goddess. As for her father, he was so exhausted when he reached shore that he could only lie upon the sand. The waves washed over him, carrying him to the bottom of the ocean, where he still lives with his daughter.

Sedna is not pretty to look at. Her sinister appearance terrifies any human who tries to enter her house. Her door is guarded by a dog or a seal, according to various versions of the myth. Sedna observes with her left eye; in the empty socket of her right eye, ugly black hairs stick out. Enormous and immobile, she is loath to leave her vast stone mansion and remains housebound. Her father assists her, leading the dying from their beds to Sedna's realm, the underworld. When the suffering see her, they know they will not live much longer.

Sedna's role is to watch over human beings, who often violate taboos: women have miscarriages, or secretly abort their pregnancies, while men harm wild animals. When this happens, the animals become tainted and suffer. But because they come from the fingers of the goddess, she

In the frigid depths beneath the ice lives the goddess Sedna, who, as humans commit sins, is showered with dirt.

suffers horribly with them. She keeps the suffering animals shut in with her. Sedna's body and her matted black hair become covered in the dirt of man's sins, which falls on her like rain.

While she is in this pitiful condition and keeps the game with her, men have nothing to hunt, and know the fear of hunger and disease. As the absence of game continues, the shaman or witch

doctor is called in. He alone can stand the sight of the goddess and calm her fury. The shaman's ceremonial visit to Sedna is carried out in the dark, while he stands in the center of an assembly. He invokes the spirits, and gradually achieves a state of ecstasy. While his assistants sing in chorus, the earth opens beneath him and his soul disappears, reaching the depths of the sea.

In Sedna's realm, the shaman encounters many obstacles: to penetrate the domaine of the goddess, he must elude first the dog guarding its portals and second Sedna's father, who mistakes him for a corpse. At last the shaman arrives before the goddess, who is half smothered by the dirt of men's sins and raging against them. At the sight of him, Sedna draws near and shakes her hair over him. He speaks soothingly and begins to comb her hair, which she cannot do because she has no fingers. The dirt falls out and with it the goddess' anger. When Sedna's good humor is restored, she frees the sea animals.

Another method of improving bad hunting conditions involves summoning the goddess to just below the place where the ritual is performed, then hoisting her up through an imaginary hole. The participants hold her there, airing their grievances until she promises to release the seals. In either case, the animals reappear, hunting and fishing become fruitful once more, and order is re-established.

In the Hindu-influenced religions of Southeast Asia, from Cambodia to Bali, and in such differing countries as Laos and Java, the rice spirit is a woman. Many mythologies recount her story and she assumes many names. In the Sundanese Islands of Indonesia she is known as Dewa Sri.

Samyan Guru, chief god of the Paradise of the Blessed, wanted to build a temple. He summoned his priest, the lord Samyan Narada, and ordered him to command the gods to gather the needed materials. All the gods hastened to comply with Samyan Guru's command and departed in pursuit of the items required, with the exception of Anta, god of the underworld, who was a serpent. Anta wept cried because he had no arms with which to carry out his task. From his tears three eggs were formed. Samyan Narada ordered Anta to offer these eggs to Samyan Guru, so the serpent, carrying the eggs in his mouth, set off. A speckled eagle asked where he was going. Anta could not reply because his mouth was full. The eagle was offended and attacked the serpent. As a result, two of the eggs fell from the god's mouth.

Anta safely conveyed the third egg to Samyan Guru. A beautiful girl child emerged from this egg. Called Dewa Sri, she was cared for and raised to adolescence by Samyan Guru's wife. Samyan Guru's father, beholding the maiden's beauty, was afraid that his son might wish to marry her. This had to be avoided, since Dewa Sri was, in a sense, the chief god's daughter.

Samyan Guru's father made Dewa Sri eat of the forbidden fruit of paradise, and the maiden fell ill and died. One week later, plants started to grow on the tomb of Dewa Sri. From her head sprang coconut palms; from her legs, bamboo shoots; from her arms, shrubbery; from her veins, vines; from her hair, herbs; from her pubis, a palm tree; from her eyes and her stomach, all the varieties of plain and sticky rice — in short, every variety of plant life known to humankind was born of Dewa Sri. Samyan Guru had a grain of each kind of rice sent throughout the kingdom of Pakuan Pajajaran so that rice might be planted in the land of Java.

DEWA SRI
SOUTHEAST ASIAN CIVILIZATIONS

All the stages of rice cultivation illustrated in this painting are performed under the protection of the goddess Dewa Sri, who gave birth to the rice spirit. Painting by Imade Budi Batuan, Bali, 1981. Private collection of Nicole Revel.

Southeast Asian mythologies all agree that at that time rice did not need to be cultivated. The Sundanese version of Dewa Sri's story tells us that a queen taught the secret of cooking rice to the women of Pakuan Pajajaran and that these women could prepare a huge meal from a single grain. But one day Dewa Sri was offended and the lives of the people were drastically changed: rice no longer grew all year round, and thereafter people had to sow, harvest, and transport their food.

Numerous Thai legends describe the great ease with which people formerly received their food. Rice just appeared by magic. People had only to make sure that the house was clean and sweep the floors to receive it. One version tells us that an enormous grain, as large as a canoe, rolled in front of the house. The housewife had only to grab the quantity needed. The grain never diminished in size. Another story says the rice spirit was annoyed by a woman whose husband asked her to make the appropriate offering by cleaning the house, since the rice would soon appear. The woman was lazy and hadn't finished her housework when the rice crashed into the house. She hit the rice with her broom and it crumbled into small grains. From that day on, people have had to cultivate rice.

A similar version is found in Cambodian mythology: in early days, rice just flew into the granary. However, one day a wicked woman hit the rice with a piece of wood, and the unhusked rice ran away, taking refuge in a crevice at the foot of the mountain. Neither man nor beast could dig it out. However, an earthworm took pity on humankind and, by dint of great patience and determination, wormed his way into the crevice, where he found the rice goddess. Hearing his supplication, the goddess promised to satisfy people's hunger but declared that rice would no longer fly into the granaries. In the future, people would have to work to obtain the grain, which would grow only during the rainy season.

Humans have toiled to cultivate rice ever since, and have learned to respect the goddess. Dewa Sri likes things neat and tidy, she is fearful and

Balinese women depart to work in the rice fields, which are the goddess' domain.

This figure from Bali, made of painted leaves, portrays Dewa Sri, whom one must not annoy under penalty of seeing rice vanish from the granary. Collection of Nicole Revel.

sensitive, and she cries and grieves when rice is mistreated. Many prohibitions surround rice, from the moment of sowing to the moment of eating. For instance, one must not speak of how the rice crop is doing, under penalty of provoking the departure of the grain's soul. Similarly, when rice has been harvested, one must be careful not to say anything that might offend the goddess, else the rice will disappear from the granary. Finally, when rice is not good, it is wiser to be silent, or at least to beg Dewa Sri's pardon before mentioning the fact.

This Balinese wood carving of Dewa Sri wears a skirt fashioned from stalks of rice. Collection of Nicole Revel.

PANDORA

GREEK CIVILIZATION

Pandora as imagined by Jean Cousin in the 16th century.
She was endowed with beauty, grace, cleverness, strength, and daring;
then Zeus entrusted her with an earthenware vessel and sent her to earth.

In Greek mythology, Pandora is the first woman. Created by the gods of Olympus, she was sent to Earth with her famous "box" . . . and catatrosphe followed.

The poet Hesiod, writing in the 8th century BC, recounts Pandora's tale:

Zeus was furious. Prometheus had stolen fire from the Olympians and given it to man. To punish this arrogance, Zeus had Prometheus chained to a rock, with an eagle pecking at his liver. Then the chief of the gods exercised his limitless intelligence to invent the most cunning punishment possible for man: a woman.

Hephaestus, the god of fire, fashioned the creature from earth and water, taking care to give her a pleasing shape. The goddesses Aphrodite and Peitho and the Graces endowed her with all their charms, and the Horae, the seasons, adorned her with spring flowers. Zeus presented her with an earthen vessel containing all the suffering in the world, and in a final touch of cunning he bid her never to open it. The new creature was irresistible: woman was beautiful, graceful, clever, strong, and bold. The gods called her Pandora, "all-giving," and Hermes led her to Earth.

Prometheus, fearing the wrath of Olympus, had warned his brother Epimetheus never to accept anything from Zeus. But when the brother encountered Pandora's loveliness, he ignored the advice and took her for his bride.

Perhaps Pandora was too beautiful to be honest, or maybe she was evil by nature, or simply too curious. One day she lifted the lid of her jar. At once, innumerable scourges, plagues, vices, and other sorrows escaped into the world. In panic, Pandora slammed the lid shut — but too late. The evils were free and began to spread to the four corners of the earth; all that remained in the jar was Hope.

Why did Pandora open the jar? Both in antiquity and in modern times, several explanations have been put forward. Some versions of the myth say simply that she was created by the gods to bring suffering to humanity. Pandora is depicted as wicked and spiteful, and with her all women,

Pandora opened her box . . .

her daughters. Another version is more ambiguous, attributing Pandora's act to curiosity. But is she a passive victim of this character trait, for which the rest of humanity is made to suffer, or is hers an act of free will, a revolt against the gods, the expression of a desire to know and choose?

The less charitable interpretation of the story was exaggerated and used by the early leaders of the Christian Church to reinforce the doctrine of original sin. They inferred that the evil within her led Pandora to disobey Zeus' orders. Her story and Eve's are remarkably similar, right down to the parallel between the forbidden fruit and the jar, though they were created for quite different reasons.

The earthenware vessel given to Pandora by Zeus was called a *pythos* by the Greeks, and was made in many sizes. Smaller ones were used to

hold wine, oil, and other supplies, while a large *pythos* might be used as a receptacle for a corpse, or even as a shelter for the living. With the passage of time and the continual retelling of the story, Pandora's fateful jar came to be known as a chest or a coffer, or simply as a box. In all Western languages, the phrase "Pandora's box" describes something that appears innocent but will unleash unknown evils.

. . . and evils spread throughout the earth.

SITA

INDIC CIVILIZATIONS

Perfect bride of a perfect king, Sita was kidnapped by a demon. Her husband, Rama, went in search of her and at last recovered her after a long battle.

The *Ramayana*, or Romance of Rama, is the oldest Hindu epic poem. The bards of northern India took four to five centuries to arrive at the final version of the chronicle in verse. It was written in Sanskrit in about the 3rd century BC, translated into Hindi in the 16th century, and carried in various forms to the Indian-influenced cultures of Southeast Asia. In Thailand, for example, the tale is known as the *Ramakien*, and it is a popular subject of carvings and paintings, even in Buddhist temples. In Indonesia the saga is told by shadow-puppet theater. Wherever it is found, the story is intended to instruct as much as to entertain.

Sita was born when the king of Mithila, Janaka the Progenitor, was preparing a piece of land for a ritual sacrifice. Suddenly, from the furrow his plow had made on the sanctified land, a girl rose up. He called her Sita, or "furrow." When Sita reached marriageable age, King Janaka decided that only a prince capable of stringing the king's extraordinary bow, which he had received from the god Siva, would win his daughter's hand. Many men tried, but none succeeded until Prince Rama bent the bow so easily that it nearly broke.

On the day Rama and Sita were married, three other weddings took place as well: Rama's brother Lakshmana won Sita's sister, and the prince's other two brothers, Catrughna and Bharata, wed her cousins. The four happy couples departed for the brothers' kingdom of Ayodhya, which is north of the Ganges, not far from the Himalayas.

The demon Ravana coveted Prince Rama's beautiful wife Sita. He carried her off, fatally wounding Jatayu the vulture, who tried to prevent the abduction.

The four princes, sons of King Dasharatha, had also been born in a miraculous way. The king had not succeeded in begetting an heir with any of his three wives, so he conducted a ceremonial sacrifice to ask the gods for help in continuing his line. Answering his prayers, a supernatural being emerged from the flames with a magic potion for the wives to drink. Dasharatha's favorite wife, Kaushalya, bore Rama, while Sumitra had the twins Lakshmana and Catrughna, and Kaikeyi produced Bharata.

The gods were not altruistic in their gesture; they had their own motives for helping Dasharatha. They had been harassed incessantly by a *rakshasa*, or demon, called Ravana, king of Lanka, identified with modern Sri Lanka, or Ceylon. But the great god Brahma had arranged things in such a way that only a human could conquer the demon. So the god Vishnu incarnated himself in the body of Prince Rama to destroy the bothersome demon.

Once Rama was married, Dasharatha was ready to abdicate the throne to his favorite son. But the night before the ceremony of succession, Kaikeyi reminded her husband of a large debt that he owed her for saving his life some time previously. In payment, she demanded that he exile Rama for fourteen years and raise her son, Bharata, to Rama's favored status.

Dasharatha pleaded for Kaikeyi to reconsider, but she held firm, and in the morning Rama was exiled to the forest. He went willingly, for it was a matter of honor, but all the same it was unfortunate, for Rama possessed all the qualities required in a good king, and Bharata, who was basically a decent type, didn't really care about the throne as much as his mother did.

Sita insisted on accompanying her banished husband into the forest. Once there, the couple began to play out their destiny. Curpanakha, sister of the demon Ravana, fell in love with Rama and tried to seduce him away from Sita. He spurned her advances. Enraged, she devised a cunning scheme: she convinced her demonic brother of the unrivaled beauty of Sita, arousing

The *Ramayana*, the epic poem recounting the adventures of Rama and Sita, is the source of many folk entertainments. Here it is the subject of shadow theater in Java.

in him the desire to possess her. Ravana distracted Rama's attention with a magnificent gazelle "whose body was covered with pearls and precious stones"; while Sita was alone, the demon grabbed her by her hair and carried her off into the sky.

Jatayu the vulture tried to stop the abduction, but was fatally wounded in the attempt, and was barely able to tell Rama what had transpired before he died. Rama set off to rescue his wife, traveling south with his brother Lakshmana. Along the way, they met the monkeys Sugriva and Hanuman, who promised to help them defeat Ravana.

Meanwhile, Sita was imprisoned in a harem in Lanka, where Ravana visited her daily to try to separate her from her virtue. But she remained faithful to her husband. Sita was released from her ordeal only when Rama arrived with Sugriva, Hanuman, and their army of monkeys, who overpowered her captor. The victorious Rama

was then seized with doubt over his bride's virtue during her imprisonment. Sita underwent the test of fire and emerged victorious, but once Rama was enthroned as king of Ayodhya, his people again complained about Sita's dubious past and he was forced to exile her.

After many years and adventures they were reunited, but Sita, not trusting in Rama's faith in her, challenged him: "If my word is true, and if I know none other than Rama, let the goddess Earth open up here beneath my feet!"

The miracle occurred. An exquisite throne sprang up from the ground, and the goddess arose to take Sita in her arms and seat her in the throne. "On this seat she was seen to sink into the subterranean caverns," back to the earth whence she came.

Rama lost his perfect wife through his unwillingness to believe in her steadfastness. But Brahma consoled him: "You will be reunited in heaven, do not doubt it."

HELEN OF TROY

ANCIENT GREECE

Seductress in spite of herself, Helen brought about the Trojan War.
For ten years, she bore the burden of guilt.
Helen on the Ramparts of Troy, by Gustave Moreau.

Flighty young girl, unfaithful wife, seductress — Helen of Sparta caused the Trojan War by permitting Paris to carry her off. We must not judge her too harshly, however, for Helen was the first victim of her ill-fated beauty and passionate nature.

The most famous woman of antiquity is the subject of numerous legends and myths, but she is best known for her appearances in the Homeric epic poems, the *Iliad* and the *Odyssey*.

Helen's mother was Leda; officially, her father was King Tyndareus of Sparta. Homer relates, however, that she and her brother Pollux were really the children of Zeus, who changed himself into a swan to impregnate Leda. Tyndareus was the father only of Helen's sister, Clytemnestra, who married Agamemnon, and of their brother Castor, according to Homer.

The young Helen learned of love with a shepherd she met while out walking. He carried her off to a grotto where they spent the night, but he did not touch her because she was grimy and covered with dirt. The next morning, however, when he beheld her arising from the foam of the sea, he realized that she was as beautiful as Aphrodite. She yielded to him.

Theseus also lusted after such divine beauty. He carried her off by force to Athens and married her. When he was certain that she wouldn't leave him, he grew tired of her. Helen's very natural resentment was increased by the fact that she was five months pregnant. She swore that she would never again be a man's plaything. Fortunately, her brothers came to her rescue and brought her back to Sparta. There she gave birth to a daughter, whom she hid away and then entrusted to Clytemnestra.

Tyndareus invited to Sparta seven suitors whom he thought worthy of Helen's hand and asked her to choose one of them: Achilles, Ajax, Diomedes, Menelaus, Patroclus, Teucer, or Ulysses. Ulysses, bolder than his companions, slipped into Helen's room one night and seduced her. But he could not marry her, for he was less powerful than the other heros, and the envy such

In *The Rape of Helen by Paris* (school of Fra Angelico, 15th century),
Helen takes a last look at Sparta.
Would she return one day to the city where she had been born?

a marriage would create might have disastrous consequences for his island of Ithaca. After spending seven days with Helen, he promised her he would make amends to the suitor of her choice, should the man be offended by Ulysses' action. The next day Helen declared that Aphrodite had revealed the name of her future husband in a dream. She chose poor shy Menelaus, for his wealth and rank, and no one was more suprised than he.

Menelaus knew he bored Helen, and he had to get drunk in order to find the courage to approach her. For her part, she threw him into the arms of other women. From this unhappy marriage was born a daughter, Hermione, who was entrusted to her grandparents' care.

Meanwhile, Menelaus' brother, Agamemnon, was toying with the idea of war against Troy. He triggered an extraordinary chain of events by asking Menelaus to invite Paris, son of King Priam of Troy, to visit Sparta. Helen was presented to Paris, and everything happened just as Agamemnon had foreseen. The handsome Paris, stirred by Helen's beauty, carried her off. According to myth, their love was reciprocal and Helen agreed to run away to Troy with him. In addition, Paris had the benefit of Aphrodite's support, since his judgment had allowed her to triumph over Hera and Athena in the contest to choose who was the fairest goddess.

Agamemnon wanted war at any price. The most powerful Greek princes, bound by an oath sworn while seeking Helen's hand, could not fail to follow Agamemnon's lead in avenging Menelaus' battered honor. But they did try to avoid the conflict by entering into negotiations with Troy, only to be met with a firm refusal from Helen, who declared that she was in Troy by her own choice. The Trojan War ensued.

In the course of the ten long years of battle between the Greeks and the Trojans, Helen sometimes felt homesick and regretted being the cause of this fatal war. But Paris, with his love, knew how to comfort her. Priam had received her as if she were his own daughter. He and Hector, one of Paris' brothers, protected her against the growing hatred of those around her. In the opposing encampment, many Greeks considered her a traitor. Homer attempts to excuse Helen by saying she always showed great sympathy for her countrymen during the war.

Paris was killed. Helen, who had become the Trojans' scapegoat, quickly found herself under the protection of Deiphobus, whom she married. Ulysses, meanwhile, felt the time had come to strike a blow that would at last end the war. He devised the well-known ruse of the Trojan horse, which Priam allowed to be brought inside Troy in spite of Cassandra's prophecy. The Greeks hidden within the horse took the city and carried Helen away.

Menelaus eventually took Helen back to the palace at Sparta. There he rediscovered wine and his mistresses, and Helen rediscovered boredom. Beauteous as ever, she could not bring herself to renounce love. One day she went to the place where she had met her first lover, the shepherd. She found a young man wandering there, and with him she relived the events of twenty years earlier. After three days in the grotto, her lover told her he was Telemachus. He was seeking his father, Ulysses, from whom he had had no word since the beginning of the war provoked by that cursed Helen. Helen did not dare to reveal her identity. She left him, weeping over the fact that her last lover was the son she would have loved to have given Ulysses.

PENELOPE

GREEK CIVILIZATION

Despite her central role in the Odyssey, Penelope's admirable qualities were given scant attention by Homer, and few later poets found her worthy of note. Yet in many ways she showed more fortitude than her husband.

As the wife of Ulysses, King of Ithaca, Penelope was left behind while her husband roamed the world. He spent ten years battling the Trojans and another ten facing peril after peril, cursed by the gods: his famous adventures include his encounter with the Cyclops, his stays in the land of the lotus-eaters and the island of Circe, the terrible dangers posed for him and his ship's crew by the Sirens and by Scylla and Charybdis, and, last but far from least, his warm welcome by the nymph Calypso.

During this time Penelope heard nothing of or from him, and did not know whether he was alive or dead. The queen withdrew from the world to her private sanctuary, where men were not admitted. Ancient Greek moral values did not require that she remain faithful to her husband, yet Penelope chose to do so.

As the years passed, it became more and more doubtful that Ulysses was still alive. According to Greek custom, Penelope should have returned to her father's home, acknowledging his right to give her away in marriage a second time. Many suitors clamored for her hand, and the strife among them upset the tranquility of the island. Her son, Telemachus, said of his mother: "Her heart is torn between two desires: to maintain her household, respecting her husband's rights . . . or to marry a Greek of her own choosing." The way everyone but Penelope saw the situation, marriage would have consoled her and made it pos-

Penelope had vowed that she would not remarry until she completed her father-in-law's shroud; by day she wove, but by night she undid her work.

36

sible for Telemachus to enjoy his inheritance. It also would have restored harmony to the kingdom.

Despite the temptation to remarry, Penelope remained steadfastly loyal to Ulysses. She used her feminine wiles and devised a ruse to keep her suitors at bay: Penelope announced that before she could choose among them, she needed to complete a shroud for her father-in-law. She worked hard at the immense burial cloth by day, but returned by torchlight at night to undo her weaving. Thus Penelope bought time, hoping that the gods would eventually allow her wandering husband to return.

Her hope was not in vain. Ulysses' seemingly endless voyage was finally coming to an end. The goddess Athena had told him of the suitors who were courting his wife and his kingdom, and when at last he arrived on the shores of Ithaca, Ulysses knew that to wreak vengeance upon the suitors he would have to re-enter his palace in disguise. Accordingly, Athena transformed him into a beggar. He revealed his true identity only to Telemachus, who helped him plot his revenge.

Still disguised, Ulysses approached the palace and asked for an interview with the queen. He did not reveal his identity, but merely told her that the king still lived, then suggested that Penelope stall her suitors with yet another ruse: this time, an archery contest with herself as the prize. Ulysses' own bow was to be used — and, as he well knew, no one but he was strong enough to bend it. Since the others could not bend it, they could not string the bow and hence could not shoot. Suitor after suitor made the effort, only to be forced to withdraw in humiliation. Finally the "beggar" took his turn. Stringing the bow easily, he used it to massacre the suitors and so regained his kingdom.

Despite his prowess with the bow, Penelope still did not recognize her husband, so thorough was Athena's transformation of him (and the long years of adventure had left their marks as well). To prove his identity, she asked him to describe

Penelope in a sculpture by Antoine Bourdelle . . . symbol of fidelity and patience, but also a strong and passionate woman.

the secret of her bed, a secret that Ulysses alone knew. He told her precisely how the bed and bedroom had been crafted of very rare woods. At last the king and queen were reunited.

Ulysses' return was Penelope's triumph, the proof that she had been right to wait faithfully for him. The Greeks raised her to the status of a goddess. Eventually she became the symbol of fidelity, the guardian of hearth and home. But she also guarded her own destiny. In this, she was stronger than Ulysses, who was bandied about like a toy at

Her suitors pressed her to make a decision, but Penelope, gazing out to sea, dreamed that her husband would reappear one day.

the whim of the gods. Yet she has remained largely unsung.

The strongest image we associate with her is that of "Penelope's web," her weaving, which symbolizes work that is never finished. Underneath her seeming passivity, Penelope's strength and true passion have remained hidden through the centuries.

MEDEA

GREEK CIVILIZATION

Medea flies away in a fiery winged chariot.
Does it take her to Elysium, or, as other versions of the legend claim,
to Athens, to claim the asylum promised her by Aegeus?

Enchantress or sorceress, human or monster — for the love of an unfaithful hero, Medea killed and killed again . . .

Immortalized by the poet Euripides in the 5th century BC, Medea and her story originate with the ancient legend of the Argonauts. Jason was the son of Aeson, whose kingdom in Thessaly had been usurped by his half-brother Pelias. Jason, brought up in hiding, returned to reclaim his throne. Pelias declared himself ready to relinquish the throne on one condition: that Jason bring back from distant Colchis the Golden Fleece of the ram that had saved their ancestor Phryxos.

The thought of this adventure enchanted Jason, who did not suspect that it was a trick to get rid of him. He convinced the bravest heroes of his time to accompany him aboard his ship the Argos — Heracles, Castor and Pollux, Orpheus, and a host of others were enthusiastic about the dangerous expedition. The Argonauts encountered many perils and some paid for their daring with their lives.

When the ship reached Colchis, the heroes began to suspect they would need more than valor to accomplish their mission. Fortunately, the gods of Olympus took an interest in their fate. Hera and Aphrodite devised a way to make the daughter of the king of Colchis fall in love with Jason. The plan succeeded excellently — for Jason. Medea, the princess, possessed supernatural powers and knew all the arcane properties of plants. With her knowledge at the service of the Argonauts, their success was guaranteed.

Aeetes, king of Colchis, did not like these foreigners, but as a courteous host he offered them a feast before asking their intentions. When he understood the reason for their visit, he was enraged, yet hid his feelings. Aeetes promised to give the Argonauts the Golden Fleece if one of the heroes could pass his tests of bravery. As the impossible tests were announced, Jason became speechless. Meanwhile, Medea had slipped into the room to observe the guests. When she caught sight of Jason, Eros quickly strung his bow and nimbly shot an arrow into the girl's heart.

Fleeing to her chamber, Medea sobbed with shame. She knew that for love of this foreigner, she would betray her father. She summoned Jason and gave him a magic ointment that would make him invulnerable for a day. She explained that he could conquer the army of dragons he was to fight by throwing a stone into their ranks so they would turn on each other. When she had finished, Jason vowed, "By day, by night, I will always remember you. If ever you come to Greece, you will be venerated for all that you have done for us, and only death will separate me from you."

Jason came through the terrible tests unscathed. Medea, knowing that her father was plotting new treachery, pleaded with the Argonauts to flee as quickly as they could. After lulling to sleep the serpent that guarded her, she took the Golden Fleece and joined the heroes aboard the Argos, taking also her brother Absyrtos.

The king set out in pursuit of the heros, leading a fleet so vast that they had little chance of escape. To save the Argonauts, Medea committed the unpardonable: she killed Absyrtos, cutting him into pieces and hurling his limbs into the sea. The Argos escaped as Aeetes slowed his fleet to gather his son's remains.

On their return to Greece, Jason learned that Pelias had massacred his family. Determined to wreak vengeance, he again sought Medea's help. She used her sorcery to cause Pelias' daughters to kill their father.

Medea loved Jason so desperately that she would have given him her very soul. Euripides tells us that the couple had two sons, and lived happily until the day they voyaged to Corinth. Presented with the opportunity to ally his kingdom with Corinth by marrying King Creon's daughter, Jason forgot all his grateful promises and cast off Medea.

Overcome with pain and grief, she vowed revenge. King Creon, fearing for his daughter's safety, ordered Medea to leave Corinth with her two sons. This was a fate worse than death — what security could an exiled woman with two young children hope for? When next she laid eyes on Jason, she

For love of Jason, Medea betrayed her own father; for vengeance, she killed her own sons.

launched into a terrible attack: "I guarded the flame of your safety. Father, home, I left everything for a foreign land. I got rid of your adversaries and led Pelias to a hideous death. Where will I go? No one can help me. I am alone." Jason, demonstrating the shallowness of his character, reproached her for arrogance and told her Aphrodite had saved him by causing Medea to love him.

From this moment on, Medea devoted all her energy to revenge. She chose a gown, sprinkled it with poison sap, and delivered it to Creon's daughter as a token of her "repentance." The moment the princess donned the dress, a consuming fire engulfed her. Creon, gathering his

dying daughter in his arms, perished in pain as well.

But Medea had made an even more atrocious resolution: to kill her own sons. Versions of the story differ as to her motives. Was her intent to strike at the heart of what Jason treasured most, or to save her children from slavery? The more forgiving variation quotes Medea as saying, "I will not let them live mistreated by foreigners, nor die by a hand crueler than my own. No, I, who have given them life, will give them death too. Oh, no cowardice now; I must forget how young they are, how sweet they are, their first cries . . . "

On the roof of the palace a winged chariot awaited her and the bodies of her sons. In one version, she fled to Elysium; in another, to Athens, where Aegeus had promised her asylum.

Hercules, Orpheus, Castor and Pollux, and other heros joined Jason on the Argos in his quest for the Golden Fleece.

SHIRIN

PERSIA — CA. 580-628

"As beauteous as the moon, as sweet as the scent of ambergris," wrote Firdawsi, one of the many Persian poets inspired by the love of the beautiful Shirin and the illustrious King Khosrow II. Her passionate love for Khosrow drove Shirin to both good and evil, and even to her death.

Khosrow, crown prince of the Sassanid dynasty, had a close friend, a painter named Shapur. He told Khosrow of the marvels he had seen during his voyages. Among these was a very rich queen, spoken of as "the Great Lady," whose realm, Armenia, extended from the Caspian Sea to Kurdistan and who changed her residence according to the seasons in order to profit from the best climate. This queen's sole heir was her niece, a fairy-like child named Shirin, which means "sweetness" in Persian. Khosrow never tired of the painter's descriptions of Armenia and the incomparable princess. He sent Shapur to search for her.

When the painter arrived at Shirin's castle, he hung Khosrow's portrait on the trunk of a tree, then hid and waited. The princess, out walking with her friends, gazed on the prince's handsome face. She was so taken with the portrait that her friends, fearing she might become bewitched, burned it. Shapur painted another portrait and the same thing happened a second time, then a third. At this point, Shirin went to take down the painting. When she looked at it, the painting, like a mirror, reflected her own features. Curious, she wished to know its secret. Inquiries were made, with no result. And then one day, Shapur was found. He spoke in praise of his prince before revealing to Shirin the purpose of his errand.

The princess took one of her aunt's horses and fled the kingdom, galloping as hard as she

Shirin left Armenia to seek Khosrow even as the prince was traveling toward Armenia, where he hoped to find his beloved. Their paths crossed at a spring, but they did not recognize each other.
Khosrow Surprising Shirin Bathing.

could. After fourteen days of traveling she stopped before a spring, which she believed to be the Spring of Immortality, and bathed. In the meantime, Khosrow, who feared that his father meant him harm, fled toward Armenia. On the way he passed near a spring where a beautiful young maiden was bathing.

Shirin arrived in Mada'in, the Sassanid capital, where she was settled in Khosrow's palace to await him. After a month, impatient, she made inquiries and learned that the prince had left for Armenia. Only then did she realize that the knight who had surprised her while bathing must have been none other than the man she sought.

Khosrow passed the winter with Shirin's aunt and sent the faithful Shapur to fetch back his beloved. In the meantime, the Persian king died and Khosrow had to return to Mada'in to take his place on the throne. He saved his country from civil war and dealt out justice to the weak. While this was happening, Shapur took Shirin back to the court of her aunt.

Khosrow then had to flee Mada'in again because a traitor was plotting against him. This permitted him to go seek Shirin. They found each other at last and, according to the great romantic Persian poet Nizami, they were like "the sun and moon flirting, joined to the same sign and playing games of love."

Fate, however, had not finished playing tricks on the lovers. To seek help in recovering his throne so that he could marry Shirin, Khosrow went to the Emperor Constantine. The emperor gave him an army — but also his daughter, Maryam, in marriage.

Khosrow was reinstated on his throne and Shirin succeeded to her aunt's throne in Armenia. Unable to stay far away from Khosrow, Shirin took up residence at the border of her kingdom. There she had a canal built by the architect Farhad, who fell in love with her. Khosrow, still passionately in love with Shirin, grew jealous of Farhad. Having tried without success to buy off the architect, he made Farhad believe Shirin was dead. Farhad threw himself off Mount Bisitun after

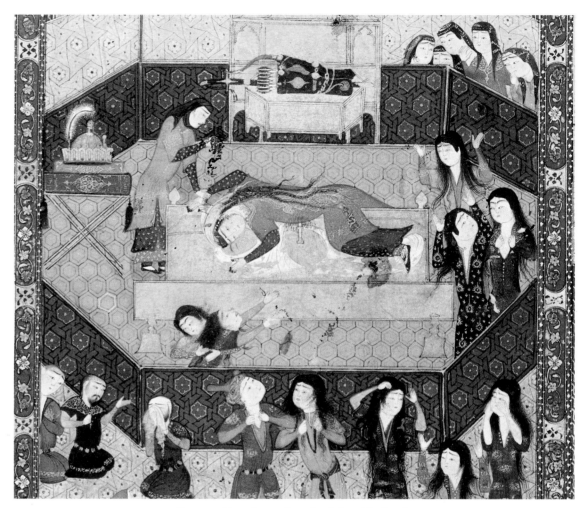

Shirin could not live without her beloved husband.
She killed herself on the day of his funeral. *The Death of Shirin.*

carving there the portraits of the two agents of his downfall.

Shirin, who despite her devotion to Khosrow had also loved Farhad, was heartbroken by this death. Khosrow repented and sent her his condolences. Then Shirin had Maryam poisoned and sent her condolences to the king. They were even, and they were both free. Overcoming his royal pride, Khosrow went to find Shirin to ask her pardon. Their story might have ended like a fairy tale: they married, Shirin proved a perfect wife and a wise counsellor, and Khosrow was a great king. But the tale ends in tragedy. Khosrow was assassinated on the order of his son by Maryam,

Prince Shiruye, who had long dreamed of marrying Shirin himself.

The queen prepared her husband's body and organized the funeral procession. On the morning of the funeral, she dressed in silk and put henna on her hands and kohl on her eyes. She had no more tears to shed, having shed them all. No one could have guessed at the sadness hidden behind her beauty. The coffin was placed in the tomb. Shirin entered, closed the door behind her, and stretched out next to Khosrow. Suddenly, the crowd gathered around the tomb heard a cry: Shirin had stabbed herself, to join her soul with that of the king for all eternity.

LA CAVA FLORINDA
SPAIN — 8TH CENTURY

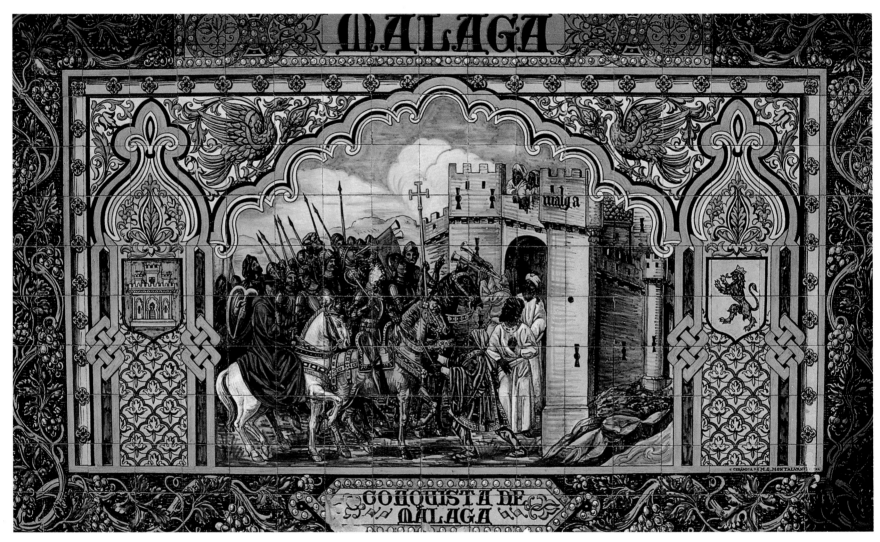

Seven hundred years after La Cava Florinda's "sin" came La Reconquista:
the Catholic rulers Isabella and Ferdinand reconquered Malaga.

Florinda lost her flower,
The king suffered his punishment;
She said that she had been forced,
He that with pleasure she consented.
And for having stolen a flower,
King Rodrigo lost Spain.

The Pax Romana had lasted four centuries when the Vandals and Visigoths invaded Spain. The latter subdued the former, formed an alliance with Rome, and founded an empire. In 701 King Witiza came to the throne. Florinda's legend — first recounted by the Arab chroniclers Razi and Abdulcasim Tarif Abdentaric, then elaborated by the Spanish — dates from this time.

Witiza's reign began peacefully enough but a sedate life was not to his taste. Lacking enemies to fight and problems to confront, he became needlessly cruel, indolent, and lascivious. He insulted the priests who criticized him repeatedly, quarreled with the pope, and closed the doors of the churches. Without faith or law, the kingdom rapidly deteriorated. According to the chroniclers, "the wicked Witiza taught all Spain to sin."

The handsome young Rodrigo, returning from exile, thus easily gathered forces and support and seized power. The whole nation was relieved when Rodrigo entered Toledo, the Visigoths' capital, and took possession of the royal palace. The relief was short-lived, however, for Rodrigo followed in the footsteps of his predecessor. Fearing he would be overthrown himself, he left a large part of the kingdom without defenses and troops in order to prevent an uprising, unaware that the danger would come from the exterior.

On the banks of the Tagus River, not far from Toledo, Rodriqo had built a palace for his wife, Elyata. One hot day, during the siesta, Rodrigo went seeking the queen in her private apartments, which like a harem were strictly forbidden to men. He came to a patio and hid himself in order to watch without being seen.

The queen was surrounded by adorable young girls who were chatting, playing, drowsing, or bathing their feet in a fountain. They were discussing who was the most beautiful. "Florinda!" cried one, who, suiting action to words, woke up her drowsing friend and half undressed her before her companions. Rodriqo, hidden in the shadow, could not believe his eyes. Never had he seen such perfection. The king lusted after this maiden, who was the daughter of Count Julien, governor

The Arab conquest departed from Ceuta, in North Africa. And King Rodrigo lost Spain for having offended a woman named Florinda.

of Tangiers and Ceuta. Julian, a Christian Berber, was allied to the Visigoths through marriage to Witiza's sister. He had entrusted his beautiful daughter to Rodrigo's care as a pledge of loyalty.

Rodrigo tried to seduce Florinda but she avoided him. One day, no longer able to remain silent, he sat next to her and asked her to extract a thorn embedded in his palm. Florinda replied that she could not find a trace of a thorn. Rodrigo took her hand and, placing it over his heart, declared: "This is where the thorn is, and only you can tear it out!" But the maiden did not respond, for she thought of him as a father. The king frequently renewed his advances, pursued her, hunted her, threatened her, and each time met with the same answer. Finally, he forced her.

Florinda wrote to her father: "You confided your lamb to the care of a lion, and your daughter has been dishonored." Count Julian had just repulsed an Arab assault when this message arrived at Ceuta. Julien vowed to take bloody vengeance on Rodriqo and the whole of Spain. First he sent a message to the king in which he exaggerated the

dangers threatening the borders so that the monarch would send all his horses and arms. Then he brought Florinda back from Toledo to Ceuta, claiming that her mother was ill. After that he sought out Muza ben Nozier, commander of the Arab army, and offered him Spain in return for his support. Muza accepted the pact.

Muza sent his governor, Tarik ben Zeyad, on reconnaissance with five ships. Upon his return, the Arab commander launched the attack on Spain. His first victory was at a place named Djebel-Tarik, "Mountain of Tarik" . . . now Gibraltar. And thus, legend recounts, to avenge Florinda's honor Spain was conquered in 711. Florinda and her family went to live in Spain afterward but she could be seen to be wasting away because of the insults she faced every day. Christians cursed her and the Moors called her *cava*, whore. One day Florinda climbed to the top of a tower, called her parents and said to them: "May this city in the future be called Malacca, in memory of the most unfortunate of women, who is going to die." Then she threw herself from the tower. The city became known as Malacca, and then Málaga. As for Rodrigo, he disappeared.

A Spanish epic poem recounts the last chapter of the story. It says Rodrigo found shelter with a hermit, who made him do penance by sleeping in a sepulchre with a seven-headed serpent. Every day the hermit would ask: "How are you, penitent, in such good company?" And Rodrigo would answer: "I am eaten, I am eaten, there where I have most sinned: Straight to the heart, spring of my ill-fortune."

Both Christian and Muslim legends recount the story of La Cava Florinda. Some believe the Spanish felt obliged to explain how and why their country fell into the hands of the Moors; they needed a scapegoat. According to Ramón Menéndez Pidal, an expert on Spanish literature, Julien, lord of Tangiers and Ceuta, did surrender to Muza and did propose that the Moors conquer Spain. No one knows why, but in order to justify this action, the story of vengeance and Florinda was invented.

ISOLDE

CELTIC TRADITION

Heroine of a Celtic legend that spread throughout Europe in the 12th century, Isolde is still fascinating because of the timelessness of her dilemma. Torn between fidelity to her husband and her fatal passion for Tristan, she ultimately chose love . . . and died for it.

Young Tristan, nephew of King Mark of Cornwall, had gone to Ireland to slay the giant Morholt, brother of the Irish queen. Stranded there, he disguised himself as a juggler to seek shelter at court without bringing the wrath of Irish royalty down upon his head. The queen hired him to teach music to her daughter, Isolde the Fair. The golden-haired princess was as cultured as she was beautiful, a lover of poetry and music.

When Tristan eventually returned to King Mark's castle at Tintagel, he could not stop singing the praises of the princess to his uncle. Tristan's enthusiasm was so infectious that the king decided to marry her. Tristan was dispatched to Ireland again, this time to fetch the bride. The Irish queen entrusted her daughter with a potion, which would unite the nuptial couple forever in love. But destiny had chosen a different union. By fatal error, Tristan and Isolde consumed the potion during the crossing and were bound together by indestructible passion.

Isolde went through with the marriage ceremony. But on her wedding night she persuaded her faithful maid Brangwain to take her place in the nuptial bed. Isolde and Tristan could not hide their love for each other, and people soon became suspicious. The earls, jealous of Tristan's favor with his uncle, saw this as a chance to be rid of him, and convinced King Mark to send him far away. Tristan went furtively by night to

When Isolde arrived at her lover's bedside it
was too late; death had already taken him.
Her only course was to join Tristan
where no one could ever separate them again.

meet Isolde near a fountain in the castle gardens, merely to say goodbye, but they were caught, accused of treason, and condemned to be burned at the stake.

Tristan and Isolde escaped and took refuge in a forest. Despite their love, they honored their vows to the king: his, that of fealty to his lord, and hers, that of fidelity to her husband. Every night they slept side by side with his naked sword separating them, a symbol of their chastity. So they lay when the king, pursuing, found the fugitive couple. Confronted with the sight of their unassailable innocence, he forgave them at once, and to let them know of his compassion, he took Tristan's sword and laid his own between the sleeping pair. Then he stole quietly away. Upon awakening, Tristan and Isolde were so moved by King Mark's gesture that they decided to return

FILM D'ARTE ITALIANA
TRISTAN ET YSEULT
Dramma Lirica

PERSONAGGI:
SIGNORI GIOVANNI PEZZINGA ..... TRISTAN
SERAFINO MASTRACCHIO Le Roi MARKE
SIGNORA FRANCESCA BERTINI ..... YSEULT
BIANCA LORENZINI ...... l'Esclave de Tristan
Societa Italiana Per Film d'Arte, Via S.Nicola da Tolentino, 78, Roma

Isolde was promised to King Mark, and Tristan was taking her to him. But on the way, the two young people drank the love potion that bound them together until death.

Madeleine Sologne brought her beauty to the role based on Isolde, while Jean Marais played the Tristan figure in Jean Delannoy's film *L'Eternel Retour*.

to Tintagel to resume the roles to which honor bound them. The king took back his queen, but sent Tristan across the sea to fight in the service of the king of Brittany.

The Breton king offered Tristan the hand of his daughter in marriage. Ironically, she bore the same name as the golden-haired Irish queen of Cornwall; she was known as Isolde of the White Hands. Tristan married her but she could not make him forget his love for Isolde the Fair.

One day Tristan was mortally wounded in battle. Desperate to see his love one more time, he sent a loyal friend to bring her to Brittany, instructing him to signal her presence or absence in the returning ship by raising a white sail or a black one. But Isolde of the White Hands overheard the conversation, and was inflamed with jealousy. When the ship bearing Isolde the Fair finally came in sight, Isolde of the White Hands falsely told Tristan that the sails were black, making him be-

lieve that his love had not come. Tristan died of despair. Isolde the Fair hastened to the castle, and, finding him dead, lay down to die beside him.

In early versions, the heroine was called Essylt and was portrayed as an Irish fairy. The tale became a favorite among poets in England, France, and Germany, and later in Italy, Spain, and Norway. Many variations evolved in the 12th and 13th centuries, some depicting the tragic couple as the chaste, innocent victims of the love potion, others holding Isolde accountable for initiating an adulterous affair. But all versions deal with the theme of fatal love.

The legend of Tristan and Isolde has inspired many replicas; the best known is Wagner's opera with its Liebestod ("love-death"). In 1943, the French director Jean Delannoy brought the legend to the screen in a modern version written by Jean Cocteau, with the unforgettable Madeleine Sologne playing the character modeled on Isolde.

THE QUEEN OF SHEBA

YEMEN OR ETHIOPIA
10TH CENTURY BC

Crowned with glory, adorned with riches, famous for her visit to King Solomon, the Queen of Sheba nonetheless remains a mystery, her origins shrouded by the centuries.

Her story is recounted in several Middle Eastern traditions, yet the Queen of Sheba's existence has never been proved. Historians believe that if she and her people lived, they inhabited either what is now Ethiopia, or the area of southern Arabia known today as Yemen. Since the two regions maintained close economic and cultural ties during the 10th century BC, when the queen's legend appears to have begun, it is hard to be sure which area knew her first.

In the Bible, the books of Kings and Chronicles describe the queen's famous visit to Solomon. Having heard of his prodigious wisdom, she traveled all the way to Jerusalem to test him with riddles. She arrived with a long train of camels bearing spices, gold, and precious jewels. During her audience with the king, she challenged him with every riddle she knew — and not a word exceeded his understanding, nor a question his ability to answer. Afterward, she visited Solomon's palace, enjoyed the bounty of his table, and attended the ritual sacrifices he made to his God. She then told him, "Everything I heard in my country about your wisdom is true, then! Blessed be Yahweh, your God, who delights you and has placed you upon the throne of Israel!" She took her leave, but not before offering Solomon gifts of gold, spices, and gems.

The Arabs called her Bilkis. She is not mentioned by name in the Koran, but its annotators frequently refer to her. One verse recounts that a messenger brought the queen a letter from Solomon, to which she replied with gifts. Because

A 16th century Persian miniature depicting the famous meeting between Solomon and the Queen of Sheba.

the king was not pleased by these offerings, she went to see him in person. She was shown into the palace, where the floor was made of crystal. Upon seeing the deep, reflective surface, she believed it to be an ornamental pond and drew up her robes to keep them dry, uncovering her ankles. In this way Solomon was able to see that, contrary to what certain demons had told him, she was not cloven-hoofed. As a result of their encounter, the queen abandoned her worship of a sun god to follow Islam. "With Solomon, I submit to Allah, the Lord of the Worlds," she vowed.

Ethiopia has its own version of the Queen of Sheba's legend, recounted in the Ethiopian saga called the *Kebra-Negast.*

The Ethiopians know the Queen of Sheba as Makeda, daughter of the governor Abu Fatuh. The governor had decided to go to Yemen, ostensibly to kill a serpent that was said to guard a fabulous treasure and demand the sacrifice of a hundred maidens a year. He took Makeda with him, thinking her beauty and intelligence might prove useful. As soon as he reached his destination, Abu Fatuh realized that the legendary serpent was none other than the local king and that it would require great cunning to overthrow him.

Abu Fatuh dispatched two of his entourage to the king's court to masquerade as ambassadors from a certain Queen of Asaba. They sang her praises, calling her a goddess from the sea, a precious gem with skin as luminous as the moon.

The queen's visit as seen by a 15th century European . . .

The king envisioned her at the center of the hundred virgins in his harem, and gladly agreed to receive her. Makeda arrived at court, accompanied by a magician — actually her father in disguise — and an eagle. The king succumbed quickly to the charms of the lovely "Queen of Asaba."

Makeda and her father seized the opportunity provided by a gazelle hunt to eliminate the king: as he took his first shot at the quarry, Makeda released the eagle, which gouged out his eyes. The blinded king fell off a cliff to his death. Makeda mounted the king's horse, and her father girded her with the skin of a snake he had killed to symbolize the dead king. As Makeda re-entered the city, the people proclaimed her queen.

Makeda reigned wisely, and the country grew and prospered. One day, a Jewish merchant appeared before her, bringing her sumptuous gifts and singing the praises of his king, Solomon. Makeda accepted the merchant's invitation to visit his homeland, and went to Jerusalem, staying there a full year. Solomon was charmed by her, but realized it would be difficult to make her break

the vow of chastity she had taken to better serve her people. He invited her to a farewell dinner and fed her very salty dishes. Then, according to a 14th century Ethiopian saga, the *Kebra-Negast,* Solomon proposed, "Let us caress each other lovingly until morning."

Makeda refused his advances and made him swear he would not touch her. He agreed, but required her promise in exchange not to touch anything in the palace. During the night Makeda woke, thirsty from all the salt she had consumed. Believing Solomon to be asleep, she went in search of water . . . and was caught with the jug in her hand. "I will release you from your oath," she told the clever king, "but let me drink this water!"

The next morning Solomon, having satisfied his desires with the beautiful queen, allowed her to leave. After returning to her country, she bore a son and named him Ibn-el-Hakim, "son of the wise man." The Ethiopians called him Menelik, "son of the king." When he reached the age of nineteen, Makeda revealed his father's identity and handed him a ring that Solomon had given her: it bore the king's seal, which would force Solomon to acknowledge his son. Menelik went to Jerusalem to meet Solomon, but in the end refused to become his father's heir, preferring instead to succeed his mother as ruler of Sheba.

. . . and in a much more modern depiction.

Murs de Babilone

Grande Semiramis et superbes   Te fourniront des fruits pour
            murailles   saouler tes entrailles.
ou l'on void des jardins au dessus et te preserveront des outrages
        des ramparts   de Mars
se vend a Paris chez P. Valran au Coin de la rue de Savoye proche les Gds Augustins   I

SEMIRAMIS

BABYLON — CA. 810 BC

"She had gardens suspended between the sky and the earth," Herodotus wrote of Semiramis. This beautiful, powerful queen built an empire and revived Babylon, whose splendor had faded under Assyrian rule.

Historians associate Semiramis with Queen Sammurramat, regent of Assyria after the death of her husband, King Shamsi-Adad V. So the legendary queen did exist, though the famous hanging gardens of Babylon, of which Herodotus wrote, are also credited to Nebuchadnezzar. Still, in Persian and Median folklore Semiramis is venerated as one of the greatest queens of all time, and the Greeks have handed down her legend.

In faraway Syria, near a city called Ashgelon, there was a lake over which reigned a goddess, Derceto, who was a mermaid. This fresh-water siren had offended the great goddess Ishtar, who punished her by making her fall passionately in love with one of the city's young men. Derceto could not resist this shameful love for a mortal and married him. But when she had given birth to a daughter, she woke from this love as from a dream, killed her husband, and abandoned the child in the desert.

Ishtar sent doves to care for the little girl. Some covered her with their wings, others stole milk and cheese from shepherds to feed her. The shepherds became aware of the losses and hid in order to surprise the thieves. Wondrous was their surprise when they saw the doves. They followed them and discovered the most beautiful little girl they had ever seen. They took her to their chief, who adopted her and named her Semiramis, "the dove child."

Onnes, an officer of the Assyrian king, met Semiramis while visiting the region and fell madly

Semiramis hard at work — an unusual interpretation of the Babylonian beauty in a 17th century French engraving.

in love with the young girl, whose beauty matched her intelligence. They married. Semiramis followed her husband to court and bore him two sons.

She accompanied her husband on many campaigns and one day, at the head of a small troop, took part in an attack on a city. Thanks to her the Assyrians were able to enter the town and win the battle. With great pride, Onnes spoke of his wife's valor in the field to the Assyrian king, Ninus. The king wished to meet this wonderful woman, and when he did, he was filled with desire for her. That evening, during a banquet cel-

Queen of a powerful empire, Semiramis found time to pursue her favorite pleasures; here she hunts lions at the gates of Babylon.

The queen and her ladies-in-waiting at a banquet in Nineveh, before the restoration of Babylon. Assyrian bas-relief, ca. 645 BC.

ebrating the victory, Ninus proposed that he give Onnes a princess of royal blood for wife in exchange for Semiramis. Onnes refused, sought out his wife, and suggested that they flee. But Semiramis had other ideas. She married King Ninus the next day and became queen. Her husband, mad with sorrow, hanged himself from the pole in his tent.

Semiramis bore a son, Ninyas, heir to the throne. The king died soon afterward; legend suggests that Semiramis forced destiny's hand by a judicial use of poison. Once on the throne, she was not the kind of woman to be content with simply governing the kingdom fate had placed in her hands. She needed to extend, to conquer, to build.

She began by transferring the Assyrian capital to Babylon in order to revive the dying but for-

merly magnificent city. She surrounded Babylon with great walls and built the hanging gardens, creating one of the seven wonders of the ancient world. Then she toured her empire, founding new cities and building new roads.

Upon her return, she realized her son was plotting to overthrow her. She so loved Ninyas — even to the point of incest, it seems — that she decided not to punish him. Instead she sent him north with an army, for according to Assyrian custom he had to gain the throne by making war.

Babylon, situated in the Tigris and Euphrates basin, was at the height of its glory. Merchandise from all over the world was sold in the bazaars, and riches spread. Semiramis wanted to undertake the conquest of India, but in the end had to admit to defeat.

In spite of all her preoccupations, Semiramis still found time for pleasures and for love. Insatiable, the beautiful queen collected lovers but managed not to shock her people, who believed her to be an incarnation of Ishtar, goddess of love. She presided as high priestess over the goddess' cult and organized sacred prostitution. Excitement

in the city reached its zenith during the celebrations dedicated to Ishtar. Under the influence of wine and incense, social barriers broke down. Unlawful love was permitted for a week, while Semiranis withdrew to the temple to perform the sacred rites.

During one such period, torrential rains came and the Tigris overflowed. Rats invaded the city and a plague struck the people, soon spreading to the court. Profiting from the panic in the populace, the priests tried to overthrow the queen. However, Semiramis' chief minister was watching over the city during the queen's seclusion in the temple. He summoned the priests to a boat, pretending to be their supporter, and drowned them. The city was perfectly under control when the queen reappeared.

Semiramis's son returned from war and she duly handed over her power to him. She meticulously put things in order . . . and then disappeared forever. Some versions of the legend say she retired to the mountains to die, others that "the dove child" was metamorphosed into a dove, the sacred bird of Ishtar.

DIDO

NORTH AFRICA — 9TH CENTURY BC

To bring about the encounter of Dido and Aeneas in the *Aeneid*, the Roman poet Virgil used literary license and dated
the founding of Carthage during the Trojan War. Illustration from a 15th century Italian manuscript.

The Tyrian princess Elissa was called Dido, "the Wanderer," by Latin historians. Her wanderings took her to the North African coast, where she founded Carthage, the city that ruled the Mediterranean for centuries. This alone would earn her a place in history, but it was as the tragic heroine of Virgil's *Aeneid* that she became legend.

The princess' story began in the prosperous Phoenician capital of Tyre, reknowned for its sailors' courage and its merchants' cleverness. When King Tyron died, he was succeeded by his son Pygmalion. Pygmalion's sister, Princess Elissa, was so beautiful that she could have chosen any husband she liked; but, following custom, she

married Acerbas, her mother's uncle.

The greedy, jealous Pygmalion coveted Acerbas' wealth, becoming more and more obsessed with the idea of possessing it as each day passed. Finally, he cut his brother-in-law's throat; but Acerbas, rightly suspicious, had taken the precaution of burying his treasure. When Elissa learned of her husband's murder, she was mad with pain and horror. She disowned her brother and swore that he would never get his hands on Acerbas' fortune.

But she kept her intentions to herself as she prepared to flee Tyre, leading her brother to believe that she would join him and live at the palace. When the king's messengers came to escort her to her new home, she convinced them to help her take some of her belongings aboard a ship first. Believing that these possessions included the coveted treasure, the servants willingly accompanied her on board — and the ship set sail.

The king discovered the ruse too late: Elissa was already approaching the coast of Cyprus. He wanted to send troops in pursuit, but was dissuaded by his soothsayers. "Elissa," they told him, "is destined to found a new city, which will surpass Tyre in glory."

On Cyprus, the high priest of Jupiter and his family joined Elissa, providing her with additional ships for her journey. And from among the many people waving goodbye to the expedition, she abducted eighty young maidens, to provide her men with wives.

When the ships arrived within sight of the African coast, Elissa knew that the land before them was their destination. She bade her companions disembark on a beach and they were soon surrounded by a peaceful, welcoming crowd. The Africans were curious to learn where the travelers came from and how they had accomplished their voyage. Once the introductions were over, Elissa asked the natives to give them a piece of land where they could rest. "The space occupied by the skin of a cow would be enough to set up our camp," she affirmed.

The Africans agreed to this bargain, and she sacrificed a cow that evening. The Phoenicians spent the next days cutting the cow's skin into very thin strips, then sewing the strips together, end to end. Elissa rolled the long, thin thong into a ball and presented it to the Africans, saying, "Here is the cow's skin, which will define the limits of our land." The thong easily encircled an

According to Virgil's epic, Dido committed suicide in despair when Aeneas departed for Italy.

area large enough for a small town. Both amazed and amused at her ingenuity, the African chief gave her the land. This is how the errant princess founded Carthage, which in Phoenician means "new town."

The white walls of Carthage soon rose on a hill between the desert sands and Mediterranean waves. The city drew inhabitants from great distances, and under Dido's benevolent authority it became rich and powerful. According to Virgil, it was favored by Juno, queen of the gods, sister-wife of Jupiter.

Dido's tragic end was immortalized by the 3rd century Roman historian Justin as well as by Virgil, but they told conflicting stories. Justin recounted how Iarbas, king of the neighboring no-

mads, fell in love with Dido and threatened war against Carthage if she would not marry him. The Carthaginian dignitaries beseeched her to sacrifice herself for her city's safety, but the queen, faithful to her dead Acerbas, interpreted their request loosely. She had a funeral pyre built at the town gates, climbed to the top, and declared, "Submissive to your wishes, I am going to join my husband." And with that, she stabbed herself.

Taking liberties with history, Virgil, in his famous epic poem the *Aeneid,* placed the founding of Carthage during the Trojan War, which actually happened some two centuries later.

In Virgil's story, Aeneas fled the flaming Troy and arrived in Carthage; his ultimate destination was Italy, which the gods had promised him. Dido organized a magnificent feast in honor of the Trojans, and listened to Aeneas' tales of their adventures and the woes of Troy. The prince offered Dido gifts; in return, she offered him hospitality for as long as it would take to rebuild his damaged fleet. For though she would not admit it, the queen had fallen victim to Aeneas' charm.

While they sojourned in Carthage, the Trojans often took part in their hosts' sport and relaxation. One day during a hunt, a violent storm broke out suddenly. As everyone searched for shelter, Dido and Aeneas arrived coincidentally at the same cave; and while the storm raged they confessed their love for each other.

With Aeneas at her side, Dido had regained happiness and hope; she reassured herself with the thought that the weather was too bad for him to take to the sea again. But the gods were against her. They called Aeneas to accomplish the noble fate they had reserved for him, to create a new nation in Italy. Resolute in the face of Dido's tears and pleading, he prepared his fleet for departure.

Dido had an enormous funeral pyre built — to burn her memories of her faithless lover, she said. At dawn she saw the Trojan fleet, sails billowing, leave the shores of Carthage. She climbed to the top of the pyre and, with Aeneas' sword, killed herself. Aeneas's last sight of Carthage was its walls, glowing red from the flames of the pyre.

"Bau-le!" The child is dead.

Pokou threw a last long look at the Komoé River, into which she had just thrown her only child, and grieved. But her people were saved. She had brought them to a beautiful country, which today is called the Ivory Coast.

Abla Pokou was the niece of Osei Tutu, the greatest king of the Ashanti. Before his rule began in the late 17th century, the Akan people were widely scattered and divided into small kingdoms. Osei Tutu united most of the tribes and took power during an immense gathering in which a seat made of gold was placed in front of him while a resounding voice proclaimed him sole ruler of the new, united Ashanti kingdom.

The Ashanti throne descended through the female line. Only a niece or sister of the king was considered worthy of giving him an heir. The fortunate chosen one, who became the queen mother, shared power with her son.

The high priest noticed Abla. He thought to make her the future first lady of the realm and trained her to fulfill this role. As the years went by, he became very attached to the surprisingly intelligent and gifted little girl. He had a feeling that her life would be something out of the ordinary, even out of the ordinary for royal princesses. But one day Osei Tutu was ambushed. Abla's elder brother assumed leadership of the Ashantis for twenty years.

Abla Pokou took her time choosing a husband. And then she was quick to repudiate him, as only a woman of her rank could do, when her belly remained disappointingly flat. Single and barren, she ended up causing trouble and uneasiness at the palace. Pregnant women avoided her look. Men were suspicious of her wit and judgment.

The king and his armies were far away at war when enemies took advantage of their absence to invade the Ashanti and march on their capital, Kumasi. Abla Pokou took over, organized the flight of the city's inhabitants — and then remained in the town, deciding she had nothing to lose but her life. She was taken hostage. Her brother returned and was furious to learn that of

QUEEN POKOU
WEST AFRICA — 18TH CENTURY

Like this woman, Pokou was of the Ashanti tribe, which lives in present-day Ghana. Her uncle, the great Osei Tutu, had succeeded in unifying the kingdom, and she had a brilliant future ahead of her.

all the royal princesses, only Pokou the barren was still alive. Still, he sent a warrior, Tano, to rescue her. Tano so successfully accomplished his task that, having brought Pokou home, he married her. Several months later, she announced that she was expecting a baby.

The king fell ill. He named a successor, then died. Unfortunately, the successor was soon assassinated by a rival, Kwissi. When Kwissi took

Pokou had to sacrifice her only child to save her people. Wooden cult statuette representing a pregnant woman.

his place on the Ashanti seat of gold, Pokou refused to support him. She preferred to go in search of a hospitable land where she could settle, accompanied by the Ashanti families, whose members felt as she did. Kwissi tried to persuade her to stay. When diplomacy failed, he sent his army to track down the runaways.

Refusing to submit to the authority of a usurper, Pokou led a band of rebels to the west. After many hardships, they reached the uncrossable Komoé River.

With Pokou in the lead, the column made its way west. They passed through interminable, dense forests, escaping the claws and teeth of the panther only to confront the jaws of giant ants and the coils of boa constrictors. They passed through regions filled with elephants and cunning serpents. After many moons of difficult travel, beset by dangers and plagued by illness, the band reach the banks of a raging river, the Komoé. They found neither ford nor canoes for crossing. Kwissi's army was still pursuing them.

The next day, they were told that the gods of the waters and the river demanded the sacrifice of a child in exchange for a safe crossing. A sick woman and her baby were brought forth, but Pokou took pity on her. In any case, she knew the gods would not accept such a poor sacrifice. She threw her own son into the waters of the Komoé.

Immediately, as if by magic, an enormous tree stretched over the river to form a bridge, and even the river animals, the hippopotamuses and crocodiles, offer their help and carried people across on their backs. Pokou and her followers were saved. When Kwissi's army tried to follow them, the bridge disappeared.

Abla became Aura, Queen Pokou. She was also called Asae, "the conqueror." From that time forth, her people have been called the Baule in memory of her child.

Tired and saddened by all she had been through, Pokou died shortly after founding the kingdom. Her niece, Akwabenua Bensua, finished her work, but perished while conquering the Youre people. Power returned to men, rivalries started up, and the Baule lost their unity.

The legend of Pokou is transmitted orally, so there are many versions of the story. But everyone recognizes Pokou's importance. To the Baule she represents what Abraham and Aeneas represent in Western civilization.

MARIANNE
FRANCE — 18TH CENTURY

"She will have her revenge — long live the sound of the guns!"
chant the peasants, workers, and intellectuals joining
forces behind Marianne in an 1894 illustration.

The French Republic could not have found a more beautiful symbol: a woman of a thousand faces, called Marianne. At first ridiculed, she has come to be adored, cherished, coveted.

In 1789, with the storming of the Bastille, ancient values were cast aside to make way for new concepts. People sought ideals like reason and liberty, which were personified as goddesses, and a popular imagery developed around these themes. In 1792, another step forward was taken: the king was replaced by the republic. Now government was accessible to all, certainly — but it was too anonymous, too abstract.

The politically active Abbot Henri Grégoire was charged by the National Convention to develop a new seal for the infant republic. He proposed a feminine representation of Liberty, "so that our emblems, circulating around the globe, present to all peoples the cherished images of republican liberty and pride." His idea was well-received, and it was decreed that "the seal of the State would be changed and bear as its personality France, with the features of a woman dressed in old-fashioned clothes, standing, carrying a spade in her right hand, and topped with a Phrygian cap or cap of liberty, her left hand leaning on a pile of weapons; at her feet a rudder."

At first she was nameless, this woman whose Phrygian cap was like those worn by liberated slaves in ancient Rome. She symbolized both liberty and the republic for which the people had fought so hard. Busts were cast of her, statues raised in her name throughout France. Her admirers felt no need to name her, but the detractors of the republic thought that if they gave her a name it would diminish her symbolism and enable them to ridicule the new government. They called her Marianne, a very Catholic and very common name combining the names of the Virgin and her mother. To their surprise, the nickname caught on, for to the people it eloquently symbolized the origins of the new regime: it recalled the streets, the most deprived social classes. To the nobility, Marianne symbolized the riffraff who did not deserve power, and they hoped she would fall ill.

Marianne as the queen of spades on
a wooden "revolutionary" playing card.

Marianne forces her way in. *Dernier Conseil des
ex-ministres* (The Ex-Ministers' Last Council), illustration
by Honoré Daumier.

Famous faces have modeled for modern
Mariannes: here, Brigitte Bardot.

Marianne on the front page, in 1891.

Marianne as a cult object:
boxes featuring her portrait.

This soon occurred. The republic faltered and was ousted by the empire, which was followed by the restoration. The republican ideas of liberty, equality, and fraternity were relegated to the closet, and Marianne with them.

In 1848, a second revolution brought a second republic, but Marianne had to wait for her rebirth until the coup d'état in 1851 by Louis-Napoleon, the future Napoleon III. The republicans then regrouped in secret societies, with her name as their password:

"Do you know Marianne?"

"From the mountain."

"The time?"

"It's going to strike."

"The right?"

"To work."

"The vote?"

"Universal."

In 1856 the writer Félix Pyat, who opposed Napoleon III, printed a "Letter to Marianne," a hymn of praise to the republic. She began to be spoken of publicly; her name became an integral element of political language. She was given a mate, in the person of Jacques Bonhomme, who symbolized the working people. With the accession of the Commune in 1871, her physical image was rediscovered, complete with red cap. In the south of France, "mariannes," small red-capped statuettes, became as popular as daily bread. They

were sold first discreetly, then publicly, and some even found their way into the town halls.

The proclamation of the Third Republic in 1875 made her almost an official figure — one who has continued to evolve without growing old. The poet Paul Verlaine would be surprised if he saw the young and beautiful Marianne of the 1990s, for in his sonnet "Buste pour Mairies" (Bust for the Town Halls) in 1881, he described her as an old woman, nearly a century old, hairless, toothless, and worn out from too wild a youth.

THE PYTHIA

GREECE
7TH CENTURY BC — 4TH CENTURY AD

For a thousand years the Pythia spoke for the oracle of Apollo at Delphi. Seated on her three-legged stool above the abyss, she was driven into a frenzy until she spewed forth the future, screamed the unknown, spit out the divine.

In her delirium — believed to be a state of divine transport — the Pythia uttered incomprehensible cries, which attendant priests interpreted as the oracle's divine prophecy. Her rantings drew multitudes craving knowledge of the fate the gods had chosen for them. The many who would undertake no action without consulting her ranged from fabulously wealthy kings, like Croesus the Lydian, to more modest individuals from Greece and Asia Minor. The Pythia's oracular pronouncements carried great weight with intellectuals, too: Plato consulted her on moral and religious matters, while Socrates reportedly received his famous dictum, "Know thyself," from her lips. For the Pythia was the voice of the oracle, and through the oracle spoke Apollo, choirmaster of the Muses, protector of science and poetry.

But the oracle's pronouncements were revered long before Apollo came forward to claim the Delphic abyss as his mouthpiece; its words were attributed to a succession of ancient deities, including the earth goddess Gaia. According to Diodorus, a Greek historian of the 1st century BC, the oracular power of the abyss was discovered by, of all things, a herd of goats. Each time they approached its edge, they began to bleat and jump about strangely. Curious, their herder approached the abyss. Immediately overcome by "enthusiasm," which in Greek means divine transport, he began to predict the future.

This miraculous phenomenon gradually acquired ceremonial trappings. Initially, people would approach the edge of the crevasse and re-

The Pythia in a frenzy.

ceive the oracle's prophecies themselves. But in their ecstatic state several fell to their deaths, so it was decided for safety's sake to install a single prophetess to tell the future for all.

Eventually Apollo appeared in Delphi and decided to take over the oracle. To do so, Homer tells us, Apollo was obliged to "kill with his powerful bow the female Dragon, the enormous and gigantic Beast." The beast in question was Python, Gaia's monstrous serpent, which guarded the oracular abyss. Pytho was the ancient name of the oracle, and "pythian" came to mean "related to the oracle of Apollo." The serpent's death transformed the Earth goddess' ancient sanctuary. The woman who prophesied there became known as the Pythia.

Chosen for life, the Pythia lived alone, isolated from all social contacts, in a house within the sanctuary. She was initially selected from among the most beautiful young maidens of the region; her family, whether rich or poor, had to be above reproach. The one chosen was considered the bride of Apollo, and had to remain a virgin. This system worked well until the beauty of one Pythia inflamed a Thessalian who had come to consult her. He kidnapped and raped her. "Following this scandal," Diodorus wrote, "the Delphians decreed that the prophetess would no longer be a maiden, but a woman over fifty years of age; she must dress, however, like a young girl, as if to recall the memory of the former prophetess."

If married, the woman had to live apart from her husband once chosen as Pythia. In addition, she had to have the pure heart and innocent mind of a maiden. As the Greek moralist Plutarch observed, "when descending into the prophetic site, she takes no art or any other learning or talent with her. It is truly with a virgin soul that she approaches the god."

Passive and docile, the Pythia was essentially a medium. Controlling her power were Apollo's priests, who noted down her incoherent remarks and turned them into calculatingly obscure prophecies.

Mediator between the gods and humans, the Pythia delivered the words of the oracle, and all antiquity listened.

It was the earth goddess who first inspired the oracle of Delphi; then Apollo took over the sanctuary and the Pythia spoke for him.

But she was the uncontested star of the ritual. She would begin by cleansing herself at the Castalian spring at the foot of Mount Parnassus; then, in the temple, she purified herself in steam scented with laurel leaves and barley. She drank water from the sacred spring Cassotis. Immaculate, with a laurel wreath around her forehead, she proceeded to the temple's subterranean rooms with her cortege of priests and consultants. This was where she encountered the god, above the famous crevasse. She mounted her tripod and the client asked his question, either orally or in writing. Perhaps affected by the carbon dioxide fumes emanating from the crevasse — for the explanation of the "divine transport" may have been that simple — the Pythia's reason began to cloud; she started ranting and raving incomprehensibly, and eventually fell into a trance. Occasionally, her attacks were so violent that she died.

The oracle began to fade in importance after the Roman conquest, but it was the Byzantine emperor Theodosius who put an end to the cult in the 4th century AD. The last Pythia carried her secrets to her grave, and today, only tourists seek advice at the sanctuary of Delphi.

THE VIRGIN MARY

JUDEO-CHRISTIAN CIVILIZATION

Mary submitted to divine will and the miracle of Jesus' birth came to pass. By atoning for Eve's sin, Mary became a near-divinity to whom people could pray when they wished to draw nearer to their Creator. *Virgin and Child* by Leonard Foujita.

A great sign appeared in the sky: a woman clothed in sunshine, the moon under her feet and a crown of twelve stars on her head. (Revelation 12:1)

The vision of Saint John gives us an image of the Virgin that has lasted two thousand years. She is called by many names: Queen of Heaven; Theotokos, the God-bearer, or Mother of God; Our Lady, the Madonna, Mater Dolorosa, Mater Ecclesiae. Under any of them, she represents one of the greatest myths of Western civilization.

If the Bible tells us repeatedly of the coming of Mary and the birth of her son, it is apocryphal texts that fill in the rest of her story. Her birth in Nazareth was itself the result of divine intervention: her parents, Joachim and Anne, had not been able to have a child, and Anne was old when an angel announced that she would give birth. The child was a girl, and the proud parents named her Mary. To show their gratitude to God, Joachim and Anne gave the three-year-old Mary to the temple. There she professed her desire to remain

a virgin, and she grew up among other virgins. When she reached adolescence, the priests wanted her to marry despite her objections.

This account from the *Protevangelium of James*, a non-canonical work from the 2nd century that reinforced the role of Mary for the early church, continues with the high priest, perplexed, consulting the Lord, then summoning young men from the family of David and promising that Mary would be given as wife only to whomever the Holy Spirit chose. The successful suitor was called

Joseph. Advanced in years, he already had three children. Soon after the couple became engaged, Mary was visited by the Angel Gabriel. "Hail, thou that art highly favored! The Lord is with thee; blessed art thou among women," he told her.

These first words of the Annunciation, to return to the canonical account, are echoed in the "Ave Maria," or Hail Mary, the prayer to Mary. The Virgin was bewildered by the angel's message: she was to have a son, Jesus; "he will be called the son of the Highest. . . . He shall reign over the house of Jacob forever, and of his kingdom there shall be no end." But how could Mary have a child, she, who, in her own words, had never known a man?

"With God nothing is impossible," the angel declared. Mary submitted to divine will, and the mystery was accomplished. Mary went to visit a cousin, Elizabeth, who, although old and reputedly barren, was also going to have a baby. Mary stayed there for three months. When she returned to Nazareth, her pregnancy was apparent.

Joseph, ignorant of the secret that Mary had shared only with Elizabeth, tried to repudiate his fiancée. But the angel appeared to Joseph while he slept to reveal the mystery to him; reassured on the score of Mary's purity, he agreed to marry her. Later, Joseph and Mary left for Bethlehem to be counted in a census ordered by Caesar Augustus. There the Savior was born.

Mary was probably part of the group of pious women who accompanied Jesus and his disciples on their journeys, although the gospels do not mention her by name in this context. It was at her behest that her son performed his first miracle, the transformation of water into wine during the wedding at Cana.

During the Passion of Christ, "When Jesus therefore saw his mother, and the disciple standing by, whom he loved, he saith unto his mother, Woman, behold thy son! Then saith he to the disciple, Behold thy mother! And from that hour that disciple took her unto his own home" (John 19:26). At Pentecost she stood among the dis-

Though she conceived without sin, she carried her child for nine months, as do all women, yet she is rarely depicted in this condition. 14th century polychrome stone carving in Lisbon.

ciples and received the Holy Spirit, personifying the church itself as the mother of all believers.

Mary remained for some time under John's care, but we do not know how or where her life ended. Relics, supposedly from the earthly remains of early church figures, abounded in the first several centuries of Christianity, but Mary's were never among them. The Assumption, her miraculous summons to heaven, is an idea developed late in Christian theology. The 6th century Byzantine emperor Maurice proclaimed August 15 a holiday to commemorate the event, but not until 1950 was it was established as church dogma by Pope Pius XII, who at the same time promulgated the dogma of Mary's Immaculate Conception, her freedom from original sin.

The cult of Mary was flourishing by the 4th century AD. In the Middle Ages it manifested itself in the concepts of virtuous woman and chaste love, idealized throughout Europe in the songs of the troubadours. The Virgin of the 13th and 14th centuries was jealous and possessive. Then, when the Franciscans conferred on her the virtues of humility and poverty, she ceased to represent matriarchy and became instead a symbol of passive and submissive femininity.

By bowing to God's will, Mary atones for the sin of Eve and receives eternal life. "Behold the

This 1908 picture from the Pao-ting region in northern China portrays Our Lady of Tung Lu, an apparition of the Virgin in the costume of the Chinese empress protecting Christians during the Boxer Rebellion of 1900.

handmaid of the Lord; be it unto me according to your word," she says to Gabriel at the Annunciation. In *The Second Sex*, the French feminist and philosopher Simone de Beauvoir wrote: "It is the supreme masculine victory that is accomplished in the cult of Mary: it is the rehabilitation of woman by the completion of her defeat."

MARIA LIONZA
VENEZUELA

An altar dedicated to Maria Lionza, a Venezuelan goddess
associated with a court of saints and significant historical
figures, who are also worshiped in her cult.

"Maria Lionza, bring me a small miracle, and I will bring you a bouquet of flowers," sings Rubén Blades. In Venezuela, one may believe in God and also worship Maria Lionza — goddess, queen, and mother.

Long ago, before the Spanish conquest of Venezuela, an Indian chief of the Caquetios tribe lived in the Yaracuy region. This chieftain had a blue-eyed daughter, who, according to superstition, would bring bad luck to the tribe. But she was so beautiful that he did not have the heart to kill her, so he hid her in his hut.

When she was grown, she emerged into the daylight and went to a lagoon, in whose waters she gazed upon her beautiful face for the first time. The lagoon's owner, an anaconda snake, beheld the virgin and fell in love with her. The serpent carried her off, but a terrible punishment descended upon him: he began to inflate and inflate, until he filled the whole of the lagoon. The waters overflowed and flooded the tribe's territory, and the Indians perished. The monster burst. The young girl became mistress of the water, the patroness of fish. Later she extended her powers over all the flora and fauna of the neighboring regions.

Other central Venezuelan legends confirm the existence of a goddess-patroness who was the object of Indian cult worship. All these legends were eventually combined into one myth, perhaps at the time of the Spanish conquest, as is suggested by this story told by Veit-Tané, the current high priestess of Maria Lionza's cult:

Thanks to her faculties as a medium, a beautiful girl from the Caquetios tribe was named priestess of an aboriginal cult. When the conquistadors arrived, she fled to the mountains and called upon her people to defend their lands, but the Indians proclaimed her to be a witch. She, however, was destined to help the Indians in their struggle. She received the supernatural forces of the Divine Being and appeared before them. When the missionaries heard of this, they told the Indians that the miraculous apparition was the Virgin Mary. They baptized her Maria de la Onza, after

A statue of Maria Lionza astride a tapir greet visitors at the entrance to Caracas. At the foot of the statue by Alejandro Colina the faithful lay offerings to win the intercession of the goddess.

a tapir-like animal of the Venezuelan jungle. The name was eventually corrupted to Maria Lionza.

The cult of Maria Lionza is a marvelous example of syncretism; it is a mixture of magical and religious rites that absorbed Christian moral values. One prays to God but at the same time one makes a pact with Maria Lionza. The saints, like spirits, serve as intermediaries between humans and the Divine Being. As a water deity, Maria Lionza protects fish, and as a daughter of the waters she attracts admirers, whom she rewards. She is the generous Earth mother who brings fertility to women and the fields. Like the Virgin Mary, she is called queen. When she takes possession of a medium, her followers recite the Hail Mary. Mary Lionza merges with the Virgin of Coromoto, the patroness of Venezuela.

Maria Lionza does not stand alone but is surrounded by a completely heterogeneous court. First, she is part of the "Venezuelan Trinity" with the Indian Guaicapuro, a great chieftain who fought the Spanish, and "Negro Felipe," a Cuban

who fought for Venezuelan independence. Next come her saints — who are various other Indian chieftains — and her vassals, masters of the rivers and the mountains. Then comes the Latin American liberator Simón Bolívar and his companion, "El Negro Primero." To this array more recent historical figures have been added, such as John Kennedy, Stalin, Hitler, and Pope John XXIII. Then there are the seven "African Powers" who come from the Cuban *santeria*, African deities assimilated with Christian saints. The influence of these powers is such that some purists maintain that Maria Lionza herself has denounced them and has forbidden her followers to work with them. The cult, which has spread to Guiana and the Andes, is undergoing diversification and now includes Hindu and Arab courts.

The cult deities are manifested through the offices of a medium who goes into a trance after swallowing and then vomiting seven glasses of warm water, then inhaling tobacco smoke seven times. An officiant called the *banco* directs the ceremony, interprets the medium's words, and prescribes to the customer. If the customer follows the *banco*'s orders, his problem will be solved or he will be healed. Maria Lionza protects people from the evil eye, and the *bancos* claim that they only appeal to her to do good, though the magic is not always "white."

To take full advantage of the magic, the customer may purchase charms, coins, or other talismans. To attract a loved one, the customer will visit a *banco* whose spirits are specialized in affairs of the heart and buy oils such as "Catch Me" and "Cling Cling," scents such as "Perfume of the Goddess," or lotions such as "The Sphere of Man." The market is flourishing.

Maria Lionza lives in a palace hidden in the mountains near the source of the Yaracuy River. She sits on a throne of serpents, with a crowned lion and a goat beside her. Her followers come to purify themselves in the spring, which is a place of adoration, and throw offerings into the river. During Holy Week, as many as forty thousand worshipers flock to the site.

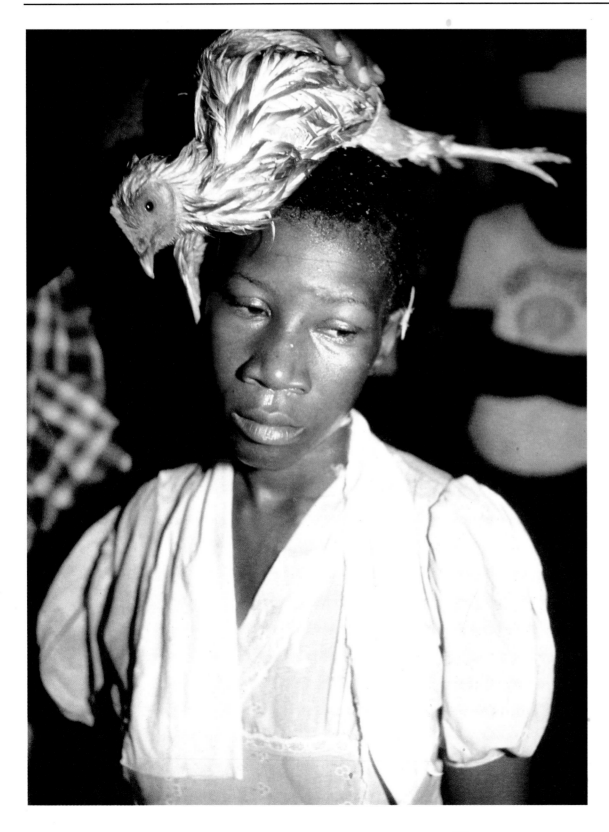

EZILI

HAITI

Although she is sometimes confused with the Virgin Mary, Ezili is to the voodoo pantheon what Aphrodite is to Olympus. She is the goddess of love, dressed all in blue.

Ezili is one of the invisibles, the loa, which came to what is now Haiti at the beginning of the 17th century when the first slaves arrived in Santo Domingo, as the island was then called. These people from ancient Dahomey, today's Benin, brought with them their myths, their gods, and their beliefs, which over time combined with other traditions.

The word voodoo comes from "vodun," which means god, spirit, or divinity in Fon, the language of Dahomey. Although rooted in Africa, voodoo developed in the Caribbean and is syncretic, a fusion of different beliefs. Voodoo practices are not easily understood by the uninitiated, but the basic tenets of the cult are simple. Through intermediaries and initiatory rites, the spirits are called up to help in daily life, resolve problems, and improve the quality of life. God is the one and only and great master, but between God and man are the dead, the spirits, and the *loa*. Ezili belongs to this last category. She may be good or evil, according to circumstances.

Originally a seawater spirit, Ezili has come to personify feminine grace and beauty. She is the goddess both of romantic and physical love, a voluptuous woman in a religion that has no concept of sin. Ezili is pictured as a lovely mulatto who lives in luxury and indulges herself in pleasure. She wears beautiful clothing and never hesitates to spend money to satisfy her desires, even to

Attractive, sensuous, diabolically seductive,
Ezili likes blue dresses, jewelry, and especially men.
She can be benevolent or malevolent,
according to the circumstances.

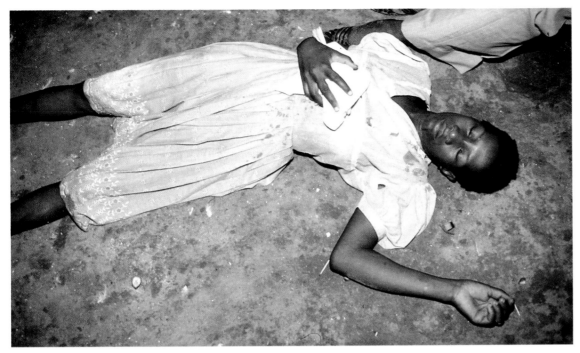

Ezili is a *loa* who takes possession of a human soul when it
enters into communication with God or when Ezili wants to contact humans.
The subject goes into a trance and "becomes" Ezili.

The chosen woman or man becomes Ezili's substitute and instrument. She can also materialize. Witnesses declare that they have seen Ezili. She appears in dreams to her followers, usually in the form of a relative or friend who acts as her intermediary. Voodoo priests and priestesses can make the goddess appear in a jug so that they may speak with her. She also has a special relationship with some of her male followers: she marries them. The poor husband has obligations he must fulfill all his life. For instance, he may not have sexual relations with his mortal wife on Thursday, because that is the goddess' sacred day.

Each *vèvè*, or symbolic drawing, represents a saint
of the voodoo pantheon. The *vèvè* of Ezili,
goddess of love, is of course a heart.

the point of extravagance. Slightly snobbish, she sometimes speaks French with an affected accent. Since she has no morals, she has an active sex life. She was the concubine of the serpent god and mistress of both the guardian of the temple and the master of thunder and lightening. Guédonibo, he who watches over the graves, unsuccessfully pursues her. Since he is black, he has no hope of success with her.

In each sanctuary a place is reserved for Ezili where her personnel things, such as her jewelry and blue dresses, are kept. During the ritual, the man or woman possessed by Ezili is led to her dressing room, where she finds everything she needs to wash and do her hair, nails, and makeup. While she is getting ready, the choir of the faithful chants:

Oh, what a beautiful woman
Is Ezili!
Oh, I shall give you a present
Before you leave, Abobo. . . .

Elizi emerges from her dressing room in all her glory. Seductively she walks forward, swaying her hips, flashing her brilliant eyes at the men, accepting a caress here, a kiss there. She looks at the women, her rivals, and laughs at them. She must receive presents, and not cheap presents, before she returns to the sanctuary, followed by her exhilarated worshipers.

In Haiti, symbolic drawings called *vèvè* fulfill the functions generally attributed to statuettes and images. Since the divinities appear in human form and as other living creatures, they do not need to be represented. Ezili's *vèvè* is a heart drawn on the ground with flour, ashes, or coffee grounds. Once assured of the divinity's presence, one may make offerings or sacrifices to her. Each *loa* has a symbolic color; Ezili's is blue. For voodoo practitioners, Christian medaillons of the Virgin represent Marie Ezili.

When the divinity wants to enter into communication with humans, she possesses someone.

Ezili is nevertheless a benevolent spirit. But beware her opposite, Erzuliégé, who is really dangerous. And the great Ezili must not be confused with Ezili-fréda, an old rheumatic woman who walks painfully on her knees, supported by a cane.

MÉLUSINE

EUROPE

Fair or dark, stern or gay, Mélusine possesses a thousand faces, each beautiful in its own way. She loves to live in the mortal world, in the palaces she has built. But beware of her: Mélusine is accursed.

The legend of this siren was already widely known when Jean d'Arras recounted it in the *Romance of Mélusine* at the end of the 14th century. According to the original Irish legend, Mélusine was a Scot; and if sometimes we find her misrepresented as a Scythian, it is because the Irish words for Scot and Scythian sound very similar. (This mistake has been made in other Irish myths as well.)

The story of Mélusine begins, of course, with her parents: One day a king called Elinas was strolling through a forest when he heard a marvelous voice singing. Following the sound, he came to a fountain. There was the singer, a beautiful woman named Pressine. Overwhelmed by her beauty and her voice, King Elinas begged her to marry him. She accepted his suit on one condition: that he agree never to see her in childbed. He promised to respect her wishes, and they were wed. The king and queen were very happy, even if their subjects occasionally wondered where such a wise, sensible queen could have come from.

Pressine gave birth to triplet girls: Mélusine, Méliot, and Palatine. Mataquas, the king's son by a prior marriage, was jealous of his stepmother and stepsisters, and set out to make mischief. He aroused the king's curiosity to such a degree that the king disregarded his oath and entered his wife's lying-in chamber. Pressine cursed him for his transgression, vowing that her descendants would avenge her.

For having broken his oath to respect her privacy on Saturdays, Raymondin lost Mélusine: she was transformed into a flying sea serpent and disappeared. Color engraving for *The Romance of Mélusine* by Jean d'Arras.

Comment melufine fen volla de raimondin en forme dung serpent du chafteau de lufignen par vne fenestre.

She fled the kingdom to take refuge with her sister, queen of the Isle of Avalon, also called the Lost Island. There she raised her daughters. When they reached the age of fifteen, she explained to them who their father was and how his action had cast them into exile.

Mélusine immediately sought revenge and persuaded her sisters to help her. She used her magic powers to imprison King Elinas inside the mountain of Northumberland. But Pressine was furious that her daughters had acted without her permission, and called down curses upon them: Méliot would be imprisoned in a castle in Armenia, with only a sparrow hawk for company. During three days each year she would be permitted the visit of a knight, but if her chastity were breached, other punishments would follow. Palatine was to join her father in his mountain prison, to await the day when a crusading knight would free her.

As for Mélusine, "every Saturday, you will become a sea serpent from your navel down to your toes," her mother decreed. The human-turned-nymph would be allowed to take a husband and live like other women, but her husband must never see her in her serpentine state.

According to d'Arras, the cursed young nymph roamed in search of a husband. In her travels, she met others like herself in a forest in the French province of Poitou. She decided to settle there, at the base of a fountain, to wait for the knight who the other nymphs prophesied would come to rescue her. The savior in question did not take long to appear, but he was in a terrible state: the knight, Raymondin, son of the count of the forest, had been hunting a boar with his uncle, the count of Poitiers. In an attempt to kill the boar, Raymondin had accidentally dealt his uncle a mortal blow. Mélusine found him in the middle of the forest, lamenting his misfortune. She was so successful in comforting him that he proposed to her, and agreed to respect her privacy on Saturdays.

Following his wife's counsel, Raymondin asked his uncle's successor to give them "as much

The sea nymph Mélusine was the victim of a curse: every Saturday, the lower part of her body took on the characteristics of a sea serpent, and she had to conceal herself from her husband on pain of banishment from the mortal world.

land as they could enclose in the skin of a stag." By cutting the skin into thin strips and laying them end to end, the couple was able to claim a vast domain, where Mélusine built fortresses, churches, towns, and palaces. As the years passed, she gave birth to ten strong boys. Each had a strange deformity — an eye in the middle of a cheek, an abnormally long canine tooth — yet they all grew up to be valiant knights.

Finally, however, Mélusine's curse caught up with them. By chance, Raymondin's brother arrived on a Saturday for a visit. As Mélusine did not appear to carry out her duties as hostess, her husband was obliged to reveal the condition imposed on him at their marriage. His brother mocked him for his gullibility, saying that Mélusine was certain to be spending her Saturdays with a lover. Cut to the quick by this accusa-

tion, Raymondin chose to break his oath rather than live with uncertainty. He descended to the cave where his wife had withdrawn, and found her in a bathtub of green marble, naked, her nether regions ending in a serpentine tail.

Horrified that Raymondin had seen her, Mélusine cursed his descendants. Lamenting, she began to change: her skin turned to scales, her

Every time one of her descendants was about to die, Mélusine would appear and utter awful cries.

arms lengthened and grew into wings, and a serpent's tail eight feet long unfurled where her feet had been. Then she took flight and disappeared into the sky, uttering desolate cries.

Overcome by grief, Raymondin ended his days in a monastery. Mélusine was doomed to reappear at the castle only to mark the deaths of each of her descendants. Thus ends her terrible story.

THE LORELEI
GERMANY

At Bacharach, a blonde sorceress there was,
Who made all men perish from love.

So the French poet Guillaume Apollinaire described the Lorelei, and so we see her, a golden-haired girl whose irresistible song attracted the vessels of the Rhine and led them to shipwreck.

Though the legend has probably lived in the hearts of Rhine sailors since antiquity, the Lorelei we know dates from the beginning of the 19th century. The famous crag overhanging the waters of the Rhine downstream from Bacharach was the subject of legends long before the Lorelei appeared on the scene, however.

Situated at one of the most dangerous passes in the Rhine, the rock inspired fear and curiosity because of its echo, which was believed to possess the powers of an oracle. When ships approached, passengers shouted questions about their fates. According to anonymous 12th century verses, dwarfs perched on the rock sent back answers through the echo. The crag also figured in the epic poem the *Nibelungenlied*. The hero, Siegfried, possessed a treasure, but the villain, Hagen, killed Siegfried and threw the treasure into the Rhine not far from the echoing rock.

In 1801, in his novel *Godwi*, the German poet Clemens Brentano published a ballad, "Lora-Lay," set in medieval times. He claimed to have created the myth by leading his readers to believe that the Lorelei was a part of popular folklore. His heroine, "so beautiful and so slender," was summoned by the bishop on account of the havoc she was wreaking among the local menfolk.

My lord bishop, make me die;
I am weary of life,
For all must perish
Who gaze into my eyes.

German legend abounds in charming feminine creatures, benevolent and malevolent, who inhabit rivers, especially the Rhine. *The Daughters of the Rhine*, drawn in 1910 by Arthur Rackham.

The young girl, victim of an evil spell that was fatal even for her, had another reason to beg for

The echo of the crag called the Lorelei was already well-known in the Middle Ages. However, it was in the 19th century that life was given to the ill-fated sorceress by the German poet Brentano.

death: her lover had been unfaithful and had left her. But the bishop, charmed like all the others, could not bring himself to condemn her to death and sent her to a convent. On her way, she climbed a rock to take one last look at the waters of the Rhine. On the horizon she perceived a sail, and thought her lover was returning.

The most beautiful of maidens is perched
Up there, marvelous;
Her ornament of gold flashes lightening
As she combs her hair of gold.
Heine

My heart with joy is full,
That must, must be my love!
And then the lass bent down
And plunged into the Rhine.

To Brentano, who was twenty-three when he wrote the tale, the poor girl was the victim of her feelings and of her own gaze. She incarnated the curse of love. This theme was popular with other Romantics, who were fascinated by her at about the same age. Both Joseph Eichendorff and Apollinaire were twenty-two when they took up the tale, and the German poet Heinrich Heine was twenty-five. Eichendorff's contribution was significant because he added to the legend. In his version, put to music by Robert Schumann, the Lorelei is dressed in black with a white veil and wears a crown of pearls in her blond hair.

In Heine's version, the Lorelei is associated with the sirens of the Odyssey whose voices called sailors to their death. There is no longer anything about her magic gaze. Brentano's notion of the siren's fatal gaze was not taken up again until the 20th century. Apollinaire, inspired by the famous rock, wrote:

My heart becomes so tender — it is my lover
approaching
And then she leaned forward and fell in the
Rhine
For she had seen in the water the beauteous
Loreley,
Her eyes the color of the Rhine, her hair of sun.

Poor sailor! How could he resist the songs of the sirens of the Rhine?

CINDERELLA

Through the intervention of her fairy godmother,
Cinderella goes to the ball dressed in magical finery.

Cinderella's tale is told throughout the world. In each of its variations, she is portrayed as a victim, rescued from her sad fate by the forces of magic and her handsome prince.

It is impossible to determine where the story of Cinderella was first told. One of the oldest written versions of the tale comes from 9th century China. A 19th century scholar counted three hundred forty-five versions of the fairy tale, and further research has since doubled the number. The same themes run through all versions: sibling rivalry, the desirability of marriage as initiation into adult life, and the concept that virtue will be rewarded. For example, Koumba, the Senegalese Cinderella, has to perform all the thankless chores while her half-sisters spend their time figuring out how to catch husbands. Through patience, perseverance, and passage of a number of tests, Koumba wins the desirable young man.

The version best known in the Western world is certainly that of Charles Perrault, first published in 1697 and adapted into operas, ballets, and Walt Disney's perennially popular animated film. In this version, Cinderella's widowed father remarries a shrew with two daughters whose stupidity is matched by their spitefulness. After the death of Cinderella's father, nothing is too good for the two conceited, oafish stepsisters, and nothing too base for poor Cinderella, who is relegated to the role of servant and cleaning woman and has only the friendship of the small animals in the house. That Cinderella might accompany her two vain sisters to the royal ball is not even considered. Yet she is kind enough to help them put on their finery and even offers to dress their hair. After her sisters depart, a fairy godmother appears to Cinderella to suggest that she, too, attend the ball. With a wave of her magic wand, the fairy transforms Cinderella's rags into an elegant gown and her wooden shoes into fur slippers — later rendered through a mistranslation as the famous glass slippers. A pumpkin becomes her coach, a rat her coachman, and six mice and six lizards the horses and footmen.

foot into the slipper and pass her off as the beauty the prince seeks. But a little bird reveals the ruse.

An older European version was written in the early 1600s by Giambattista Basile, who in his *Pentamerone* calls the young maiden "Cinder Cat." In French she is "Cendrillon" and in German "Aschenputtel." All these names indicate that our heroine is perpetually dirty, covered in cinders from the hearth. Degraded and demeaned, taunted by her peers, Cinderella is in a situation with which

Modest and submissive, Cinderella sits
by the hearth while her vain stepsisters deck themselves out.

Midnight! Cinderella must leave the ball, in spite of the prince's pleas. Fortunately, she loses the slipper that will allow her beloved to find her again.

Cinderella is the belle of the ball and dances often with the prince. The ball lasts for three evenings. On the first two, she is careful to return home before midnight, the hour when her finery changes back into its original form. On the third night, she does not notice the time passing and has to hurry away as the clock strikes twelve, losing a slipper as she goes.

The prince, enchanted by her, sends his steward the next day to seek the maiden whose foot is dainty enough to fit the tiny slipper. The sisters try in vain, but Cinderella's foot slides effortlessly into the slipper and the prince takes her for his bride. Out of the goodness of her heart, she invites her sisters to live with her at the palace, and marries them off to two lords of the kingdom.

The brothers Grimm recorded another version of the story, with several significant differences from Perrault's. Their heroine is more assertive: she tells her family she would like to go to the ball, but is refused permission. And she plays an active role in securing her fate, for rather than the deus ex machina of the fairy godmother, it is a little bird, sheltered by a tree Cinderella has planted and nurtured on her mother's grave, who grants her wish. In the Grimm tale, bad character is as justly rewarded as virtue: during Cinderella's marriage procession, the two stepsisters each have an eye gouged out by doves.

In a Scottish version called "Rashin Coatie," the stepmother mutilates her own daughter, cutting off her heel and toes in an effort to stuff her

children can identify. But her story should also inspire young listeners because she is amply rewarded in the end for her kindness and generosity, patience and perseverance. And in that light, her arduous toils can be seen as initiation rites, required before she can achieve her destiny.

SHEHERAZADE

Every night, Sheherazade told King Shahryar a story,
taking care not to complete it before dawn.
She kept him on this merry-go-round for a thousand and one nights.

Sheherazade . . . the sound of her name conjures up images of magic carpets airborne on their way to the mysterious Orient of *The Thousand and One Nights*. The legendary heroine has served as guardian of these enchanting, fabulous stories for more than a thousand years.

Popular tales retold and embroidered upon throughout the Arab world for centuries, *The Thousand and One Nights* came originally not only from Arab countries but also India, Persia, and possibly Greece. A 9th century Arab historian found some of the stories, including the one about Sheherazade, or Shahrazad, in a Persian anthology called *Hazar Afsanah* (A Thousand Tales). New tales may have been included as recently as the 16th century, but the literary device of Sheherazade as narrator has always been preserved. Here is how, according to the first night's tale, Sheherazade came to recount these adventures:

Embittered by an experience with feminine infidelity, Shahryar, a king in Central Asia, devised a way to avoid further betrayal. Each time he married, he murdered the bride after the wedding night, ensuring that no wife would have time to be unfaithful. Terror reigned in his kingdom, and all young maidens hid from him. One day the vizier in charge of finding new brides went home greatly distressed because he could no longer persuade anyone to marry the king. His daughter Sheherazade told him, "By Allah, O my father, give me in marriage to this king — either I shall die, and be a ransom for one of the daughters of the Muslims, or I shall live, and be the cause of their deliverance from him."

The clever young girl had devised a strategy for conquering the king's bitterness, using her talents. For she "had read various books of histories, and the lives of preceding kings, and the stories of past generations." She was very eloquent and a delight to listen to.

Sheherazade married Shahryar. On their wedding night, she used his insomnia as an excuse to tell him a story. At dawn the tale had not ended, and the king, curious, allowed her to live another night to complete the story. She finished it early the next evening, and immediately began another . . . and so it went, for a thousand and one nights, during which Sheherazade won the king's love and, unknown to him, bore him three children. When she told Shahryar about them, he had already succumbed to her: "O Sheherazade, by Allah, I pardoned thee before the coming of these children, because I saw thee to be chaste, pure, ingenuous, and pious."

Shahryar's profound change of heart, his reawakening to love, made him want to share this

A costume for Sheherazade designed by Léon Bakst.

joy with others. He told his brother Shahzaman what had happened, and Shahzaman promptly proposed to Dunyazade, Sheherazade's sister. A lavish celebration was organized for the two couples. And Shahryar, wishing to immortalize the cause of his happiness, had *The Thousand and One Nights* put into writing. It is stated there: "And he and the people of his empire continued in prosperity and delight and happiness until they were visited by the terminator of delights and the separator of companions" — death.

Sheherazade disarmed the king with intelligence, charmed him with gentleness, conquered

"In you I have found a woman who is pure, pious, chaste, gentle, honest, complete in all regards, ingenuous, subtle, eloquent, discreet, cheerful and wise," Shahryar said to his bride.

Sheherazade as seen on the French screen in the 1960s in *Scheherazade*, by Pierre Gaspard-Huit.

him with perseverance. Hers was a victory of mind over might, of wisdom over cynicism — a woman's victory.

Her story proves the power of poetry and the strength of words to awaken desire. For centuries she has represented Oriental femininity. The West came to know her through Antoine Galland's 18th century French translation, and above all Sir Richard Burton's definitive English rendering in the late 19th century, but also through writings by authors as varied as Théophile Gautier and Edgar Allan Poe, and through the music of Nicolai Rimsky-Korsakov.

Sheherazade's tales touch on all the great themes of humanity: love, nostalgia for times past, cruelty . . . As "The Tender Tale of Prince Jasmine and Princess Almond" tells on Night 998,

Love was before the light began,
When light is over, love shall be;
O warm hand in the grave, O bridge of truth,
O ivy's tooth
Eating the green heart of the tree
Of man!

The spirit of Sheherazade reigns over all tales of the desert.

JULIET

ITALY

The lovers of Verona tried to defy hate, but their star-crossed love could end only in death.

Juliet Capulet became one of literature's most famous women thanks to William Shakespeare's tragedy *Romeo and Juliet*. Forever living, she is a worthy incarnation of the woman who loves.

At the beginning of the 15th century, Luigi da Porto transported the legend of the two unfortunate lovers from Sienna to Verona and gave the heroine and hero new names: Giannoza became Giulietta and Mariotto became Romeo.

In two novellas da Porta emphasized the young people's passion and especially Juliet's fearless yet chaste love. The story attracted Matteo Bandello, who rewrote the tale adding further details. This version was translated into French and then into English. In this form it reached Arthur Brooke, a 16th century poet who freely reinterpreted the tale in *The Tragicall Historye of Romeus and Juliet*. Shakespeare used Brooke's version as a source for

his plot but refined and remodeled the characters. In his hands, and through his genius, an original work and the Juliet we know today came into being.

The action takes place over five days in 1300 AD, in beautiful Verona, a city divided by the hate between two important families, the Montagues and the Capulets. Young Romeo Montague, who thinks he is in love with a girl named Rosaline, goes to a masked ball given by the Capulets and meets Juliet, who is betrothed to Paris. Romeo asks himself: "Did my heart love till now? Forswear it, sight! For I ne'er saw true beauty till this night." Juliet, in learning the identity of the young man who has charmed her, cries out: "My only love sprung from my only hate! Too early seen unknown, and known too late! Prodigious birth of love it is to me, that I must love a loathèd enemy."

This sudden and spontaneous love changes their lives. During the night Romeo visits Juliet. She consents to a marriage, which takes place the next day in the greatest secrecy. That very day, Romeo intervenes in a quarrel between his friend Mercutio and Lady Capulet's nephew Tybalt. But Mercutio is killed by Tybalt, whom Romeo in turn kills. Realizing that his action condemns him to exile, he spends a furtive night with his wife and leaves for Mantua.

Juliet then learns that her father has fixed the date for her marriage to Paris. Taken by surprise, Juliet agrees to a plan proposed by Friar Lawrence. She will drink a potion that will make everyone believe she is dead but will wear off after forty hours. Friar Lawrence will tell all to Romeo, who will come to her burial vault and take her to Mantua with him. Juliet drinks the potion but, in an unfortunate chain of coincidences, Romeo does not receive the friar's message and is told his beloved has died. He procures poison and returns to Verona. When he arrives at the Capulet vault that night, he encounters Paris and kills him. Then Romeo kisses Juliet for the last time and swallows the poison. When she awakes, she finds his body. Juliet kisses Romeo for the last time and fatally stabs herself. The two families, seeing the catastrophe born of their hate, reconcile over the bodies of their children.

Romeo and Juliet are the ideal couple. From the moment they meet, they think and act as one, a unity made larger by innocent love born in the midst of hate. Juliet is the ideal woman. Although she is chaste and pure, she is capable of defying paternal authority because her love is true.

The famous balcony scene from Shakespeare's play has been rehearsed, recited, and played innumerable times.

Olivia Hussey was fifteen, about the age of Shakespeare's Juliet, when she played the part in Franco Zeffirelli's film. It was the first time such a young girl had appeared in the role.

Of the two lovers, Juliet has the stronger character. She knows how to act alone as an independent human being, whereas Romeo surrounds himself with advisers. Thoughtful and wise, Juliet also proves intuitive. Love transforms this shy child of fourteen into a mature woman, yet she does not lose her freshness or her youthful dreams. Juliet faces both life and death courageously. Her death, joined with that of Romeo, demonstrates the triumph of love over hate.

One of Shakespeare's most popular plays, *Romeo and Juliet* has inspired countless imitations in many languages and genres. The tale was transposed, transported, and set to modern song by Leonard Bernstein in *West Side Story*. Other composers have used the story too — Niccolo Zingarelli, Vincenzo Bellini, and Charles Gounod in opera (Zingarelli's had a happy ending!), Hector Berlioz as the theme of a symphony, Peter Tchaikovsky for an overture, Sergei Prokofiev for a ballet. In these many forms Juliet continues to live and die before our eyes.

THE LITTLE MERMAID

DENMARK

Many writers have speculated on what mermaids dream about.
The unforgettable creation of Hans Christian Andersen dreamed of a mortal prince . . .

The Little Mermaid, gazing out to sea, seems lost in her memories — as if the heroine of Hans Christian Andersen's tale, frozen in bronze, is reliving her story over and over.

She was the youngest of the six daughters of the sea king, and dwelt among the wonders of the deep. Her grandmother's tales of the land aroused in her the desire to see its perfumed flowers, and its singing fish, which lived in trees and flew through the air! She was anxious to reach the age of fifteen when, like her older sisters, she would be permitted to visit the surface of the water.

At last her turn came. The lovely mermaid, with eyes as deep blue as the sea itself, swam all the way up to the foam. She came near a superb three-masted sailing ship and, through the waves, saw a young prince celebrating his birthday with much merriment.

Soon a storm arose — no trouble for the agile mermaid, who enjoyed the rough waves, but for the ship and its crew, disaster. The masts broke, the ship foundered, and the sailors sank into the ocean depths . . . all save the young prince, who was cradled in the safety of the mermaid's arms throughout the night. In the morning she laid his unconscious body on the beach, hiding to see what would happen. Soon some young maidens appeared and led the awakened prince into a nearby dwelling. Nothing remained for the Little Mermaid but to return home with her sorrow — for she had fallen in love with the mortal prince.

Her grandmother explained to her that humans died quickly, with only their souls granted immortality, while mermaids and mermen lived three hundred years before being transformed into sea foam. How could she even think of living as a human? But the Little Mermaid was not convinced. Overcoming her fear, she approached the sea witch to ask her advice. The witch offered her a potion that would transform her fish tail into legs and enable her to breathe air. But at what price! Each of her light, graceful steps would cause her terrible pain, and she would never be able to rejoin her family as a mermaid. "Only if the prince marries you will you achieve immortality of the soul," warned the witch. The sea princess accepted these conditions, then discovered that there was yet another price: the witch demanded her tongue in payment for the potion.

The next day, the prince left his castle, descending the marble steps that led to the sea, and there found the naked, unconscious girl. She awoke and felt a burning pain where her fish tail had been . . . but she had legs, and her prince was looking at her, asking her where she came from. Mute, she could only gaze at him with her big, blue, solemn eyes. He took her to the castle and had her dressed in sumptuous clothing.

"The found child," as the prince called her, was the loveliest of all the maidens at the castle. She slept at the prince's door, accompanied him on his rides, and climbed the mountains with him, despite the agony her feet caused her at every step. Her sisters came to visit her every night, waving to her from the sea.

The time came for the prince to marry. He was extremely fond of the Little Mermaid, but did not consider marrying her — even though she reminded him of the girl who had found him on the beach, when he was shipwrecked. The prince had fallen in love with that girl and had dreamed of her ever since. However, he knew he was des-

The Little Mermaid was ill-fated, for she who lived under the sea wanted only to settle on land beside her handsome prince.

tined to marry the princess of a neighboring kingdom. The prince set out by boat to meet his bride without much enthusiasm, accompanied as usual by "the found child."

What a surprise when, upon reaching their destination, the prince's boat was met by the maiden who had filled his dreams. She was the princess he was to marry! On their wedding day, the Little Mermaid carried the princess' train, knowing that she would die and become sea foam before the sun rose again. The wedding party and crew returned to the boat that evening to continue celebrating. The Little Mermaid danced gaily with all the sailors, but she was sick at heart. As the merrymakers drifted off to bed, she remained alone on the deck to await daybreak — and her death.

Suddenly her sisters emerged from the waves, shorn of their hair. They had given it to the sea witch in exchange for a magic dagger. The Little Mermaid had another chance: if only she would

use the dagger to kill the prince before the sun rose, she would become a mermaid once more, with three hundred years left to live.

The Little Mermaid crept close to the sleeping couple . . . and threw the dagger into the sea; her love for the prince would not allow her to kill him. Then she dove into the waves, ready to die, for dawn was breaking. But soon she realized that she was still alive, floating in the air among spirits that no one could see or hear. She had become one of them, a creature of the air. The Little Mermaid had suffered so much, and was still so dedicated to doing good, that she had been saved.

Andersen's fairy tale, published in 1836, ends here, but the Little Mermaid's story continues. In 1909, the Danish ballerina Ellen Price created the title role of *The Little Mermaid* with the Royal Danish Ballet in Copenhagen. In the audience was one of her most fervent admirers: Carl Jacobsen, a brewer and a great patron of Danish art. Jacobsen was so moved by the performance that he persuaded the dancer to pose for the sculptor Edvard Eriksen. Jacobsen presented this statue of the Little Mermaid to the city of Copenhagen in 1913, a year before his death.

Edvard Eriksen's statue of the Little Mermaid is to Copenhagen what the Eiffel Tower is to Paris.

CARMEN

SPAIN — 19TH CENTURY

In a letter dated September 21, 1845, Prosper Mérimée wrote: "You will shortly read an amusing little piece by your humble servant, which would have remained unpublished if its author had not been obliged to buy a pair of pants." Two weeks later, *Carmen* was published in *La Revue des Deux Mondes.* Mérimée could hardly have suspected that the tale, and especially its gypsy heroine, would become so beloved.

"She wore a very short red petticoat, which revealed white silk stockings, worn through in several places, and dainty shoes made of Moroccan leather and laced with ribbons the color of fire." This is how Mérimée's Carmen, a worker in the Seville cigarette factory, looked to the corporal Don José. A flirt, she responded to men's compliments by "making eyes at them, her hand on her hip, as brazen as the true gypsy she was." When Carmen attacks a fellow worker with a knife, Don José has to arrest her. On the way to prison, Carmen uses all her charms to seduce the corporal, even speaking to him in his native Basque. He can not resist her, so he allows her to escape.

For this weak indiscretion, Don José is stripped of his rank and imprisoned for a month. Yet he cannot stop thinking about, and longing for, the beautiful woman who brought him trouble: "If sorceresses really exist, she is one." In a gesture of generosity, Carmen gives him a file and a gold coin concealed in a loaf of bread to help him escape. But the honest José chooses to complete his sentence.

After his release, Don José is assigned to guard the colonel's door the evening when Carmen and her dance troupe are scheduled to entertain there. "She was decked out this time like a shrine, dolled up, covered with gold and ribbons." Don José knows he loves her, and feels jealous even of the officers who toss flowers at her dancing feet.

"Brazen, like the true gypsy she was,"
in the Carlos Saura film.

Later he searches for Carmen, just to spend the day with her. When he leaves her that evening he asks if he can see her again. "When you are not so innocent," she replies. " . . . Cats and dogs don't get along well for very long. Perhaps, if you followed the law of Egypt, I could become your 'romi,' your gypsy wife." She loves him "a little"; but if he wants a closer relationship, he will have to take up the gypsy way of life.

Don José allows himself to be led on by the tantalizing woman. One day, in a jealous rage, he fights and kills a lieutenant. According to Carmen's way of looking at life, the best way out of his predicament is to join a band of smugglers. José can think of no other solution; he follows her advice, believing that if he embarks on this new life "of hazard and rebellion" he can at last possess this devil of a woman.

José and Carmen live as *rom* and *romi*, or gypsy man and wife, but Carmen does not like being ordered about: "What I want is to be free and do whatever I please!" He dreams, meanwhile, of leaving for the New World, where they could make their living honestly. "We were not made to plant cabbages," she retorts. Carmen is tired of this bothersome love, annoyed by José's jealousy. She becomes enamored of a bullfighter named Lucas; Don José learns of their affair at a bullfight in Cordoba. But even after Lucas is killed by a bull, Carmen refuses to follow José to America. "It is over between us," she tells him. "As my *rom*, you have the right to kill your *romi*; but Carmen will still be free." She throws her wedding ring to the ground and Don José stabs her.

"Daughter of Satan," liar, sorceress, dangerous, incapable of fidelity — Carmen has little to redeem her. Mérimée himself may have scorned his creation. "A woman is a devil," he wrote as early as 1827, expressing the traditional misogynistic view. And love, the sole moral value Carmen believes in, can only lead to her death. The fatalism of the story inspired Georges Bizet to write one of the world's best-known operas.

Carmen debuted at the Opéra-Comique in Paris on March 3, 1875 — that is to say, on the third day of the third month. This detail is important because three months later, it is said, Bizet died at his home at the very moment when, in the third act of the thirty-third performance, during the "Card Trio," the "merciless card that always says Death!" was turned over.

The opera was at first considered immoral. The story of the loose woman and the weak man who loved her so unrelentingly held little appeal. The music also broke with tradition. Its "bad taste" would come to be appreciated later, when it was recognized as a prototype of musical realism,

The first flesh-and-blood Carmen: the French mezzo Célestine Galli-Marié, who created the role for Bizet.

"We were not made to plant cabbages," Carmen told Don José; "our destiny is to live off non-gypsies." A scene from the Francesco Rosi film.

CARMEN
La plaza de toros.

Carmen and her lover traveled through the mail via this 1905 postcard.

verismo, the Italian movement that contrasted with Romanticism.

Carmen has not ceased to seduce — quite the contrary. As the years have passed, more and more people have come to admire her for her true worth. She has been a huge favorite of the movie industry since its early days. She was the uncontested star of 1983 — that year, three directors with very different styles interpreted her character and story. The Italian Francesco Rosi adapted the opera, the Spaniard Carlos Saura made "a play within a play" using flamenco ballet, and the Frenchman Jean-Luc Godard took liberty with the story in *Prénom Carmen* (First Name: Carmen), using only its main themes: the world of society's dropouts, the difficult relationships between men and women, the permanence of death.

ALICE

ENGLAND — 19TH CENTURY

Lewis Carroll's heroine leads us through magical lands, where everything is topsy-turvy, strange, and muddled: the world of the imagination.

Who was she, Carroll's well-bred, curious Alice, who ventured into "Wonderland" and "Through the Looking Glass"? In her, the author rolled into one many of his young female friends: Dolly Argles, his favorite Gertrude Chataway, Mary Brown, Agnes Hull, Edith Jebb, Mary Macdonald, and, of course, the Liddell sisters, Edith, Lorina, and Alice.

All in the golden afternoon
Full leisurely we glide;
For both our oars, with little skill,
By little arms are plied . . .

On July 4, 1862, while boating on the River Isis near Oxford, the Reverend C.L. Dodgson first told the Liddell sisters the story that would one day become *Alice in Wonderland.* His introductory verses to the book pick up its history:

Ah, cruel Three! In such an hour,
Beneath such dreamy weather,
To beg a tale of breath too weak
To stir the tiniest feather!
Yet what can one poor voice avail
Against three tongues together?

The tale pleased Alice Liddell so much that she immediately began to badger her friend to put it in writing. Dodgson continued to recount the story to his young friends, embellishing it with every retelling. Finally, he began to write it down. His diary tells us that he wanted his heroine to be kind and gentle, courteous and trustworthy, but above all, extravagantly curious and open to outlandish ideas. Under the pen name Lewis Carroll, Dodgson published *Alice in Wonderland* in 1865.

Deep in Wonderland, Alice had strange adventures and met fantastic, illogical, grotesque characters such as the March Hare and the Mad Hatter.

Here is the story of Alice's dream voyage through Wonderland:

Alice was sitting, bored, with her older sister one day, when suddenly a White Rabbit appeared, complaining that he was late for an important appointment. Intrigued by the talking rabbit, she followed him into his burrow, where she fell "down, down, down . . . 'somewhere near the centre of the earth,'" onto a pile of leaves. Following a path, Alice discovered a magical world where mysterious happenings were the norm. When she drank from a bottle labeled "Drink me" she shrank to a height of ten inches; when she ate cake labeled "Eat me" she grew to giant dimensions. In her frustration at these inexplicable events, Alice began to cry. The rabbit passed by, dropping a pair of gloves and a fan in his haste. As soon as Alice picked them up, she shrank again, becoming so small that she had to swim to keep her head above the surface of the lake of giant tears she had shed. Rabbits weren't the only talkative animals in Wonderland; mice and birds chatted with her as well, but she frightened them away when she spoke of her cat, Dinah. Alice eventually regained her normal appearance by following the advice of a caterpillar sitting on a mushroom, smoking from a hookah, or water pipe.

She then met a duchess, who handed her a baby that turned into a pig. And then came the famous Cheshire Cat, who appeared and disappeared at will, leaving his enormous smile hanging in the air. There followed the Mad Hatter's tea party, where three or four guests sat at an enormous table set for a crowd, and changed places whenever they felt like using clean dishes. Finally, after a game of croquet played with flamingoes for mallets and hedgehogs for balls, she realized that the threats of the Queen of Hearts held no danger because . . . "You're nothing but a pack of cards!" she shouted. The living cards all assailed the little girl and she woke to find her sister brushing fallen leaves away from her face.

Wonderland is the kingdom of nonsense, where Alice discovers the absurdities of the adult world. There readers can reimmerse themselves in childhood, which Carroll preferred to maturity. There logic takes on the peculiar quality that came to be known as Carrollian (" . . . said the Cat: 'we're all mad here. I'm mad. You're mad.' 'How do you know I'm mad?' said Alice. 'You must be,' said the Cat, 'or you wouldn't have come here.'") and characters talk endlessly, in an explosion of mad words. At the bottom of the rabbit hole, Alice discovers herself and learns the importance of communication.

The tale did not achieve immediate popularity, but captured the public's imagination after the publication in 1871 of the second part of Alice's adventures, *Through the Looking Glass*. In this tale, Alice walked through a mirror and found herself on a huge chessboard. There she met the twins Tweedledum and Tweedledee, became a queen in the chess game, made the White Queen vanish into a soup tureen, turned the Red Queen into a pussycat . . .

Alice's creator intended her to be a kind of model child, kind, courteous, trustworthy, and very curious.
Illustrations by Arthur Rackham.

Anon, to sudden silence won,
In fancy they pursue
The dream-child moving through a land
Of wonders wild and new,
In friendly chat with bird or beast —
And half believe it true. . . .
Thus grew the tale of Wonderland:
Thus slowly, one by one,
Its quaint events were hammered out —
And now the tale is done.

Lewis Carroll liked to photograph his young friends.
Here is a portrait he made of Alice Liddell,
who inspired the fictional Alice.

ROXELANA

CONSTANTINOPLE — 16TH CENTURY

In the Ottoman empire, the sultan customarily chose his concubines from a harem of slaves.
Roxelana, however, managed to get Süleyman the Magnificent to marry her.

Roxelana's secret? She made the master of time and the shadow of God on earth, Süleylan the Magnificent, laugh. Contrary to custom, he married her and made her the first lady of the Ottoman Empire. He loved her to the end.

Europeans knew of her as Roxelana. In Constantinople she was called Rossa, translated as "the redhead" because of the color of her hair, or as "the Russian" because of her origins. Some believe she came from the Caucasus, where she was kidnapped by Cossacks and turned over to Greek merchants. Others say she was a Polish Catholic captured by Tartars during a raid. Still others say Tunisian buccaneers captured her off the coast of Provence, where she had been born ten years earlier.

Roxelana was taken to the slave market in Constantinople and purchased for the sultan's harem. Süleyman had inherited the vast empire of his father, Selim, and was now the world's richest prince. His seraglio had to reflect the Great Turk's position. There he kept his concubines, his favorites, and the four *kadines*, his chief consorts, one of whom would bear his heir. The sultans of the great Constantinople, where milk and honey flowed, these fierce warriors, these great conquerors, had the blood of slaves in their veins.

Roxelana received the teachings of the Koran and learned singing, dancing, embroidery, and all the other things she must know to serve her master and lover well. She was such an enthusiastic and amusing person that her compagnons gave her a pretty nickname, Khourrem, which means "laughing one" or "joyous one." At the end of two years she spoke Turkish, Arabian, and Persian and was admitted to the presence of the *sultana valide*, the queen mother.

One evening when Süleyman was making the rounds of the harem, he stopped before her and threw her his handkerchief. According to custom, she was expected to return it to him when night fell. A few hours later a eunuch came to lead her to the sultan's apartments. When they awoke the next day he did not send Roxelana away imme-

After becoming the sultan's legal wife, Roxelana worked to ensure her sons' future. Only one of them survived her; Selim succeeded to the Ottoman throne eight years after his mother's death.

diately but listened further to her stories. Decidedly, this young girl amused him greatly.

According to the Venician ambassador, Roxelana was "not beautiful, but graceful." She captured Süleyman's attention with her charm, and in so doing attracted the jealousy of the senior *kadine*, Gülfem, whose son Mustafa was considered the heir to the throne. The sultan made certain his laughing one was by his side during festivals and processions, and wrote her love poems during his conquest of Hungary.

One day, irritated by the laughter of her rival, the neglected favorite threw herself at Roxelana, scratching her face and tearing her hair and clothes. That evening Roxelana refused to appear before the sultan, saying that the fight had left her too tired, that her face and body were disfigured by scratches, and that her pride was hurt. When he heard this, Süleyman went into a towering rage, broke with Gülfem, and sent her and Mustafa to a far province. Roxelana had won.

The only thing she now had to do was rid herself of Ibrahim, the grand vizier, in whom Süleyman had placed his confidence. The extraordinary influence of this Greek slave, married to a sister of the sultan, had made him a rich and powerful man. Ibrahim was as much in her way as she was in his. Roxelana managed to convince the emperor that such a friend was dangerous. Ibrahim was assassinated in 1536. From that time on, the laughing one was the only person to benefit from the sultan's affections, and was in addition the first lady of the harem since the death of the *sultana valide*.

Roxelana's influence continued to grow. She told her master that she wished to give part of her fortune to charitable works, but Islam did not accept the gifts of slaves. Süleyman obligingly freed her, and she had a hospital and a mosque built. Now, however, as a free women, she could no longer give herself to the sultan outside marriage; this was forbidden by the laws of the Koran. What could Süleyman do but marry her?

Ottoman chroniclers, certainly shocked, do not even mention the event, but the marriage is recounted in the *Journal de la Banque Saint-Georges* of Geneva: "The most extraordinary thing happened this week, absolutely without precedent in the history of the sultans. The great lord Süleyman took for wife a Russian slave called Roxelana and there was much rejoicing. . . . Everyone talks of this marriage but no one knows what it means."

With the help of the grand vizier, Rüstem, Roxelana set about ensuring her sons' future. Mustafa and his family disappeared. Cihangir, one of Roxelana's sons, so loved his half-brother that he died of grief. Süleyman himself greatly suffered from this loss. Roxelana's two other sons, Selim and Bayazid, quarreled, and Bayazid was strangled to death in prison in 1561.

Roxelana had died in the arms of her husband in 1558, surrounded by honors, and so never knew her son's fate. The survivor, Selim, suceeded Süleyman eight years later. He was the first of a long line of idle sultans who contributed to the empire's decline.

MADAME DE POMPADOUR

FRANCE — 1721-1764

A young middle-class woman — a nobody, but beautiful and smart — scaled the social ladder to become the mistress of King Louis XV of France. And while it is true that the Marquise de Pompadour ruled a world of pleasure and illusion, she wielded considerable influence in more serious matters as well.

When Jeanne-Antoinette Poisson was only nine years old, a clairvoyant told her she would one day hold the affection of the king (and many years later the marquise would send this same fortune-teller six hundred livres in thanks). But fate could not have taken this course without the help of many whose paths crossed little Jeanne-Antoinette's.

Her father, François Poisson, had made a fortune, but fraudulent business dealings earned him a long exile starting in 1725. During his absence, his wife became the mistress of a tax collector, Le Normant de Tournehem, who lavished money and attention on her little daughter. Jeanne-Antoinette had an excellent education and grew up to be an enticing, witty woman. As his ultimate gift to her, de Tournehem gave her in marriage to his nephew, Charles Le Normant d'Etioles. The young bride frequented fashionable salons, where she met Voltaire and other distinguished men of letters. Her wit and beauty stood out.

In time, the moment arrived for her to make her debut at court. King Louis XV was not a happy man; dissatisfied with the company of his queen, Maria Leszczynska, he had been moving discontentedly from one brief affair to another when he met Jeanne-Antoinette. She became his mistress in February 1745, and soon received a royal warrant granting her the title Marquise de Pompadour. An estate was purchased for her, and her husband was quietly gotten rid of.

Energetic and ambitious, Madame de Pompadour focused her many talents on raising her status in the king's entourage.

Making a name for herself at the court of Versailles was no easy job. While Madame de Pompadour had no trouble entertaining the king, the rest of the court rejected her as an insolent bourgeois upstart. Playing on her name — *poisson* means "fish" in French — her detractors caricaturized her in *"poissonades"* such as this:

The great lords are sinking lower,
The financiers are getting richer
And the Fish are getting bigger;
This is the reign of the good-for,
good-for, good-for-nothings . . .

Micheline Presle played an insolent Madame de Pompadour in the film *Si Versailles m'était conté* (Scenes from Versailles).

The young woman was quite self-possessed. While attending to the king's pleasures, she also worked to increase her power and influence. The creation of her Théâtre des petits appartements, where she sang and acted, gained her a great many admirers. She busied herself in many activities, amassed wealth and property, built palaces, and hired young artists to decorate them. She became known for her exquisite taste and her eye for attractiveness; the "Pompadour style" was born. She patronized letters as well as the arts: the encyclopedists received her support, as did her old friend Voltaire, who, with her help, became a member of the Académie Française and official historian of France.

Granted a seat at court in 1752, Jeanne-Antoinette was honored again when she was named lady-in-waiting to the queen four years

Court scene at Versailles, from an 18th century fan:
Cadet de Gassicourt presents his son to the king while everyone whispers that the child is really the illegitimate son of Louis XV himself.

later. Her popularity and influence had outlasted her sexual charms, for by this time she was no longer the king's mistress. She remained his favorite, however, and as such had the responsibility for arranging his pleasure, even if she did not personally provide it. She procured young mistresses and took care of the inevitable "details" — childbirth, allowance for mother and child. . . . Always occupied with a thousand things, she still found time to practice poetry and engraving, to found the Sèvres porcelain factory, and to invest a fortune creating France's military academy.

An astute businesswoman, Madame de Pompadour also kept abreast of political and diplomatic intrigues. Her influence on foreign affairs has been exaggerated, however; in these matters she often acted as the king's intermediary, but rarely more. The "king's coquette" was not always popular with Parliament, who accused her of having a bad effect on the public finances.

Madame de Pompadour's reputation began to suffer. She was briefly expelled from court after an assassination attempt against the king, but was soon recalled. Later she was blamed for instigat-

ing the Seven Years' War, when most likely she had merely expressed support for it. She had once shown a keen interest in military matters, but when the king confided to her his torment over the defeat of her protégé the Prince de Soubise at Rossbach in 1757, she is famously reported to have expressed her utter lack of interest in the course of events by uttering the old proverb, "Après nous le déluge" — roughly, "After us, the heavens can fall!"

The world, and the court, had lost their fascination for her. The king neglected her and the Duc de Choiseul, her lover, disappointed her. Seriously ill with lung congestion, she settled her affairs and called for a priest. When he was preparing to depart, she said to him: "Just a moment, monsieur le curé, we shall leave together." The king mourned her. Voltaire called her a philosopher. And shortly after Madame de Pompadour's burial, the grieving queen, offended by the shallow emotions of the courtiers, wrote: "As for the others, she is no more talked about than if she had never existed. That is the way people are. Loving them is a waste of time."

AIMEE DUBUCQ DE RIVERIE

MARTINIQUE 1762 — CONSTANTINOPLE 1817

From aristocrat to harem slave: is Aimée's story truth or fiction? Painting by J. B. Hilair, 1787.

Legend or history . . . ? Fate led a young girl from Martinique to a position next to the Ottoman sultans. While her cousin Josephine enjoyed power and glory thanks to her husband, Napoleon Bonaparte, Aimée Dubucq de Riverie took her place in the annals of the Ottoman Empire behind closed doors, within the shadow of the seraglio, hidden by veils.

Or did she? Aimée de Riverie's story is filled with mystery. She disappeared during a sea voyage between France and Martinique in 1788 and apparently reappeared under the name of Nakshidil in the impenetrable harem of the Great Turk. Legend quickly became part of the tale of this young aristocrat who was made a slave but triumphed by becoming a sultana. Were Aimée and Nakshidil the same woman? The dates of their respective paths, although close, do not precisely coincide. However, popular imagination and novelists' pens have overlooked this small detail to present us with a larger than life heroine. Here are the outlines of her story:

Aimée grew up among the sugarcanes of her family's plantation on the French Caribbean island of Martinique. She was a carefree and happy child, frolicking in the fields with her governess and the slaves' children or playing with her cousin Josephine. One day the cousins consulted a fortune teller, who revealed things about their respective futures that hardly seemed believable: Josephine would become a queen, and Aimée would live and reign in a sumptuous palace!

When Aimée had finished her preliminary education her parents sent her to France to complete her training. After many years at a convent school in Nantes, the time came for Aimée and her governess to go home to Martinique. The two women set sail to return to the pleasures of their far-away island.

Aimée must have thought this would be her final voyage: they were shipwrecked. The arrival of a Spanish ship bound for Majorca barely saved the passengers from drowning. Aimée's adventures had only begun, however, for just when she believed she was safe, pirates captured the ship.

In the closed, veiled world of the harem, female slaves plotted incessantly to influence the empire's destiny.

son to be Mahmud II, sultan of the Ottoman Empire.

Nakshidil thus became the *sultana valide*, or queen mother. She left the seraglio and took up residence in a palace on the shores of the Bosporus. She acted as an adviser to her son, especially when Napoleon proposed an alliance with the Turks against Russia. Aimée had detested Napoleon ever since his campaign in Egypt; perhaps she also bore in mind his repudiation of her cousin Josephine. Mahmud instead concluded a peace treaty with the czar, a strategic move that permitted him to send his troops to fight Napoleon.

Mahmud, influenced by his mother, was a reforming ruler ahead of his time. At the end of her life, Nakshidil asked her son to build her a tomb with an adjoining fountain where visitors might refresh themselves. In this tomb lies the enigmatic blond whose life, or legend, continues to fascinate us.

They conveyed the booty — men, women, and goods — to Algiers. Aimée was received by the dey, the governor of this Ottoman province, who realized that the aristocratic, beautiful, blue-eyed blond was a prime piece of merchandise. There was no question of selling her on the slave market or even of keeping her for himself. He made a present of her to Sultan Abdulhamid I.

Thus did a blond slave arrive in Constantinople, where the eunuchs of the imperial harem awaited her. They covered her with a white cloth so that none might gaze upon her, and took her to the palace. The doors of the seraglio swung shut upon the slave and her past. She started a new life in a closed world governed by the workings and hierarchy of the harem, a world where female slaves plotted incessantly to influence the empire's destiny.

The chief steward of the harem took her under his wing, saw that she got a proper Oriental education, and gave her the name Nakshidil,

"image of the heart." She was introduced to the languages of the court and the laws of the harem.

Nakshidil soon won the heart of the old Sultan Abdulhamid, who made her his favorite and even, it is said, his counselor. She bore a son, Mahmud, who might one day ascend the throne; thus she became a *kadine.*

Abdulhamid died in April 1789 and his nephew became Selim III. For eighteen wonderful years, Nakshidil was at Selim's side. She shared his life and took part not only in his happiness but also in his policies. Then in May 1807 Selim was overthrown and his cousin Mustafa took the throne. Nakshidil and her son, Mahmud, were confined in a room and Selim in his apartments.

Meanwhile, the former sultan's partisans were plotting to restore him to the throne. When they invaded the palace on July 28, 1808, Mustafa ordered his three prisoners slain . Selim was killed, but Nakshidil and Mahmud escaped. Later that day the victorious rebels proclaimed Nakshidil's

Amber O'Shea played Aimée
in Jack Smight's 1988 film *The Favorite.*

This scene from colonial Lima recalls Micaela Villegas'
origins. Of modest background, she decided
to climb the social ladder, determined to better herself.

MICAELA VILLEGAS

PERU — 1748-1819

Micaela Villegas, mistress of the viceroy of Peru, was known throughout Lima to be witty, charming, elegant, vivacious — and sharp-tempered. The vulgar nicknamed her La Perricholi — "mongrel bitch" — and the French made her known as La Périchole throughout the world.

Micaela was of modest background, one of six children of Spanish and Indian descent. An intelligent girl, she had a fervent imagination, a good memory, a flair for singing, an inclination toward comedy, and a taste for music. Naturally, she looked to the theater. Her parents permitted her to pursue this career, for although they were respectable their financial situation was precarious. Micaela dreamed, watching the magnificently dressed and perfumed young ladies of Lima's high society.

An actor, impresario, and theatrical director called Maza opened the doors for her career in exchange for her favors. She appeared in dramas, comedies, farces, and religious plays. Micaela adored this world and was happy to be part of it. At twenty she was a known actress, loved her work, and was attracting both the admiration of men and the jealousy of women, who cattily said she was ugly.

Micaela Villegas was not a beauty but even with her faults she personified grace. She was stocky but extraordinarily vivacious, her eyes were dark and sparkling, her hands and feet were tiny, and she had thick brown hair. Above all, she knew how to attract men.

Although highly sought after, she had not yet reached the height of her ambition. Then one evening, destiny knocked on her dressing room door. Viceroy Manuel de Amat invited her to the palace for a private interview on condition that she tell no one.

Don Manuel de Amat y Junyent, then in his sixties, was a nobleman from Barcelona who had a sense of propriety. He had come to Lima several years earlier to take up his post as viceroy and governed with a firm military hand, imposing measures such as the death penalty for thieves, the expulsion of foreigners without work, and severe tax-payment controls. The population was hostile to him, but that didn't worry Micaela. She decided to accept his invitation even though she was invited by the back door. He treated her like a lady and she became his mistress.

From this time on the young woman's life changed dramatically. Every evening the members of Lima high society applied themselves, like the viceroy, to going to the theater to applaud her. The more she was admired and desired by some, the more she was envied, detested, and slandered by others. To the aristocracy she was simply "His Excellency's plaything" and to the opposition she was corrupt. In the villages, however, women thought of her as a goddess. They had nothing to reproach her for, not her fine clothes, nor her aristocratic manners, her arrogance, her quick and sometimes vulgar language.

Micaela flaunted her position, sitting on the viceroy's lap and even nibbling from his plate at luncheons. Such behavior, however, did not prevent great ladies from asking her for favors, which she always obtained from the viceroy. Amat's adoration for his young mistress reached its height in 1769, when she bore him a son. He was nearly seventy at the time.

The viceroy had imposed further unpopular measures, increasing taxes and expelling the Jesuits. To distract public attention, he increased public entertainment. Micaela continued to appear on stage, by choice. However, her capricious behavior had begun to annoy her lover. One evening when her performance was not up to standard, Maza told her that a rival actress could do better. She grabbed a whip and struck him. Shocked, members of the audience shouted: "Out! To prison with her!" Amat, fearing that his enemies would take advantage of the situation and attack him, broke off his liaison with Micaela. The viceroy's anger cooled after two years and

In Jean Renoir's film *Le Carrosse d'or*, taken from *Le carrosse du Saint-Sacrement* by Mérimée, Anna Magnani played the character inspired by Micaela. Jacques Offenbach's opera *La Périchole* was also loosely based on this story of an act of charity.

Micaela returned to the stage, where she asked her public's pardon in a song. Everyone cheered.

The incident that earned her a kind of immortality went something like this: Micaela wanted to go to a festival in a new four-horse carriage, accompanied by her lover and their son, Manuel. The viceroy gave her the carriage, the horses, two footmen, and a lady-in-waiting but refused to go with her. On her way to the festival, her path crossed that of a funeral procession led by an old priest who could barely walk. Micaela made him take her place in the carriage and followed on foot. When he wanted to give the carriage back to her, she refused. The priest asked her name so that he might pray for her. She replied: "La Perricholi!" The story became legendary, and Prosper Mérimée used it in his work *Le carrosse du Saint-Sacrement*.

Amat was replaced as viceroy and left Peru in 1776. He was accused of embezzlement and various other crimes but was acquitted for lack of proof. La Perricholi was the subject of rumors, attacks, and insults. She continued in the theater, however, becoming an impresario and working with Vincente Echarri, whom she married.

When the liberator of Peru, General José de San Martín, arrived in Lima at the head of his troops in 1820, Micaela had been dead for a year. But her granddaughter went to kiss the liberator, and several days later the son of La Perricholi, as a citizen of Peru, signed his country's declaration of independence.

WALLIS WARFIELD

UNITED STATES 1895 — FRANCE 1986

She was not beautiful, but she became one of the most elegant women in the world, and also one of the most talked-about. For Wallis Warfield, a king gave up his throne.

Wallis was born in Blue Ridge Summit, Pennsylvania, before her parents had made their union legal. Despite this, she received a respectable middle-class upbringing in Baltimore, with her grandparents bearing the costs of a good private school after her father's early death. At school, little Wallis stood out because of her saucy disposition and her fierce will to be first in everything and to monopolize attention. When she ceased to be the center of attention, she would make herself faint to capture it again. Her prominent cheekbones and angular features were not beautiful, but with her liveliness and her elegant, impeccable attire, she captivated nonetheless.

At eighteen she made her debut at a cotillion for debutantes in Baltimore. Here she began her quest for a rich, handsome husband. While visiting friends in Pensacola, Florida, she met Earl Winfield Spencer, a navy pilot who seemed to fit her requirements. But the evening after their wedding in 1916, she discovered that he was an alcoholic. His career suffered as a result, and his quick temper and jealousy made Wallis realize this was not the man of her dreams. She wanted a divorce, but her family advised her to wait.

In 1920, the Prince of Wales, who would become Edward VIII, visited Colorado, where the Spencers lived. Wallis dreamed of attending the banquet held in his honor. But the Spencers were not on the guest list.

Spencer was sent to China in 1922; Wallis remained at home and mingled with the diplomatic crowd, where her conduct often caused scandalized gossip. Like other officers' wives, she began to transmit confidential documents for the military. Eventually she was sent to Europe, then in 1924 to join her husband in China. There,

The romance that rocked the British Empire — Wallis and Edward smile in the wintry sun minutes after their marriage at the Chateau de Cande at Monts, France, on December 15, 1937.

according to a dossier assembled much later by the British secret service, Wallis frequented the "houses of song," which were said to be luxury brothels, and indulged in other pastimes that gave rise to gossip and speculation.

When she returned to the United States she obtained her longed-for divorce, in 1927. In New York she soon met Ernest Aldrich Simpson, an English shipping tycoon. After he extricated

At age twenty-two, Wallis was the wife of the rich and handsome navy pilot, Lt. Earl Winfield Spencer.

himself from a prior marriage, the two were wed in 1928, taking up residence in London. Wallis adapted to the English climate and was introduced into London society by her husband's sister. She numbered among her friends Lady Thelma Furness, then the mistress of the Prince of Wales. Inevitably, one weekend in November 1930, the Simpsons were invited to a house party attended by the future King Edward, who to his family and friends was known as David.

The first evening, Wallis went unnoticed by the royal guest of honor. But at lunch the next day, she sat next to the prince. Courteously, he inquired about her comfort and asked if she did not suffer from the absence of central heating. Wallis replied that she adored cold houses, adding that she was disappointed in his conversational gambit. When the prince asked why, she told him that all American women arriving in England were asked that same question, and that she had expected more originality from the Prince of Wales. Her show of independence surprised him and aroused his curiosity.

Despite her status as a divorcée, Wallis soon succeeded in being presented at court. The same evening, the Simpsons were invited to dine at the home of Lady Thelma in the company of the prince. Then they began to receive frequent invitations to his summer home, Fort Belvedere. Wallis' attraction for the prince grew; gradually, their friendship became a deeper sentiment.

In 1934, Wallis and David traveled together to Spain and France, where the attentions of photographers caught them by surprise. Their relationship became obvious; the prince, visibly in love, did not hesitate to break the rules of protocol to appear at her side at receptions. She made an elegant companion.

The British government began to take note, and worried that Wallis fostered pro-Nazi sympathies, which did not appear to displease the prince. The secret service kept close tabs on her and assembled a dossier. In January 1936, King George V died, and the prince was proclaimed King Edward VIII.

After his coronation, Wallis became a state problem: there could be no question of the king marrying a divorcée. She was prepared to forego marriage, but he preferred to give up the throne. On December 10, 1936, he abdicated, asserting that it was impossible for him to uphold his responsibilities as king without the help and support of the woman he loved.

The couple was married in France, in a castle in the Loire Valley, after Wallis' second divorce.

He had been created Duke of Windsor and she thus became his duchess, but she was explicitly denied use of the title "Royal Highness." No member of the royal family attended the wedding.

In 1940, Prime Minister Winston Churchill offered the duke the governorship of the Bahamas. During the five years the couple spent there, Wallis devoted herself to Red Cross work. After World War II and a period of further travel, they settled down near Paris, on the edge of the Bois de Boulogne.

The duke and duchess were the jewels of the jet set, but the British royal family steadfastly shunned them. Edward's mother, Queen Mary, died in 1953 without ever having agreed to receive Wallis. Finally, twelve years later, Queen Elizabeth II paid the couple a visit in a hospital where her uncle was to undergo an operation.

The dignity of the duke and duchess won them the respect of the world, with Wallis' elegance and good taste a legend. The passage of time seemed to have no effect on her face. Edward died in 1972; when his body was taken from France to England for burial, the Duchess of Windsor was at last received with the utmost grace and attention.

After the funeral, Wallis sought assurance that there would be sufficient room for her to be buried next to her husband. Upon her death in 1986, her wish was granted.

Even when the Duke and Duchess visited London, as here in 1963, the British royal family shunned them.

PHRYNE

GREECE — 4TH CENTURY BC

By posing for the sculptor Praxiteles,
Phryne opened wide the doors of glory and immortality.

Though she had achieved great wealth, fame, and adulation, Phryne the courtesan suffered from the contempt in which moral society held women of her profession. To avenge herself on her detractors, she elevated herself to the status of a goddess on the strength of her beauty alone.

Her given name was Muesarete. She was born in the town of Thespae, whose patron was the god Eros. Of modest station, she sold capers at the town market to help support her family. At a very young age she learned to use her charm and beauty to sell her merchandise — even though she was nicknamed Phryne ("toad") for her sallow skin.

At about age thirteen, Phryne left for Athens to try to make her living playing the flute in religious celebrations. On her arrival, she was described as a little girl "with blue eyelids, short hair, and pointed breasts, dressed only in a belt from which hung yellow ribbons and black iris stalks." Very soon she learned to unfasten this belt after the banquets ended and the music and dancing ceased. She settled among the courtesans, where she learned to like liberty; and she wanted to become rich, like her companions. So this girl of about fifteen, who till then had though of Love only as the god of Thespae, launched into a career in the erotic arts as a hetaera, one of the class of highly cultivated courtesans of Greece.

She did not have to wait long for success. Phryne was so lovely that she needed no embellishment and could dress simply in a tunic, with a veil to cover her hair. She withdrew into her villa, ceasing to frequent the public square as soon as her reputation was sufficient to attract customers. The Athenians, intrigued by her air of mystery, were willing to give their fortunes for her attentions. Phryne excelled in the arts of love, but granted her favors only for a king's ransom.

After Alexander the Great attacked and destroyed the nearby city of Thebes in 336 BC, it was decided that it would be too costly to rebuild it. The young courtesan offered to pledge her now immense fortune to bring the fabled old city in her native region back to life. But her money was refused, considered tainted. Phryne promised

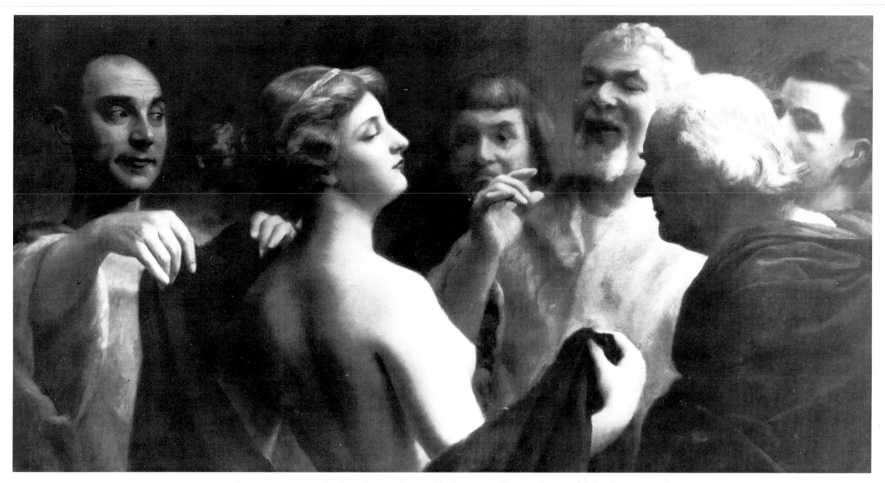

"Who among you would dare deprive the world of the one who served as model for the immortal
Aphrodite of Cnidus?" asked Phryne's lawyer, revealing her nude perfection.

herself that one day those who had mocked her would scoff no more.

She paid a call upon Praxiteles, an Athenian sculptor who was quickly becoming famous. Without saying a word, Phryne undressed before him, displaying to his amazed eyes the perfect figure of a living statue. Such pure beauty could only be divine — it must be that of the goddess Aphrodite!

The courtesan became his muse, inspiring to its fullest the genius of Praxiteles. With Phryne as his model, he created such masterpieces as the famous Aphrodite of Cnidus, which broke with tradition by portraying the goddess entirely nude. It drew admirers from far and wide. The courte-san-cum-muse was adored, and became known as Phryne-Aphrodite. Praxiteles was not the only artist to find inspiration in her perfection. After seeing her emerge from the sea after bathing, Alexander's court painter, Apelles, made his *Aphrodite Anadyomene* (Aphrodite Rising From the Sea) in her image.

But the young woman, who continued to shut herself up like a hermit, had become too well-loved: she now aroused the jealousy of certain Athenians. They conspired against her, accusing her of blasphemy, the gravest of all crimes. At her trial, the orator Euthias tried to condemn not only Phryne but all the hetaerae, accusing them of corrupting youth, and insulting the gods by claiming adoration for themselves. Despite a brilliant speech in her behalf, Phryne's defense counsel, the great orator Hyperides, could tell he had not outdone Euthias. So he suddenly tore off Phryne's tunic, asking: "Who among you would dare deprive the world of the one who served as model for the immortal Aphrodite of Cnidus?" This spectacle moved the judges to leniency.

Toward the end of her life, Phryne returned to her native Thespae, taking with her a statue of Eros with gold and marble wings, which Praxiteles had given her. She offered the statue to the temple in the old city, and visited there every day to worship her god. She died with her forehead resting on Eros' foot.

LAILA

CENTRAL ARABIA — 7TH CENTURY

The melodious name of the wise, beautiful Laila means "night." The poet Qays lost his mind for love of her, and in his dark madness wrote inspired verse. His "Madman's verses" made Laila a legend.

Thirteen centuries ago in the Arabian desert, it was not unknown for poets to die of love. While the bards Omar and Imroul-Qays were telling of their adventures and of women's sensuality, other poets became troubadors of courtly love: there was Jamil, who vowed an impossible passion for Buthaima, and Kuthaiyir, with his love for Azza. And there were the many poets of the Banou Uzra tribe, acknowledged experts on the subject. But by their own admission, the Uzra were surpassed in the expression of love when a new poet emerged in the Banou Amir tribe. This was Majnun Laila, "Laila's Madman," whose eloquence raised his beloved far above the ranks of her poetic peers, and inspired a literary tradition around her.

I fell in love with Laila at the time when she
*   wore her hair shoulder-length,*
And we, her companions, had not yet seen her
*   two breasts take shape.*
We were young and guarded the flocks.

The poet met Laila near Mount Tawbad, where their families led the lives of nomads. They were cousins, and grew up not far from each other. Qays was a handsome young man, intelligent, strong, excelling in the art of rhyme. He was the youngest and favorite son of a rich lord. From a less affluent family, Laila nonetheless possessed all the grace and beauty desirable in a girl, and loved to listen to poetry.

Or — well, perhaps that's not exactly how it was. There are so many versions of Laila's tale; as

Majnun, Laila's "Madman," dedicated his time to celebrating his beloved through poetry.

early as the 10th century a writer called Abdul Faraj had collected many of them into a book. Some say that Laila and Qays weren't cousins, weren't even of the same tribe, that Qays sought her out because he had heard of her beauty. Small matter — what counts is that the two young people fell passionately in love.

There was nothing to prevent their wedding — nothing save the sheer mundaneness of the idea. Qays' love was too intense to be bound into the banal convention of marriage. His passion surpassed ordinary limits; it surpassed even his reason, as this anecdote, immortalized for the stage by the Egyptian Ahmed Chawqi, shows:

Qays came to fetch wood in Laila's camp, and talked to her while playing with the cinders.

"How many times have I asked the dawn if you sighed in the middle of the night? How many times have I questioned the winds which I thought had stirred the perfumed folds of your dress? Or a gazelle who has stolen the black from your eyes?"

"Leave the fire, young man!" the beautiful girl replied, "You are in danger. A flame has set the right sleeve of your coat on fire." But he didn't feel the flame; his love burned far hotter, so that he nearly fainted.

Qays was mad with love: he proclaimed it in the face of the world, in verse, yet had not yet made a formal request for Laila's hand in marriage. This mocked convention, transgressed social norms — it dishonored Laila's family, who could no longer allow a union that had been discussed publicly before they had a chance to give formal approval. Qays lost his beloved because he had created a scandal. But he still had the words, the poetry she had inspired in him:

Am I forbidden to see her?
Will they make it a crime
For me to go where she lives?
I will always have rhymes!

When Laila was given in marriage to another, Qays went completely insane and came to be called Majnun, the Madman. He wandered alone, naked, in the desert, reciting his verse to an audience of wild animals. He became especially fond of the

Some say Laila was a little girl when she met Qays.

company of gazelles, because they reminded him of his beloved. They became used to him and he protected them from hunters.

Responding one day to a visitor's question, Majnun said that he did not love Laila. "Love is the intermediary which joins two separate people. But it is not needed here, for Laila is me, and I am Laila," he explained. For his love was purified, absolute, mystical. Still later poets would use similar words to talk of love for God: "I am he who I love and he who I love is me," El Hallaj, a great Sufi, or Islamic mystic, wrote a century later. Still later Persian poets, such as Nizami and Djami, compared the love for Laila to the love of God in their verse.

Qays' family sent him to Mecca, in a last desperate attempt to bring him back to sanity. But the Madman, instead of hearing the voice of God there, thought he heard Laila's name:

This cry, it was Laila's name without Laila.
And I felt that a bird was flying out of my heart.

On the subject of Majnun and Laila's death, the many versions of the story contradict each other. But no one doubts that the survivor died of grief, shortly after his beloved. "My pain and my remedy, it is you, my life and my death are in your hands alone."

He was led by love of his "Night" into the darkness of insanity, but his inspired words immortalized both his beloved and the very idea of the divinity of mad, exalted passion. Much later, and a very long way from Arabia, the 20th century French author Louis Aragon was inspired by Majnun Laila to write "Le Fou d'Elsa" (Elsa's Madman), in which he says:

I have given you the place reserved for God, that the poem
Forevermore shall rise above the litanies.

The legend of Laila was born in the desert.

BEATRICE

ITALY — CA. 1265-1290

Did Beatrice really exist or was she only a dream? The little girl glimpsed in the streets of Florence became the muse of Dante Alighieri, the woman who informed the poet's life and work.

Dante was a young boy when he first saw the nine-year-old Beatrice. "She appeared dressed in a most noble color, a soft and true red, girdled and dressed as was fitting for her youth. . . . Since then I say that Love governs my soul which was so soon married, and love took on me such assurance and lordship through the virtue bestowed on it by my imagination, that I must do all love wills."

This platonic love — devoid of carnal desire or the will to possess — that Dante dedicated to Beatrice was the wellspring of his imagination. Although he would have to wait nine years before meeting her again, he thought only of her and lived only to see her. "That exquisite lady appeared before me, dressed in the whitest white, between two gentle ladies of more advanced ages; and in passing through the street, she turned her eyes in my direction, timidly; and then in her infinite courtesy, which is today rewarded . . . she greeted me, in a most virtuous manner, and it seemed that then I could glimpse the boundaries of bliss."

Beatrice was dead when Dante recounted this episode in *La Vita Nuova* (The New Life), a collection of poems inspired by her. She had become "the glorious lady of his thoughts" who nourished his heart, his soul, his work. He vowed to consecrate to her a poem worthy of her great virtues. She became the inspiration and guardian angel of his great *Commedia*, or *Divine Comedy*. In this immense poetic fresco, Dante portrays himself at the age of thirty-five and tells how Beatrice shows him the way to Paradise: lost in an obscure forest, he is prevented by three terrible beasts from

For Dante, Beatrice was "the glorious lady of his thoughts." Illustration for *The Divine Comedy*, School of Venice, 14th century.

Dante encountering Beatrice in the streets of Florence:
"That glorious lady appeared before me, dressed in the whitest white."

reaching a hill that is just in sight. Beatrice sends Virgil to him, and the Roman poet guides him on the path to salvation.

The beauty of his muse, which he extols in all his writings, symbolizes the beauty of the soul. Beatrice is the mediator between heaven and earth, between the human and the divine. In her most sublime idealization, she is identified with theology. Dante has thoughts only for her when an-

other "lady," later identified with philosophy, tries to comfort him after Beatrice's death. For Dante, the purest, most ethereal, mystical love, which leads to completion and redemption, is expressed through adoration of a human being.

In Beatrice, Dante created one of Western culture's most perfect pictures of idealized womanhood, a theme cherished by the troubadours of courtly love and the Romantic poets. And yet he

probably never met the little girl or the young woman he glimpsed in the streets. She may have existed only in his imagination. No one knows.

Some say Beatrice was the daughter of a Florentine nobleman, Folco di Geri de Pardi. If this theory is true, Beatrice was a married woman and the mother of a family who apparently died without ever never knowing of the extraordinary love she had inspired.

MONA LISA

ITALY — EARLY 16TH CENTURY

Thanks to Leonardo da Vinci, the smile of this virtually unknown woman is one of the most famous in the world.

She is present, yet far away; grave, yet ironic; simple, but disturbing. Behind La Gioconda's smile hides the enigma of the human soul. But what has Mona Lisa been looking out at for all these centuries?

Leonardo da Vinci began this portrait, destined to become perhaps the most famous painting in the world, around 1503. Although many have tried to prove that their own heroines were the subject of the work, it is now accepted that Mona Lisa Ghevardini, wife of the Florentine Francesco di Zanobi del Giocondo, modeled for the painting. But very little else is known about this woman, except that she was nearly thirty when she posed for her portrait. The time and circumstances in which it was painted are also shadowy. The one

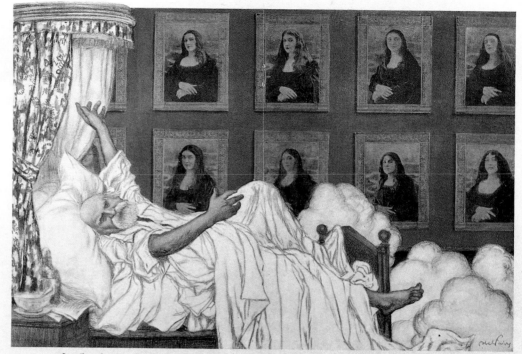

Le Cauchemar du Sous-Secrétaire d'Etat : Vision fugitive... et toujours poursuivie... !!!

The caption of this editorial cartoon by Abel Faivre reads,
"The Under-Secretary of State: a Fleeting Vision Still Pursued."
The poor man's nights were haunted when La Gioconda was stolen

La Gioconda has inspired many interpretations, such as Gérard Vulliamy's *Le Cygne de la Joconde* (La Gioconda's Swan).

undisputed fact is that Leonardo was its creator.

According to Giorgio Vasari, the great historian and art critic of the time, "Leonardo undertook to execute, for Francesco del Giocondo, the portrait of Mona Lisa, his wife; and after toiling over it for four years, he left it unfinished." Vasari thought the painter had come as close as art could to imitating nature; he found the portrait so vibrant that it seemed to have a life of its own. To produce the smile that Vasari called "a thing more divine than human," the artist hired "persons to play or sing; and jesters, who might make her remain merry."

Claiming that the painting was unfinished, Leonardo refused to deliver it to Francesco, and instead sold it to one of his patrons, François I of France, for four thousand gold ecus. The king's men later had to stop the artist from giving it to the Duke of Buckingham, who wanted to take the Mona Lisa back to England.

Like a favorite courtesan, *La Gioconda* sojourned at each of the great courts of France in turn: Fontainebleau, Versailles, the Tuileries, in Napoleon's private chambers, then in the great gallery of Napoleon's museum, the Louvre.

The painting was already reknowned at the turn of the century, when theft made it even more famous. At 8 A.M. on August 21, 1911, an Italian painter employed by the museum stole the Mona Lisa and attempted to sell it in Italy. The crime was discovered and Italy returned the painting to France — but not before displaying it in a series of exhibits to crowds of fans. Since then, the Mona Lisa has traveled to the United States, the Soviet Union, and Japan, with equal success.

She has been examined from every angle, her measurements carefully calculated. Some have speculated that she was pregnant at the time of the portrait, while others have claimed she was asthmatic. But no one has ever penetrated the mystery of her smile.

MUMTAZ MAHAL

INDIA — 1593-1631

Mumtaz Mahal, the "chosen one of the palace,"
was the most beautiful of the Mogul queens.

"A teardrop of love on the cheek of time": that is how the poet Rabindranath Tagore described the Taj Mahal. Shah Jahan shed this splendid tear for the love of Mumtaz Mahal.

The lovestruck emperor descended from an illustrious line of Asian conquerors: Genghis Khan on his father's side and Timur on his mother's, as well as Babur and Akbar. But even with this glorious heritage, he was not strong enough to withstand the onslaught of a woman's beauty.

Prince Khurram, as Shah Jahan was known in his youth, was the son of Jahangir, emperor of Mogul India. The prince was about fifteen years old when he went to one of the fairs held periodically in Agra. It was common for Mogul princes and princesses to meet and converse there freely. On this occasion, an astonishingly beautiful girl caught the prince's eye. She was Arjumand Banu Began, granddaughter of Jahangir's prime minister and descendant of a learned Tehran family. She had received the faultless education customary for daughters of noble lineage. At the sight of her, Prince Khurram fell in love. He told his father that he wished to marry her and, as was customary, Jahangir requested her hand from her father, Asaf Khan.

The couple became betrothed in the traditional way. The young people waited five years before marrying on April 12, 1612. By this time Khurram was twenty years old, and already had two children by his first wife. His bride was nineteen. Upon her marriage, she was called Mumtaz Mahal, or "chosen one of the palace." Khurram married one more time, but Mumtaz was unquestionably his favorite of his three wives.

In 1622-1623, Prince Khurram began a rebellion because one of Jahangir's wives was scheming to replace him as heir with her own candidate. He and his father were reconciled after three years of virtual civil war. Mumtaz Mahal accompanied and sustained him during this difficult time. Jahangir died in 1627 and Khurram took the throne, becoming Shah Jahan, "King of the World."

But it was not an easy world to rule, for times were hard and the Indians, burdened by taxes and

98

periodically devastated by famine, had grown rebellious. The emperor was cultured — a lover of literature, music, painting, and architecture; but all these talents, and even his prowess as a soldier, could not make him a good ruler. In the absence of reliable advisors, Mumtaz Mahal became his most important supporter. As guardian of the royal seal, she was privy to all important decrees and decisions made by her husband. Intelligent, refined, profoundly religious, she was also a great philanthropist and humanitarian. She frequently used her considerable influence with her husband to obtain leniency for the condemned.

Shah Jahan could not bear to be separated from Mumtaz Mahal, and took her with him even on his military expeditions. All the historians described her as the most lovely of the Mogul queens.

The historians also acknowledged that she knew how to enhance her natural beauty with cosmetics and shampoos made of rare herbs, and with massage treatments using perfumed oils. Thus Mumtaz preserved the full flower of her youth through the births of thirteen children.

Her fourteenth childbirth, in 1631, killed her. Knowing she was about to die, the queen begged her attending daughter, Jahan Ara, to call the emperor so she could see him one last time. Shah Jahan hastened to her side and held her as she breathed her last, his heart broken. He refused the customary bejeweled, embroidered imperial garments, preferring to wear only the simple white of mourning. He stopped listening to music, and lost interest in the affairs of the kingdom. "The empire has no flavor," he would say, "even life has no more taste at the moment." He may have dreamed of abandoning the throne to become a beggar, to seek refuge in a religious life, but the kingdom was a sacred charge, which one could not relinquish at will.

The grief-stricken king threw his whole soul into building the Taj Mahal: "Taj" being the contraction of "Mumtaz," and Mahal meaning "palace." It is possible that he designed the mausoleum himself, as legend tells, for he had often given his opinion to master architects on other

The emperor Shah Jahan erected an exquisite tomb
for his favorite wife as a pledge of his undying love for her.

A dream in stone,
in memory of a woman: the Taj Mahal.

structures. Artists came from all over Asia, and possibly even from Florence, to assist in creating the most beautiful tomb in the world. Precious stones were brought from Egypt and Arabia, sapphires from Tibet, moonstones and topazes from Baghdad, lapis lazuli from Sri Lanka. The pure white marble for the walls was brought to Agira by elephant caravan. More than twenty thousand people worked for twenty-two years to complete the fabulous tomb and its mosques, gardens, and walls.

It is said that Shah Jahan had intended to have a replica of the Taj Mahal built in black marble for himself, linked to the white tomb by a bridge of marble. Before he could begin such a project, however, his son by Mumtaz Mahal, Aurangzeb, imprisoned him in the fort of Agra and proclaimed himself emperor in 1658. As Shah Jahan was dying, they say, he asked for his deathbed to be placed on a balcony where he could contemplate his masterpiece and dream of his beloved.

AISHA

ARABIA — 614-677

Aisha was still playing with dolls when the Prophet Mohammed took her to wife. The little girl grew up near him, knew how to make herself loved, and stayed his favorite wife. After his death, she played an important political role, which culminated in the famous "Battle of the Camel."

The Prophet was approaching the age of fifty; his wife, Khadija, who had been a source of strength, had died and he thought of remarrying. A matchmatcher suggested two politically advantageous choices: Sawda, a widow nearing thirty, or Aisha, a girl of six. Mohammed asked the go-between to negotiate for both. Since Abu Bakr, Aisha's father, was a faithful friend and one of the first converts to Islam, the Prophet decided that a marriage would strengthen their bonds.

Aisha herself recorded that "the Messenger of God married me when I was six years old and the marriage was celebrated when I was nine. We came to Medina and then I had the fever for a month." This was several months after the Hegira, the flight of the Prophet and his followers from Mecca in 622; Abu Bakr had also moved his family from Mecca.

One day, Aisha's mother came to fetch the child as she was playing with friends. "She made me go into a house where I found ladies who said: Happiness and blessings! Good luck! My mother gave me into their keeping. They washed my hair and made me beautiful. And I was not afraid except in the morning when the Messenger of God came and they gave me to him." After a simple ceremony, Aisha settled with her toys in a room of Mohammed's house, which later became the mosque of Medina. The Prophet came to see and play with her, which must have distracted him from his worries. Aisha was very pretty and intelligent, and had a good memory.

The favorite wife of the Prophet Mohammed, Aisha became "the Mother of the Faithful" and a figure especially respected by Sunni Muslims. *Memories of Times Past: Mohammed and His Family*, 17th century.

Several years later an unfortunate incident — which might have been called "The Queen's Necklace" — harmed Aisha's standing. The Prophet, who by then had six wives, chose his favorite to accompany him on a campaign against a tribe that was preparing to attack Medina. On the last evening of their return journey, Aisha went a little distance from the camp, either to perform her ablutions before prayer or to answer a call of nature, depending on who is telling the story. The next morning, as everyone was getting ready to leave, she realized she had lost a necklace. She went to look for it, and when she returned the army had left without her. They had put her litter onto her camel, thinking she was inside. Aisha stayed where she was, waiting for them to notice her absence and come look for her. Shortly before daybreak a man from the rearguard, Safwan, found her and took her back to the troop.

This inadvertent adventure caused libel and slander. In particular, Abdallah ibn Ubayy, chief of the anti-Mohammed faction known to Islam as the Munafikun, or hypocrites, proclaimed: "Aisha may be excused for what she has just done, because Safwan is younger and more handsome than the Prophet." Such statements bothered Mohammed and he grew cool to Aisha. When she realized she was being slandered, she took sick and fled to her parents. In the meantime her husband tried to sort out the truth. Ali, who had married the Prophet's daughter Fatima, counseled him to get rid of Aisha: "There are lots of women in the world. If in your heart you are not sure of this one, choose another." Aisha, already Fatima's enemy, never forgave Ali for these words.

Mohammed went to see her. Aisha, convinced that an innocent victim did not have to repent, put herself in God's hands. She was right to do so, for the Almighty revealed seventeen verses to his messenger on the subject of Aisha's innocence and the slanders against her (Sura 24 of the Koran).

The Prophet fell ill in 632. When he felt death approaching, he asked to be put in Aisha's room. She took care of him until he died.

The Prophet was in the habit of taking one of his wives along when he went on a compaign.
Caravan of Pilgrims in the Desert, engraving by Just L'Hernault.

Childless and a widow at about age eighteen, Aisha, "the Mother of the Faithful," could not remarry. Her father, Abu Bakr, succeeded Mohammed as the leader of Islam for two years. He was followed as caliph first by Omar and then by Othman, whom Aisha opposed. However, when Othman was assassinated in June 656, she denounced the murder and joined forces with Talha and Zubair to avenge him. At the head of a thousand troops from the Prophet's tribe, the three took the Iraqi city of Basra.

Ali, now caliph, whom they refused to recognize, marched against them. The struggle was long and bloody. On December 13, 656, the day of what became known as the "Battle of the Camel," Aisha was in the front lines. Much later the Andalusian writer Ibn Abd-Rabbih would tell us that Aisha said: "Oh my people, silence! I have maternal rights over you and am entitled to speak. Only accuse he who is untrue to his god. The Prophet, on him all blessings, died on my bosom and in my arms. . . . " Astride her camel, she revived the courage of her troops with her speech, and they continued to fight ferociously. Ali could see what she was doing. According to the historian Tabari, the caliph said: "As long as those men see that camel standing they will not quit." He sent two men to capture it. One of them cut off the hand of the man holding the reins, but another of Aisha's followers picked them up. His hand was also cut off. Seventy men in all lost their right hands. In the end, Ali ordered his men to cut the tendons of the camel carrying Aisha's litter. When the camel fell, the army from Basra fled.

Ali had Aisha led back to Medina with the greatest respect. In time they were reconciled. Ali was eventually assassinated, but Aisha lived another twenty years. The conflict in which both had participated resulted in the great schism that divided Islam into Shiah, the sect that supported Ali, and Sunnah, which had opposed him.

POPE JOAN

ITALY — 9TH CENTURY

The Rogation Day procession was fatal for Pope John VIII,
who was taken to be a saintly man until "he" gave birth. 15th century
miniature for *The Decameron* of Giovanni Boccaccio.

On credulity, error, and ignorance,
Priests have skillfully built their power;
I want to declare and prove today
That a woman likewise had her hour.

Voltaire.

Saeculum obscurum and hardly glorious, the Dark Ages of the 9th century did, however, witness the accession of a very interesting pope, called John VIII. Not the John VIII who reigned over the Church from 872 to 882, and was poisoned to death. No, our John VIII died in a much more unusual way, at least for a pope: he was finished off by the crowd after enduring a difficult childbirth.

For this John VIII was really Joan: "A woman succeeded Leon IV for two years, five months and four days," wrote Johannes Duns Scotus in the 11th century. Many other chroniclers gave their own versions of the incredible story of Pope Joan — they were so widely told that when the Church tried to erase her from the pages of history, they could not get rid of her. Instead of disappearing into obscurity, she evolved into legend, and for the Church her story became an allegory on the character flaws of the "true, only, and unique" John VIII — which is to say, the other John VIII. The Church's interpretation became so widely accepted that perhaps only a search of the Vatican's secret archives could root out the truth.

Happily, people of spirit and courage have taken up the cause of Pope Joan, and through an abundant literary tradition have restored her credentials. She was reinstated not only by Voltaire, but earlier by the Italian Giovanni Boccaccio, and in our time by Lawrence Durrell, in an adaptation of a Greek treatment of the story. And some of the scholars who now declare the whole legend entirely apocryphal do admit, even so, that it may have been inspired a 10th century Roman woman senator who reputedly controlled the elections of the popes. Here is an amalgam of several versions of Pope Joan's story:

Joan was born in Mainz, of a peasant mother who died soon after, and an Irish father, an extremely learned monk who taught theology in the monasteries and gave his daughter the best possible education. She was a gifted pupil, passionate about the humanities, arts, and theology. As they went from monastery to monastery she wore men's clothing for comfort while traveling.

After Joan's father died, the beautiful orphan continued her travels and her studies. Greek, physics, and philosophy soon held few secrets for her. One day, she met a young Benedictine monk, a man of spirit and heart, with whom she formed a great spiritual bond. They became lovers, and left together to journey across Mediterranean Europe to Greece. For discretion's sake, Joan dressed in the same clothing as her companion, and called herself "John." Athens bowed to the erudition of this young monk and his gift for argument. We do not know if her lover died, or if "John" left him, but she arrived in Rome alone.

Theological success found her easily. With her eloquence and virtue, "John" shone as she taught rhetoric, philosophy, and theology. Italy was then in real need of such a light. Pope Leon IV chose "Friar John" as his personal secretary; when the pope's health failed, the vote favored "Father John." *Vox populi, vox Dei:* on Leo's death, "John" became Pope John VIII.

After being ordained and enthroned with great ceremony, "John" began her papal career to everyone's satisfaction. Her renown was such that the chroniclers called her "the New Solomon." In her piety, she disbanded her predecessor's corps of concubines, appointed bishops, had churches built, sent the old Emperor Lothair to finish his days in a monastery, and crowned his son Louis II ruler of the Holy Roman Empire.

However, after several months the pontiff became bored with her new employment. Boccaccio wrote that she "fell into licentiousness and allowed [her]self to be courted, then seduced, by Lambert of Saxony, ambassador in Rome, who, his passion appeased, disappeared courageously and at the right moment." There was talk of a cardinal, too.

These dalliances eased her heart for a while. But soon her beautiful face became sad again, as if burdened by profound worry. She seemed ill for a time, then grew fat; she dressed in heavy, full garments, abandoned pontifical activities, shut herself up in her apartments. She went out only to take part in a Rogation Day procession to the Lateran Palace, where the crowd awaited her.

This ceremony proved fatal to the sovereign pontiff. When the faithful pressed around her to acclaim her, she collapsed suddenly, doubled up with pain on the ground — and gave birth. No one believed it was a miracle; they cried, "Sacrilege!" The pope was a woman! Thus the Holy Father perished on the day she became a mother, a victim of the anger of the crowd and hatred of the clergy.

For some time after this, the sex of each pope was carefully checked before he was enthroned. The person appointed sat on a chair with a hole in the bottom, the *stercoraria*, and the cardinals filed past him one by one, each in turn sliding a hand under the chair, so as to be able to declare: *"Testiculos habet et bene pendentes!"*

When the child appeared,
everyone realized the deception put over by Pope Joan.

SAINT TERESA OF AVILA

SPAIN — 1515-1582

The sole woman proclaimed a doctor of the church (the title given to Roman Catholic theologians of outstanding merit and holiness) Teresa of Avila is the greatest of the Catholic mystics. Her complex personality and the honesty of her writings also make her the most fascinating.

She was born in a village of the province of Avila, "the land of kings and saints." Teresa was of aristocratic Castilian blood on her mother's side, and of Jewish descent on her father's; her paternal grandfather had converted during the Inquisition. To those who questioned her breeding she would say: "I am a daughter of the church."

Her first mystical experience, at about age seven, led her to attempt running away from her parents to achieve her dream of becoming a hermit or being martyred by having her head cut off by Moors in the Holy Land. As an adolescent, she devoted herself to reading not only the lives of the saints but also romances of chivalry.

At sixteen she was pretty, coquettish, and in love with one of her cousins. She was thinking of marriage but her father had other ideas; she was sent for schooling to the Augustinian convent in the town of Avila. Although she entered against her will, she had only one idea when she came out in 1532: to return. Her mother had died and her brothers were leaving one by one for the New World, so she took over the household duties. But finally, ignoring her father's wishes, no longer able to resist her desire to take religious vows, she ran away.

Teresa knocked on the door of Carmelite Convent of the Incarnation and three days later, on November 2, 1535, she took the veil. Not long after, she fell ill and was taken to a healer who only made her worse. According to one version of the story, she was taken home and died.

Her intelligence and the strength of her faith made Teresa of Avila exceptional even among saints.

Her family took turns watching over her body. On the third day, her brother fell asleep and a candle fell, setting the room on fire. The body almost burned. The next day, tradition has it, Teresa revived. Her religious philosophy is based on the theme, "Oh that I die to not die."

During her long convalescence, Teresa read the *Third Spiritual Alphabet*, a masterpiece of Spanish mystical literature, which would help her achieve the "Prayer of Quiet." She recovered, but by some accounts was left partially paralyzed and occasionally suffered muteness from which she would recover only after taking Communion.

A sociable person, Teresa loved company and the latest news; even in her piety she liked to charm and to please people. At the convent she was considered a phenomenon and received many visitors — especially, in some versions of her life, one gentleman from Avila. She received a first warning: "Christ appeared before me and with great severity let me know how much he regretted it." She saw the man again and Christ appeared a second time. She felt that she had lost the Prayer of Quiet and went through a serious crisis, disciplining herself with fasting and flagellation.

In 1555, when Teresa was forty, she had a decisive experience: upon seeing a statue of Christ, she received knowledge of her humanity and threw herself to the ground in tears. She later had more visions and heard voices. Her confessors, however, did not understand that she was having mystical experiences, and she was thought to be possessed. These were troubled times, abounding with false visionaries and fanatics. In 1574 a rival went so far as to denounce her, and the following year, as a result of the dispute in the Carmelite order over the strict rule that Teresa advocated, she was forced to withdraw to a convent in Castile.

Many times Teresa reportedly experienced the phenomenon known as transverberation: she saw an angel who drove a javelin of gold into her heart, leaving her "filled with a great love of God." By some accounts she was also subject to levitation and asked the sisters to pin her to the ground to stop her. She reputedly went through this expe-

Saint Theresa of Avila knew and described many mystical experiences, such as the feeling that an angel was driving a golden spear through her heart.

rience once with her friend and fellow reformer and mystic, Saint John of the Cross, who was said to levitate whenever he spoke of the Trinity; one day, as the two mystics began to discuss just this subject, John was propelled to the ceiling even though he kept a tight grip on the chair he was sitting in, and Teresa soon joined him.

Teresa knew "spiritual marriage" with God. In one version of her life, this came about because, during Communion one day, John of the Cross found her "greedy" and gave her only half a host. The Lord appeared in her innermost soul, held out his right hand, comforted her, and told her she would watch over His happiness like a wife: "My honor is now yours, and yours is mine."

She compared this union to that of two wax candles joined so closely that they make one double light.

In her writings, Teresa attempted to explain her mystical state through images and metaphors. In her autobiography she wrote: "I will say nothing of which I do not have wide experience," and described the path that led her to an intimate, almost physical relationship with God.

But her work also went outside literature. She reformed the Carmelite order, founded some fifteen convents, extended her reforms to the monasteries with the help of John of the Cross, and worked for church unity.

The ramparts of Avila, chief city of the "land of kings and saints."

When Teresa died at the age of sixty-seven, she was, according to some versons, in a state of ecstasy and afterward the wrinkles on her face disappeared as if by miracle and her skin became like that of a child. Seven years later when she was exhumed for relics her body was reputedly intact. At the fifth exhumation, tales say, her heart was taken from her and found to be cracked in two because the angel had transfixed it so many times.

Salome

Galilee — 1st Century AD

The legend of Salome, given only a few scant lines in the
gospels of the New Testament, was a huge success
with Symbolist and Decadent writers and
painters, such as Gustave Moreau.

Matthew and Mark related the story of this Jewish princess in a few lines in their gospels. Over the centuries, Salome has fascinated painters and poets, who have portrayed her as splendid, mysterious, and exotic — and also as perverse and diabolical. But the episode that has gained her eternal infamy actually arose from her mother's malevolence, rather than her own:

Salome's parents, Herod Philip and Herodias, divorced and Herodias married Herod Antipas, the Roman-appointed tetrarch, or king, of Galilee, who was also the half-brother of her first husband. John the Baptist opposed this union, saying: "It is not lawful for thee to have thy brother's wife." The king threw him into jail. Mark's gospel recounts that "Herodias had a quarrel against John, and would have killed him, but she could not: For Herod feared John, knowing that he was a just man and an holy, and observed him; and when he heard him, he did many things, and heard him gladly" (Mark 6:19-20).

Herodias brooded over her lust for vengeance, awaiting the right moment. Her opportunity arrived during the king's birthday banquet. "Herodias' daughter came in, and danced, and pleased Herod." The king promised to give her whatever she desired as a reward. Salome consulted her mother, and at Herodias' request announced to the king: "I will that thou give me by and by in a charger the head of John the Baptist." Despite his distress, Herod could not break the promise he had made in front of all his guests, so he sent a guard to John's prison to carry out the deed. The guard "beheaded him in the prison, and brought his head in a charger, and gave it to the damsel; and the damsel gave it to her mother."

After this episode Salome married King Aristobulus in the year 54 AD. The Roman emperor Vespasian gave her the land of Chalcis in Greece, where she became queen. According to the Byzantine historian Nicephore, Salome died around 70 AD in tragic circumstances. In the dead of winter, she was crossing the Rhône River, which was blocked with ice. It broke under her weight and, as she fell through, the ice severed her neck.

During the 4th century, the popularity and veneration of John the Baptist increased — and with it the infamy of Salome. Saint Jerome attacked her character, and the church fathers held her story up as an example of the evils that dancing could lead to. From this time forward, her name would forever be associated with immorality.

Salome's dancing so delighted Herod, he offered her anything she desired. She asked for John the Baptist's head.

The legend of Salome inspired painters and sculptors as early as the year 1000. Since then, scenes of her performance for Herod's guests have been adapted to each contemporary style in its turn. She was depicted doing handstands in the 12th century and was called a tumbler. Her name was well-known during the Italian Renaissance, but then was almost totally forgotten until the Symbolists, Romantics, and Decadents rediscovered her in the 19th century.

"Her pale and passionate face radiated all the charms of the Orient and her rich dress also called to mind the tales of the sultana Sheherazade,"

"Through a delicate blue veil hiding her bust and head one could see the lights of her eyes, the tinkling jewelry of her ears, the white of her skin," wrote Gustave Flaubert in *Herodias*.

wrote Heinrich Heine in *Atta Troll*, his poem devoted to Salome. The German poet showed a fascination with the exoticism that would later inspire many other writers, including Gustave Flaubert in *Trois Contes* (Three Tales): "She danced like priestesses from the Indies, like Nubians from the waterfalls, like Lydian bacchantes. She swayed in every direction, like a flower being tossed about in the wind." He describes in minute detail this quintessential Oriental dancer: "Her eyelids half-closed, she twisted her middle, swung her belly about in undulating movements, made her breasts quiver; her face remained motionless and her two feet moved ceaselessly."

Oscar Wilde, in his play *Salome*, written in French for Sarah Bernhardt, emphasized the violent desire Salome felt for John the Baptist, whom she called Iokanaan. "I am in love with your body," her lines read. "Neither roses from the garden of the Queen of Arabia, nor the feet of dawn tram-

pling leaves, nor the breast of the moon when she lies down on the breast of the sea—there is nothing in the world as white as your body! I will kiss your lips, Iokanaan. I will kiss your lips!" Indeed, she does kiss the lips of the decapitated John, imposing on him in death what he would not accept from her alive. In Wilde's drama, it is Salome's unrequited passion that pushes her to the fatal act: she becomes mad with desire.

The Decadent writers and artists of the end of the 19th century continued to present Salome

Salome was sometimes portrayed as nearly satanic.

in this perverse light. In the Richard Strauss opera inspired by Wilde's play, Salome appears draped in the seven veils that have since become inextricably part of her image, obscuring her from clear view. Because, as the French Decadent novelist Joris-Karl Huysmans notes, "Neither Saint Matthew, nor Saint Mark, nor Saint Luke, nor the other evangelists dwelt upon the dancer's extraordinary charms or her acts of depravity. She remains in the background, lost, mysterious and swooning, in the distant fog of the centuries, elusive to those with unimaginative and precise minds, only accessible to the unhinged, made visionary by their neurosis."

COUNTESS ERZSEBET BATHORY

HUNGARY — 1560-1614

Erzsébet Bàthory did not wish to grow old. To preserve her skin against the ravages of age, she bathed in blood — the blood of young girls whom she killed slowly in the dungeons of her castle. And the whiter the skin of "the Bloody Countess," the blacker her soul became.

The brutal customs of the feudal system remained firmly embedded in 16th century Hungary, which, conquered by the Turks, had remained untouched by the progress of the Renaissance.

Erzsébet was born into the noble Báthory family, already infamous for its excesses. Some were distinguished by their good deeds, others by their penchant for lewdness and violence. Even in her childhood, Erzsébet, or Elisabeth, had sought the company of the worst elements of the family — that of Aunt Klara, for example, who had four husbands, killed the first two, and lived a wild life before coming to a tragic end: she was captured by a pasha, raped by the whole of his garrison, and stabbed, and her young lover was roasted on a spit. Erzsébet's Uncle István, King of Poland, suffered from "crises of the brain," a widespread affliction among the Báthorys: epilepsy. Some were plainly mad.

Erzsébet's destiny was linked with that of a much quieter family, the Nadasdys. At the age of eleven, she was officially betrothed to Ferencz Nadasdy, and the following year was sent to live with her future mother-in-law. Custom required that her family-to-be take care of her education until her marriage. Erzsébet did not show much interest in the austere life led by the Nadasdys, nor in learning the duties of mistress of the house. She preferred to go riding.

It was a grand wedding. After more than a month of celebration, the couple left to settle at

This turn-of-the-century Hungarian postcard shows Erzsebet Bathory, who found an excellent wrinkle remedy: she bathed in human blood.

Csejthe, as Erzsébet wished. She loved this sinister castle, set on a hill near a deep forest reportedly inhabited by witches and werewolves. In the Carpathian mountains on the Austro-Hungarian border, occult arts and superstitions of all kinds happily cohabited with the ancient cults of the sun and the moon. Erzsébet would hide her darkest secrets in the immense dungeons of this castle.

After a time, she grew bored. Her husband went to fight against the Turks, leaving her alone with guests she found unpleasant. She would have liked to entertain her own family, but the Báthorys, too odd for the tastes of the Nadasdys, were carefully kept away. Her visits with her husband to the court at Vienna were her only diversions, and Ferencz's weakening health put an end to these. By that time Erzsébet had four children and was nearly forty years old. But the beautiful brunette with the steely gaze, who bleached her hair in the Venetian fashion, still looked young. She spent whole days at her toilet, and hours contemplating her reflection in her favorite mirror. No wrinkle yet furrowed her satin skin, the envy of all who saw her.

She believed she owed her resistance to the ravages of time to the atrocities she committed. According to one version, the countess had slapped one of her servants until her nose bled, and by accident the blood splashed onto Erzsébet's face: she thought that it had made her skin whiter, more translucent. From that day on, she bathed in human blood.

In the popular account, she was helped by two toothless old witches, Jollona and Dorko, and by a hideous hunchback. There was also Darvulia, who chose the "bleeders" and who initiated the countess in the pleasures of inflicting pain.

The monstrous band had more than six hundred victims. They sought tall, young virgins, attracting them to the castle by promising them employment. The girls were imprisoned in dungeons to await their tragic fate. They were tied up tightly and beaten; their bodies were pierced with needles, and cut with razors; finally the veins in their arms were slit. "The mistress always rewarded

Another postcard displays the castle of Csejthe, in whose dungeons the countess tortured young virgins before bathing in their blood.

The "Bloody Countess" tale in a comic book by George Pichard.

the old women when they had tortured the girls well," one of her companions said at her trial. "She herself tore out the flesh with pincers, and cut between the fingers. She had them led onto the snow, naked, and sprayed with icy water. She sprayed them herself and they died of it."

The carnage may have begun before the death of Ferencz Nadasdy in 1600, but it reached its climax after that date. Erzsébet had an "iron maiden" constructed like that used in torture at Nuremberg. Blinded by her mad passion for the pain of others, she was no longer content with the red blood of servants, but wanted the blue blood of noble victims. She took fewer and fewer precautions to conceal the horrors she committed.

Inevitably, her atrocities were discovered. Her accomplices appeared without her at the trial in 1611; every effort was made to avoid bringing scandal on the illustrious Báthory and Nadasdy names. But all the evidence spoke loudly against Erzsébet herself: witnesses, objects of torture, and a little notebook wherein she had noted the names and characteristics of her victims. Her accomplices were executed; she was condemned to life imprisonment in her castle; she lived there three more years, uttering neither appeal nor repentance.

The 19th century Austrian writer Leopold Sacher-Masoch, whose novels gave birth to the term masochism, retold the countess' tale in a short story. Since then, she whom the Hungarians called "The Beast" has appeared in literature, on the stage, and on screen.

Mata Hari

NETHERLANDS 1876 — FRANCE 1917

An exotic dancer with a gift for seduction who loved money and military officers, Mata Hari was reputedly a godsend to the German secret service, which made her into the dangerous Agent H21 of World War I. The spy with the velvet eyes had all Europe at her feet.

"Take care of my Gerda! She may be intelligent but she is a good girl. Later, perhaps, you'll make her a deaconess." The pious and respected Mrs. Zelle, pronouncing these words on her deathbed, was never to know how different her daughter's destiny would be. At the age of fourteen, Margaretha Geetruida found herself the only woman in her family and responsible for raising her three brothers. Then her father, a prosperous hatter, remarried and placed her in a convent, where she proved brilliant at languages. At eighteen she left the convent and rapidly shed her Catholic upbringing. She frequented Amsterdam nightspots and twisted men around her little finger.

In 1895, Gerda married — as the result of a practical joke. She read an advertisement by a Dutch army captain, on leave from India, looking for a wife. She immediately replied, sending her photo. For Gerda, an officer was "a kind of artist associated with the brilliant career of arms" and she adored them all, regardless of nationality. In fact the advertisement was a joke played by some friends of Rudolph MacLeod, a woman-chaser in his forties. But he was so struck by Gerda's portrait that he wished to meet her. The tale is classic: they fell in love, she got pregnant, they married, and he resumed chasing women.

After the birth of a second child, the couple joined Rudy's regiment in Sumatra. Gerda's life was impossible. Rudy drank, treated her like a domestic slave, beat her, wouldn't let her go out. During an official diner, Gerda attracted the attention of the local sultan, who asked her to his

Behind the features of Mata Hari,
"eye of the day," was the eye of Berlin.

palace. She sneaked out, hoping to ask for money to leave Rudy, and came back after spending the night with the sultan, sure that he would help her.

But before she could leave, her son died — later Mata Hari claimed that he was poisoned and that she had strangled the murderer with her own hands — and her husband left her, taking their daughter. Gerda was alone when she gave birth to her third child, a daughter by the sultan. She didn't want to live with the sultan but he offered her money if she would leave him the baby. So she abandoned the little Banda, returned to the

Gerda presented herself in Paris as "the first dancer of Java" and, after a struggle, met with success.

Netherlands, and divorced.

In 1905, free at twenty-six, Gerda went to Paris, intending to establish herself as a sacred dancer from Java. She called herself Mata Hari, which in Malay means "eye of the day," the sun. Her career did not flourish at first, and she lived off the generosity of her lovers. Finally she met the industrialist and Asian art collector Emile

The story of the dancer-spy inspired the cinema. Greta Garbo played Mata Hari in the film of the same name.

Guimet. Fascinated by the woman and the artist, he organized a recital for her. Nearly naked, Mata Hari danced — "lithe as the serpent hypnotized by the sound of the flute," according to one critic — and was a sensation.

After enjoying success in many European capitals and an easy life thanks to her lovers' money, she was annoyed to realize her fame was fading. "If Paris has ceased to adore me, I shall go to Berlin!" she declared. There she passed herself off as a natural daughter of the Prince of Wales and a Hindu princess. According to one account she attracted the notice of the chief of police, who realized she would make a good spy. Mata Hari apparently accepted his proposal and, after a brief training period, became Agent H21.

In 1912, Europe was on the brink of war. Her first assignment was to ensure that French journalists supported Germany. When war broke out she was sent to the Netherlands and reported from there until she obtained authorization to enter France again in July 1915. Thanks to her network, the Germans were informed of Allied sup-

plies and movements. She then went to Vittel, where a great counteroffensive was being prepared. This strengthened French officials' suspicions about her. But Mata Hari's influence stretched as far as the French War Ministry, for her career as a courtesan was at its peak.

Watched by the Italians when traveling in Spain, interrogated by the British secret service when visiting England, and followed by a French agent when in the Netherlands, Mata Hari may have decided to defect to France to calm suspicion. But a last trip to Madrid, where she met a German friend, was fatal. She was arrested shortly after her return to Paris in February 1917. Her protectors could do nothing. She was accused of spying and condemned to death in a closed court. Her version of affairs was that she was a double agent. Historians of the war still argue about how much actual spying she did, and for whom.

The rumors surrounding the dancer's death were even more fantastic than those about her life. One of her lovers reputedly thought of an escape based on the opera *Tosca*. Her seventy-five-year-old lawyer tried to save her by claiming she was pregnant by him. It was said that on the eve of her execution she danced an appeal to the god Siva and ate a last supper of filet mignon and champagne. She went before the firing squad on July 17, 1917.

Her daughter Banda, still in Asia, learned later of the legend of Mata Hari. Banda reportedly joined the Japanese secret service when Japan invaded Java in World War II, then worked in China for the CIA before being caught and executed in 1950.

Mata Hari on the day of her execution.

ANNE BONNEY AND MARY READ
THE CARIBBEAN — 18TH CENTURY

Two women who made every sailor in the Caribbean tremble:
Anne Bonney and Mary Read, who served aboard The Implacable.
Anne and Mary in the Antilles, 19th century Italian engraving.

When the English boarded The Implacable, the pirate sloop of the notorious Jack Rackham, the two pirates who defended themselves the most fiercely were Anne and Mary, the beautiful buccaneers.

Anne Bonney, or Bonny, was the natural daughter of a serving girl and a lawyer from Cork, Ireland. Her father, who was married, passed her off as the orphaned son of a cousin so that he could take care of her. Things might have gone on peacefully like this, but the lawyer was caught while committing adultery and, to avoid the scandal, left Ireland abruptly. Taking his mistress and their daughter, still disguised as a little boy, he settled in South Carolina and became a prosperous planter. His mistress died and he took charge of educating his beloved daughter, who turned into a healthy little savage.

Although basically kind, Anne was temperamental. One day she went so far as to stab her English maid. When she was old enough to dream, her thoughts turned to the high seas and pirates, yet she fell in love with a simple sailor who dreamed only of safe harbors. Against her father's advice, she married Jim Bonney and moved to the Bahamas, but quickly tired of him when he refused to join a band of pirates. Soon Anne found a lover more to her taste in the colorful Captain "Calico Jack" Rackham, or Rackam. She easily persuaded the buccaneer to take to the seas again, left her home and husband, and weighed anchor aboard The Implacable.

Anne took to wearing men's clothes again. Booted, she wore the trousers of a sailor, a shirt belted with a red and white silk scarf, and a grey felt hat. A cutlass, hand pistols, and cartridge belts completed the picture. Since clothes do not a pirate make, she practiced swordplay regularly with Rackham. The pirates accepted her as one of their brethren. Warlike and fearless, even capable of cruelty, she was always the first to board a prize vessel and came to be considered her lover's equal.

Following a venture to pillage a Cuban hacienda, Anne and Jack sailed south toward Maracaibo, Venezuela, searching for a ship to sack. They fell upon a Dutch corsair. A young, still beardless Englishman was among the crew. He immediately agreed to join the pirates. His charming manners and the fact that he didn't drink like the rest of the men attracted Anne and exasperated Jack Rackham. Then Anne discovered that the newcomer was a woman.

No one on board had suspected Mary Read's real sex until Anne developed a fondness for the supposed handsome young man. In an effort to seduce him, she disclosed that despite her attire she, Anne, was a woman. An embarrassed Mary was obliged to reveal that she was, too.

Mary Read's English mother, married to a sailor who was often absent on voyages, had con-

Anne Bonney took the place of her lover, Jack Rackham, and proved to be the better captain.

ceived her out of wedlock. To hide this from her family, she substituted Mary for the year-old son she had recently lost. Called John, Mary was dressed and raised like a boy. At thirteen she learned why she wasn't quite like the other lads but decided to keep up the subterfuge, which gave her much freedom.

She became a lackey, a sailor, and a soldier, first in the Flemish infantry and then in the cavalry. She fell in love with a handsome Flemish trooper, and, having told him her secret, married him. They opened a tavern and lived happily until he died. After that she once again took to wearing masculine and military clothes. Finally, tired of this life, she set off for the Caribbean.

In the beginning only Anne and Jack knew Mary's secret. The two women became the best of friends — and more, by many accounts, though when the crew captured a prize and a charming

young carpenter aboard signed on to join them, Mary promptly fell very much in love with him. Yet she didn't dare say anything until after a violent quarrel arose between the young man and another pirate, a strapping fellow who provoked the carpenter into a duel. Fearing that she might lose her loved one, Mary turned his antagonist's anger upon herself and arranged her own duel with him before he and the carpenter could fight. As proficient with pistol as with sword, Mary killed her adversary, and her carpenter did not have to risk his life. She loved him even more after this incident and finally showed him her breasts as a proof of her love and good faith. They married in pirate fashion aboard The Implacable and had a short but memorable time together.

Both Anne and Mary wore the pants in their marriages. Rackham thought more of drinking than commanding, so Anne often took his place. As for Mary's carpenter, he preferred provisioning the pirates and left the fighting to his wife.

In October 1720 the pirates aboard The Implacable were surprised by an armed British sloop sent by the governor of Jamaica to capture them. Most of the male pirates were drunk. Anne and Mary defended the ship while their companions hid in the hold. They were overcome in this unequal battle, and all the pirates were taken to be judged in Jamaica.

On the day of his execution, Rackham, who had dared to plead not guilty, was allowed to talk to Anne for a last time. She said: "I'm sorry to see you here, but had you fought like a man, you wouldn't be hanged like a dog!" Since both women said they were pregnant, their executions were deferred. Anne escaped, thanks to her father, but Mary ended her days in a cell, thinking of her beloved, the only pirate who was released.

At least, that's one version of the story. Anne and Mary, unheard of before their trial, afterward attracted biographers like flies, and details of their lives vary in every account. Almost nothing verifiable is known about them, including Anne's eventual fate.

BONNIE PARKER

UNITED STATES — 1910-1934

This is the story of Bonnie Parker, the golden-haired girl who, for love of Clyde Barrow, embarked on a life of crime. She predicted her fate better than anyone else:

Some day they'll go down together;
And they'll bury them side by side;
To few it'll be grief —
To the law a relief —
But it's death for Bonnie and Clyde.

Nothing in Bonnie's childhood prepared her to become a public enemy and legendary outlaw. She was raised by a gentle, conscientious mother, whom she adored. Her father died when Bonnie was four, and Mrs. Parker moved to the Dallas area with her children, to be nearer to her relatives. Bonnie's cousin Bess remembered her as a star pupil who won prizes in composition, spelling, and recitation. The excellent student was fascinated by acting and cultivated her natural ability to make people laugh. She hoped to become an actress, a circus acrobat, or an opera singer when she grew up.

As an adolescent she had plenty of boyfriends, but did not go out on her first real date until she was fifteen. She married Roy Thornton when she was only sixteen, but continued seeing her mother every day, so Mrs. Parker suggested that the young couple move in with her in 1926. Bonnie stayed in her mother's home until the spring of 1932, when she left with Clyde Barrow.

Roy had neglected his wife, often disappearing without explanation for days at a time. Bonnie shed many tears over him, until she went to work as a waitress and discarded her despair. In 1929, she left Roy and lost her job. And then one day, in a friend's kitchen in West Dallas, Bonnie Parker met Clyde Barrow.

Bonnie had this photograph taken as a joke, but it appeared in all the newspapers and spread the idea that "Public Enemy Number One" was a hard woman.

Bonnie fell in love with the charming young man, unaware of his unfortunate habit of "borrowing" cars and cracking safes, which earned him occasional prison terms. Clyde was between jail terms when he met Bonnie, and he was enchanted by her. His sister Nell described Bonnie as a charming, doll-like woman, with wispy blond hair, delicate skin, a seductive mouth, and extraordinary blue eyes. And Bonnie's mother liked Clyde, too; she thought him very handsome with his wavy brown hair, his sparkling dark eyes, and his dimples.

Clyde soon wound up in prison again, but Bonnie believed that at heart he wasn't a criminal, and set out to show him that they could be happy living peacefully together. Her tactics were a bit

For love of Clyde Barrow, Bonnie embarked on a life of crime. Fascinating characters and a vivid story tempted Arthur Penn, who directed the film *Bonnie and Clyde* with Faye Dunaway as Bonnie.

misguided, however: to bring him home to her sooner, she helped him escape by smuggling a gun to him in prison. Clyde was recaptured a week later, and this time was imprisoned for eighteen months. When he was released in 1932, he was twenty-three years old and two toes poorer: he had asked a fellow prisoner to chop off his two

Bonnie and Clyde's car, pockmarked by bullet holes during the last bloody police attack.

big toes with a hatchet so he would not have to work in the fields.

It was clear that Clyde would never change, so Bonnie had only two choices: give him up, or join him in a life of crime. Bonnie loved him and chose the second route, knowing full well that it could lead only to early death for both of them. During their first armed robbery, she was arrested and spent three months in prison, where she wrote "The Ballad of Suicide Sal." In the meantime, Clyde pulled off a hold-up — and the police thought Bonnie was involved. This was how the legend started. From then on, whenever a crime was committed in the area, Clyde Barrow was accused and it was said that the "golden-haired girl" was his lookout and drove the getaway car. Thus began their long flight through the Southwest.

When Clyde was released from prison, his brother Buck joined the "Barrow gang" along with his wife Blanche, a timid woman who really wanted to go home to her parents. Bonnie, Clyde, and their companions W.D. Jones and Ray Hamilton had developed bad habits: they committed robberies when they needed money, kidnapped policemen for the fun of it, and visited their families whenever they could. In fact, they lived like hunted animals, and were only happy because they were together. Bonnie blamed outside forces for their fate; she felt that society had given them no choice.

The press hounded the Barrow gang, sometimes reporting that they were in several places at the same time, claiming they were capable of anything. Bonnie was portrayed as a cigar-smoking, submachine-gun-toting moll because of a photo she had posed for as a joke. She hated this image.

The police in all the Southern states were hot on their heels. They tried to trap the gang in a bloody battle in Missouri. The next attempt, in Iowa, was even bloodier: Buck was killed, Blanche was captured, the three others were wounded and barely escaped. Bonnie and Clyde lived less than a year more, staying mostly in their car because the dragnet was closing in on them. Betrayed by the father of a friend, they were taken in ambush on May 23, 1934, near Gibsland, Louisiana, by a Texas posse. Their captors, wanting to be absolutely sure they were dead, fired over fifty times into each of the corpses.

When the citizens of the area learned what was happening, they rushed to the spot to collect souvenirs of the famous criminal lovers. They tore off Bonnie's dress, cut off her hair, and ransacked her purse. In Dallas, twenty thousand people gathered to see their bodies, and their funeral drew crowds of spectators. As the ceremony ended, airplanes swept low over the cemetery to drop flowers onto their open grave.

"It's death for Bonnie and Clyde."

MARIA BONITA

BRAZIL — 1908-1938

The *cangaceiros*: bandits who were loved by some and hated by others.
A scene from one of Brazil's best-known films, *O Cangaceiro*, by Lima Baretto.

Quick, quick, Maria Bonita!
Wake up and make the coffee!
Day is about to break
And the police are already about!

The Brazilian bards sang the glory of Maria Bonita; poets wrote of her romance with the highwayman Lampião; filmmakers immortalized their adventures. All of this fed the legend of Maria Deia, known as Maria Bonita, "Pretty Mary."

"She was a small, nicely rounded, dark-haired woman," one companion recalled. "Her dark chestnut hair was long and shiny; she had beautiful teeth. She was really very pretty and none of the photos I have seen do justice to her beauty."

She grew up near Jeremoabo, in the state of Bahia, one of eleven children. Her father, Joao Casé, was a wealthy landowner. When she married, Maria left her father's *fazenda*, or big farm, Malhada do Caiçara, to settle nearby with her husband, José, a shoemaker. But while she lived with José, she dreamed of Lampião, the great *cangaceiro* of nearly mythic reputation.

The *cangaceiros* were armed men who lived outside the law. They had become a sort of mafia that "protected" the *fazendeiros* and defended the population, much like Robin Hood and his merry men, in the popular imagination. Thanks to his prowess with weaponry and to astute alliances with politicians and *fazendeiros*, one of these rebels had achieved mastery of the entire *sertão*, an immense region of northern Brazil. He was Captain Virgulano Ferreira da Silva, alias Lampião, "the lantern." A brigand, certainly, but also a poet and musician, he angered the police and excited the hearts of women. But seduction did not interest Lampião; he preferred to visit prostitutes occasionally rather than court young ladies at length.

Pursued by a detachment of police, Lampião took refuge one day at Malhada do Caiçara. Forewarned of his arrival, Maria told one of his companions that she wanted to meet the great bandit. This aroused Lampião's curiosity. The following day, they went to visit Maria. One of the many versions of this legend tells that she recognized him as soon as she opened the door:

"He's the one I love," she said immediately. "Will you take me with you?" And Lampião replied, "Whatever you want." She dressed quickly for travel, packed up a few things, took leave of her husband with a simple "Goodbye," and left with the *cangaceiros*.

Maria Bonita followed her lover everywhere. Both ended up dead by violence.
A scene from another Brazilian film, *The Black God and the White Devil*, by Glauber Rocha.

Maria Bonita left husband and family to live with Lampião, the great *cangaceiro*. Their legendary love inspires the Brazilians, who revive it in the *litteratura de cordel*, popular stories that are sold hanging from a string.

What could her poor husband do? Nothing. Maria even had her parents' blessing. As for Lampião, the shy, solitary bandit, he found himself with a wife. This pleased his companions, for it meant they could now bring their wives along, too. The gang of Captain Virgulano joined with a gang of wives, who followed them and lived precariously in the wilderness. The women were not idle: they gave first aid after attacks, sewed, and did the cooking in the makeshift settlements. In the evenings, they enlivened camp life with their dancing and singing. And sometimes they had babies. During labor the women would be taken to trustworthy allies to be properly cared for. Lampião was solicitous about these matters and did not leave Maria during childbirth. She had several children, but only a daughter survived.

Unlike her female companions, Maria joined her husband in combat. Generally, she stayed at Lampião's side, urging him to be prudent, but on occasion she took part in the struggle with the pistol she wore in her belt. A journalist who tried to make a film about the *cangaceiros* reported, "I have just spent six months with the gang; I have never seen her thwarted, nor frightened. . . . She accompanies Virgulano everywhere; she rides up and down rocks and hills; never did he hold her hand to help her; it was not necessary." Maria was known as a gentle, calm woman, but she could react violently to the contemptuous "ladies" whose houses the gang invaded: she would snatch their earrings — and their ear lobes with them.

During the last four years of his life, Lampião quieted down somewhat. Maria urged him to abandon his perpetual flight, and to settle down on a *fazenda*. But Lampião had sworn to live with a gun in his hand when his father was killed by a rival family aided by the police — and anyway, it would have been very difficult for this wild old dog to learn tame new tricks. He compromised by trying to make their life more secure. Lampião set up headquarters at Angico, a veritable fortress in the mountainous region of Sergipe, and from there controlled smaller bands which ventured out to make attacks. He relied heavily on his lieutenants, and ceased to be heard of. Rumors spread that he was dead, but the police remained vigilant.

In June 1938, the police captured a trader, one of Lampião's allies, and forced him to reveal the location of the bandits' den. According to the official version, forty-eight military policemen encircled Lampião's refuge at dawn on July 28, 1938, and killed all the bandits living there at the time — Lampião, Maria Bonita, nine men, and one other woman. It seems unlikely that the police accomplished this so easily, after twenty years of vain pursuit. More likely, the trader was forced to poison the gang, while the police took credit for the "victory."

The corpses were decapitated, and their heads displayed on the church steps in Santana do Ipanema. Later, those of Lampião and Maria Bonita were exhibited in a museum in Bahia. As for the treasure of jewels and gold coins that Maria Bonita was rumored to have amassed during her seven years as a bandit — it was never found.

Boadicea, Queen *of the Iceni.*

BOUDICCA

BRITAIN — 1ST CENTURY

Some women in history are figures of legend even though we know almost nothing about them, neither their place nor date of birth, and little about their looks or their beliefs. Boudicca is one of these. We have no precise idea of the path she took to become a part of history and a symbol of Britain. Yet the very fact that we know so little about the woman adds to the mystery and significance of the legend that surrounds her.

Boudicca, or Boadicea, was the wife of Prasutagus, king of the Iceni tribe. She bore him two daughters. Had she born a son, we would probably know even less about her. But she did not; and the schemes of Agrippina, a woman Boudicca would never meet, changed the course of history in the British queen's remote corner of the Roman Empire, what is now roughly the county of Norfolk.

Agrippina, fourth wife of the Emperor Claudius, was at the focus of the empire and of power. To further the interests of her son Nero, she provoked an estrangement between Claudius and Britannicus, his son by his third wife, Messalina. Agrippina's tireless gift for intrigue was effective. Nero became emperor following the assassination of Claudius (tradition has it that the murderer was Agrippina). Shortly afterward, at the instigation of his mother — who was using Britannicus as a threat — Nero had Britannicus assassinated. Not even Agrippina escaped the cruelty and abuse of power that marked her son's reign; ultimately she was killed at his order.

In Britain, Prasutagus realized his death was imminent. Worried about the stability of his kingdom, he thought of a scheme that he believed must prove infallible. He left his private wealth to his two daughters and to the Emperor Nero, thinking that this would oblige Nero to respect

In her homeland, Boudicca's legend grew until she personified British spirit. Today her statue guards the entrance to London's Westminster Bridge.

BOADICEA.

Boudicca led the Iceni to revolt against Roman injustice.
When they failed, she chose to die like a warrior and a queen.

his will. He was wrong. The historian Tacitus tells us that after Prasutagus' death in 60 AD the Roman army flogged Boudicca and raped her daughters, if not with Nero's approval then at least with his silent consent.

Nero had no reason to respect the last wishes of a barbarian king whom he considered his subject. No one could have foreseen the far-reaching consequences of outraged innocence.

Having neither husband nor son to protect her, Boudicca decided to defend her daughters' inheritance. With infinite patience, and sustained by anger and a sense of injustice, she first appealed to the pride of the Iceni. She called for vengeance and protested against the excesses of Roman rule. She incited the Iceni in the name of freedom. Ultimately she raised an army one hundred and twenty thousand strong, ready to break the yoke of Roman rule.

The governor of the province, Suetonius Paulinus, was abroad and Boudicca seized her opportunity. In 60 or 61 AD, rebellion burst out in the whole of East Anglia. The surprise attack was a massacre. According to Tacitus, the Iceni killed seventy thousand Romans and local sympathizers. They sacked Camulodunum (Colchester), Verulamium (St. Albans), and Londinium (London), as well as numerous military outposts, before Suetonius returned. He quickly organized a counterattack. Even though the rebels had annihilated the Ninth Legion, the superiority of the Roman forces and the reinforcements called up by their leader was so great that, following a fierce battle, Suetonius reconquered the province.

Boudicca had failed, but she did not submit to the humiliation and torment that would surely have followed Suetonius' triumph. Instead, she chose the fate of warrior and queen, probably death by poison at her own hand. According to tradition, her daughters joined her.

Boudicca's story is brief, sad, and violent. Perhaps that is one reason her memory has persisted over the centuries. Imagination may give her any aspect, any age, any personality. She exemplifies courage and the capacity of women to adapt to changed conditions despite the constraints of marriage and motherhood. She was neither the first nor by any means the last to demonstrate that women could bear arms, fight ferociously, and face up to the cruelty of battle. But she caught the imagination like no other.

Though Suetonius' decisive victory over Boudicca served to put an end to British rebellion against the Romans and solidify the empire's grasp, it was Boudicca's valiant defeat that lived in memory. In her homeland, her legend grew until she came to personify the resilient British spirit and the determination that "Britons never will be slaves."

Several localities in and around Greater London claim the honor of being the site of Boudicca's last battle. Thomas Thornycroft's bronze statue of the queen and her rearing horses, which guards one end of Westminster Bridge, is a favorite landmark for Londoners and visitors alike. By proving that righteous indignation can overcome weakness and that no task is too great where justice is at stake, Boudicca gained immortality.

AL-KAHINA

ALGERIA — 7TH CENTURY

The clairvoyant war chief Al-Kahina fought the Arab invasion from her stronghold in the Aurès mountains of what is now Algeria.

Clairvoyant, queen, and war chief: that was Al-Kahina, who succeeded in uniting the Berbers and, as their leader, ferociously fought the Arab invaders. Historical figure or legendary, she remains the symbol of Berber identity.

In the middle of the 7th century, the newly Islamized Arabs undertook to conquer Ifrikiya, the eastern part of the Mahgreb or northwest Af-rica. It was a jihad, a holy war sanctioned by the Koran with the aim of converting the conquered populations to the new faith. The peoples to be subjugated were the Byzantines, who occupied the eastern regions of present-day Algeria, and the Berbers, who lived throughout Ifrikiya. More than fifty years of fighting would pass before the Arabs achieved their goal.

In 670, Ukba the Nafi founded Kairouan, in what is now Tunisia. It was the first Arab town on African soil. But his conquest was short-lived, for in about 683 he was killed by Kosaila, the chief Berber. Kosaila died only about three years later, leaving an enormous void in tribal leadership. A chief was needed to lead the Berber resistance. Al-Kahina became that chief.

Who was she? "Al-Kahina," her nickname ("the clairvoyant" or "the sorceress"), had been given her by the Arabs because she claimed to hear demons and read people's minds: "That woman forecast the future, and nothing she announced failed to take place," remarked the encyclopedist Nuwairi. Others have read "Kahina" as a feminine version of *kohen*, Hebrew for priest, inferring from this that she was Jewish. Others say she was a Christian. There is no proof of her religion, or even of her true name: Dihya, Dahya, Damya, Damiya? Many variations exist.

Born in the Aurès mountains, Al-Kahina belonged to the Jarawa, a subgroup of the nomadic Zanata tribe. It is said that she married a Greek, to whom she bore a son. That would support the idea that she was Christian, and also explain her influence on the Byzantines. Al-Kahina also bore a second son, fathered by a Berber.

Upon the chief's death, Al-Kahina proved herself a worthy successor by unifying all the Berber clans, greatly increasing the number of warriors fighting the Arabs. A new Arab conqueror, Hassan ibn An-Numan, laid siege to Carthage in about 695, firm in his intent to take his conquest deeper into Africa. He ran into Al-Kahina.

According to the historian Ibn Idhari, when Hassan asked the Kairouan villagers who was the most powerful prince in Ifrikiya, they replied: "It is a woman called Al-Kahina, who lives in the Aurès; all the Romans fear her and all the Berbers obey her; with her killed, the whole of the Maghreb will yield to you and you will no longer find rivalry or resistance."

Hassan set off to attack her. Warned of his approach, Al-Kahina demolished her fortress at Baghaia so it would not fall into enemy hands. Counterattacking, she was victorious in a desperate battle on the banks of the Nini River. From then on, that waterway was known as the River of Affliction by the Arabs. The Berbers took prisoners. "Al-Kahina treated them kindly and sent them all away, with the exception of Khaled Ibn-Yezid, of the Cais tribe, a man distinguished by his rank and bravery, whom she adopted as a son," Nuwairi tells us.

Al-Kahina was a Berber, like these women from the Biskra area in Algeria.

The Arab Hassan retreated and set up camp to the east of Tripoli, where his caliph ordered him to stay. After about five years, Hassan was ordered to resume the struggle. Seeing that the invaders were returning, the Berber queen decided to employ the "scorched earth" tactic, rendering the area useless to the conquerors. Arab historians exaggerate the consequences considerably: "This accursed Kahina ruined all that," wrote Ibn Idhari, referring to important towns, villages, and fortresses of Ifrikiya, "and then numerous Christians and natives, crying for vengeance against her, had to flee to Spain and other islands." It is certain that her measures did not meet general approval, and some of the Berbers rallied to Hassan's cause to save their homeland. Al-Kahina's action had destroyed the hard-won Berber unity; the prophetess within her knew she was conquered.

The Arabs advanced. The story goes that one day Al-Kahina entered a state of ecstasy and, her hair loose, beat on her chest, crying that the end of the war was near, that Hassan's troops would conquer, that she would die. Refusing the shame of flight, she insisted on fighting to the end. Yet she summoned her sons just as her adopted son Khaled was informing them of her prophecy — and counseled them to surrender to Hassan.

Was it weakness? Treason? Let's call it clairvoyance. For by encouraging her sons to join the enemy, Al-Kahina was not only protecting her lineage, she was also giving her sons as a legacy to a civilization that would spread throughout the whole of the Maghreb.

The Berber queen fought her last battle in 702, near a well that bore her name for many years. Her sons were allowed to join Hassan's camp, on condition that they provide him with twelve thousand warriors; this they did. At the head of Al-Kahina's Berbers, her sons joined forces with the Arabs and completed the conquest.

JOAN OF ARC

FRANCE — 1412-1431

A simple farm girl, she answered a divine summons to take up arms against the English invaders and lead her dauphin to his throne. For this act of courage she was denounced as a heretic and burned at the stake. And now she is a saint, often used as the symbol of French nationalism: Jeanne d'Arc, Joan of Arc.

Legend calls her a shepherdess. While it is true that Joan sometimes took care of animals, she was the daughter of a prosperous farmer in the small parish of Domrémy, on the border between Lorraine and Champagne. Pious and charitable, she divided her time between various household and farm tasks. Most likely she was in the garden of her father's home when she first heard the voice of the Archangel Michael. He was followed by a vision of Saint Catherine, patron saint of young girls, and then by Saint Margaret of Antioch, the martyr whose statue watched over the Domrémy sanctuary. Joan's life was turned upside down.

The voices exhorted Joan to deliver the kingdom of France from its English invaders and their Burgundian supporters, and to lead the dauphin Charles to Reims to be crowned. At first she resisted the appeals, believing that a thirteen-year-old girl could not accomplish such a thing. The voices increased in their insistence, and at last in 1428 she gave in, seeking out the French captain at Vaucouleurs as the voices instructed. Half-amused, half-angry, he sent her home. She came back the next year. This time the captain relented; after taking the precaution of having her exorcised, he entrusted Joan with a sword and sent her with an escort to join the dauphin in Chinon.

It was in February 1429 that Joan began the dangerous journey to her prince's side, crossing a France impoverished by the Hundred Years' War. She dressed like a man, in surcoat and tight hose, and slept among her six male comrades. They

Joan of Arc is frequently used
to symbolize French nationalism.

respected her vow of chastity because she radiated such goodness.

When she arrived at Chinon, Charles was in a precarious position. If the English took Orléans, his chances of being crowned king were gone forever. There is no doubt that only the urgency of his plight convinced him to see Joan. That, and the fact that a prophet had said, "A woman was the ruin of France, another will save her."

To test her, the prince disguised himself and mingled among his guests. Joan knew immediately which was her "gentle Dauphin," and bowed to him, saying she had come in the name of God to have him crowned in Reims. Then she proved to him the divine authority for her mission by revealing a secret sign, or, in some accounts, by telling him what prayer he had addressed to God

Joan knew that she would soon be taken captive, but didn't hesitate to try to relieve the Burgundian siege of Compiegne.

the previous All Saints' Day. She still had to undergo three weeks of testing in Poitiers to prove the authenticity of her faith to the theologians. Finally she was allowed to leave for Tours, where she was granted the first emblems of her rank as *chef de guerre*: the white armor she was so proud of, and a standard bearing the image of Christ and the French coat of arms. To complete this outfit, a sword was discovered in the chapel of Saint Catherine of Fierbois, as her voices had foretold.

Battling to deliver Orléans from the invaders, Joan impressed her compatriots with her courage and initiative. She also had to evade all the traps

She was burned at the stake, like a witch.

set by her own captains in their efforts to reduce her to a symbolic role. This seventeen-year-old, having forced the English to retreat, entered the city in triumph and began to outshine even Charles himself in the honor accorded her. Several months later, on July 16, 1429, she reached Reims, where the dauphin was crowned King Charles VII in full pomp and circumstance.

Still stirred to action by her voices, she had every intention of battling until all France was recovered, but support was lacking. Charles VII's efforts to keep her at court by plying her with gifts did not make her mission easier. Joan finally took up arms again at the head of a hundred men, knowing her voices had foretold that she would be captured. On May 23, 1430, she was taken captive by Burgundian troops while fighting for Compiègne, and was sold to the English.

Joan's trial was held in Rouen the next year, under the authority of Bishop Pierre Cauchon.

Accused of heresy and witchcraft, she defended herself simply and courageously, maintaining that her voices had not lied to her. When asked during the trial whether she was in a state of grace, she replied: "If I am not, may God grant me that state, and if I am, may God keep me there." Under pressure, however, she was forced to sign a statement renouncing her claim to divine inspiration, which she later retracted. She was finally declared a relapsed heretic, turned over to the English, and burned at the stake in the old market square in Rouen. The list of her crimes was carved on the stake to which she was bound:

Joan, who is called the Maid of Orleans, a pernicious liar, an abuser of people, a soothsayer, superstitious, a blasphemer, presumptuous, an infidel, a boaster, an idolater, cruel, dissolute, a conjuror of devils, an apostate, a schismatic, a heretic.

Charles VII, who had done nothing to save Joan, conducted an inquiry almost twenty years later. Her name was cleared in 1456, and she became a national hero and a thorn in the flesh of Franco-English relations. And in 1920, Pope Benedict XV declared Joan of Arc a saint.

Ingrid Bergman played Joan in the film *Joan of Arc*.

Malintzin, the young Indian girl who opened Mexico's doors to the Spanish conquistadores, wanted to free her people from the domination of the Aztec Empire. She was accused of treason.

The Aztecs were despotic rulers whose cruelty was especially evident in their religion, which advocated human sacrifice. The peoples they had conquered still remembered older, less bloodthirsty beliefs. They venerated the god Quetzalcoatl, the plumed serpent, born of a virgin. But he had abandoned them and set off to the east in a canoe, promising to return one day.

Malintzin was born in the province of Coatzacoalcos, a part of today's Veracruz region. The "zin" ending to her name denotes not only respect and affection but also indicates her noble origins; her father was the village's chieftain. He died when she was eight and her stepmother sold her as a slave at the fair in Tabasco, in order to ensure her half-brother's inheritance. She went from hand to hand and finally found herself in the house of the chieftain of the Tabasco region. Although she only spoke her native tongue, she had a gift for languages and quickly learned the Nahuatl spoken by her masters.

When Hernán Cortés and his men arrived on the Mexican shores and set out to conquer the territory, the chieftain of Tabasco was defeated. He met with Cortés many times and agreed to pay him a tribute consisting of gold and virgins. Malintzin was chosen as a part of this precious gift. She became Cortés' slave and was called "Malinche" because the Spanish could not pronounce her name. In the Spanish conqueror Malintzin saw a bearded white god who came from the sea, from the east, and she recognized him as Quetzalcoatl — he had returned!

Cortés wanted to march on the capital, Tenochtitlan, dethrone the Aztec emperor, Montezuma, seize his riches, and convert the Indians to Christianity. Malintzin devoted herself body and soul to this god who was going to rid the subjugated Indians of the Aztec tyrant and revive a religion of love and peace. To be more useful to him, she learned Spanish and became

LA MALINCHE
MEXICO — EARLY 16TH CENTURY

Malintzin saw in Cortés the serpent god Quetzalcoatl, returned to liberate his people from the yoke of the Aztec. She loved him and opened the doors of her country to him. Lienzo de Tlexca, a 16th century Mexican manuscript.

The chieftain of Tabasco offered young girls to Cortés as part of his tribute to the conqueror. Malintzin, whom the Spanish called Malinche, was among them.

his interpreter. She guided him through the country, drew up maps, and cared for him and his soldiers when they were struck by fever. She regularly acted as his emissary to spread the good word and persuade the Indians to welcome their savior. She went to battle at Cortés' side; during one conflict, when some of the Spanish were killed, she hid the bodies so that the people would not realize that the white gods were mortal. In the evening, she would take Cortés in her arms and tell him about the history and customs of her people. Then she would watch over the sleep of her god, who was also her lover, a fact that seemed quite natural to her.

The Spanish troops finally arrived at the gates of Tenochtitlan. Though Malintzin was by now beginning to doubt that Cortés was a god, she saw in him destiny's instrument, fashioned to drive out the oppressor. She agreed to participate in her country's destruction in order to save it. Montezuma, who knew well the legend of Quetzalcoatl and also saw the resemblance between the god and the conqueror, was easily talked into surrendering to Cortés. Malintzin even approved when Cortés forced Montezuma to attempt to mediate in the bloody fighting between the

Detail from "Colonial Domination," mural by Diego Rivera in the National Palace, Mexico.

Indians and the Spanish; the emperor's subjects turned on him and fatally wounded him. But when all the Aztec dignitaries were executed she discovered that Cortés was as unjust as Montezuma.

After the battle, Cortés decided he had no further need of Malintzin. Though she was carrying the child of the god she had so worshiped, he gave her to a conquistador named Jamarillo. After Cortés' death she went with Jamarillo to

After his vicory over Montezuma's troops, Cortés brought about the Aztec emperor's death. Gift From Montezuma to Cortés. Codex Vurdobonensis, early 16th century.

Spain. Called Dona Marina, she was received at the Escorial, the royal palace, with all the honors due the princess she really was. Bernal Diaz del Castillo, a chronicler of the Americas, wrote: "Cortés could do nothing without her. Dona Marina was a noble woman. She had great influence over all the Indians of New Spain."

After Mexico won independence from Spain in 1821, the Mexican people vilified Malintzin. Yet she should be rehabilitated, for she believed in a just cause and she did not passively submit to the Spanish; by adopting their values and ways, and by communicating her own to them, she paved the way for cultural crossbreeding.

DONA BEATRICE

CONGO — 1684-1706

In the 17th century, ambassadors, missionaries, soldiers, and merchants flocked to Central Africa. Italian engraving, 1825, taken from an engraving of 1700, showing the Congolese king receiving Dutch ambassadors.

The young Congolese woman known as Dona Beatrice, or Saint Anthony, was convinced that the saint lived through her. Missionaries found her dangerous because she established a popular cult and preached national unity. Like Joan of Arc, Dona Beatrice died at the stake.

When the Portuguese explorer Diogo Cão, or Cam, landed at the port of Mpinda at the mouth of the Congo River in 1482, he opened the doors of the region for the missionaries, soldiers, and merchants who quickly followed. They poured into the Kongo kingdom, which encompassed parts of today's Congo, Zaire, and northern Angola. Missionary followed missionary, each trying to beat the baptismal record of the last, and they succeeded in gaining the confidence of the Kongo kings. But by the end of the 17th century clan rivalry was tearing the country apart. The capital, which the missionaries called São Salvador, had been destroyed and deserted. The king, Pedro IV — who, like his recent predecessors, had taken a European name — had fled to the mountains.

Pedro IV had everything needed to unite the kingdom, with one notable exception: courage. He was a descendant of the Kimpansu by his mother and of the Kimulaya by his father. This doubly royal descent could rally most, but not all, of the kingdom's chieftains. Pedro tried to retake the capital but failed, and quickly returned to the shelter of the mountains.

At around this time a girl of aristocratic birth named Kimba Vita, later baptized Beatrice, was growing to maturity. As a missionary, Lorenzo da Lucca, wrote: "This is her life story, as she told it to me in private abjuration at the time of her death.... When she was a child, often did appear to her two white children who played with her, pearl rosaries in their hands. She then became the concubine of two men, successively I believe. They could not peacefully live with her, for she was proud. She was also *nganga marinda*, a priestess or medicine woman of a superstitious or fetish sect called Marinda, or whatever devil is called by this name."

126

The missionaries' religion spread, but a young woman named Beatrice interpreted Christianity
in her own way and founded the Antonian cult. *Baptism of a Congolese king*, Milan, 1690.

Obviously, the missionary did not altogether approve of Kimba Vita. She was dangerous for the Catholic Church and the Portuguese settlers. At the age of twenty, while King Pedro remained in hiding, she was called on to restore the Kongo kingdom — and called not by just anyone, she claimed, but by the Portuguese-born Saint Anthony of Padua himself. She told a Capuchin monk, Bernardo di Gallo, that "God had sent Saint Anthony, the first saint of the Franciscan order. First he was sent to the head of a woman in Mugeto, but because the village didn't want to keep him, he left and went to an old man's head in Sohio. He left there because the missionary father wanted to beat him." He finally went to Dona Beatrice's head "to preach to the Chibango and was received with applause and joy." Kimba was ill when he came but was revived by the saint's soul and started to preach.

For two years Dona Beatrice, aided by an old woman, Fumaria, was a thorn in the missionaries' sides. She founded the Antonian cult, built a church, spread her dogma throughout the country, and attracted many followers. The Portuguese missionaries saw this "false Saint Anthony" as a rival to their power. She became a minor queen, surrounded by disciples, and urged the people to follow in her path, burning both fetishes and the cross, which she claimed fulfilled the same functions as a pagan cult object. Bernardo di Gallo wrote: "She also changed the Salve Regina in a fashion that I know not whether to call diabolical or blasphemous." But the worst was that she urged the people to drive the whites out of the kingdom.

Dona Beatrice tried to bring Pedro around to her way of thinking but did not succeed. The weak king preferred the idea of having himself consecrated by the pope — an honor proposed by Bernardo di Gallo. This would formalize the Catholic Church's grip on the country and bury the popular movement created by Beatrice, who had succeeded in allying herself with many great chiefs. Bernardo waited for an opportunity to condemn her for heresy.

The cult leader's position seemed unassailable — she had reputedly performed resurrections and other miracles, and had acquired an army of followers ready to sacrifice themselves for her. Yet she brought about her own destruction. She fell in love with her "Guardian Angel," a man named Barro, who in the cult was called Saint John. "The Virgin of the Congo" became pregnant and that was the end of her career. She fled with Barro. Her followers thought she had gone to visit God and would soon return. The king's men, how-

King Pedro IV of the Kongo kingdom preferred
to ally himself with the missionaries rather than follow
the resistance movement started by Beatrice. The "false
Saint Anthony" was burned at the stake. *Congolese king
receiving missionaries*, Milan, 1690.

ever, uncovered the truth when they found her with her lover and baby.

The missionaries encountered no difficulty in bringing her to trial, and the sentence was pronounced by her own brethren. In July 1706, Dona Beatrice and Saint John were burned at the stake. Their son was baptized — Jerome. The missionaries had refused to name him Anthony; they wanted to be sure that the memory of Dona Beatrice would die with her.

CREEK MARY

NORTH AMERICA
18TH-19TH CENTURIES

Amayi, at the head of the Creek warriors, launched the attack against Savannah — she had learned that Indian and white man could not live together in peace. And then, after defending the territory of her forebears, she fought for that of her brothers the Cherokees as well.

When her brother Machichi, chief of the Muskogee Creeks, was killed in a skirmish with pioneers, Amayi took his place. She was the "Beloved Woman" of her people and well-liked by the whites of Georgia as well. She married one of them, John Kingsley, and took his name. However, she is best known to history as Mary Creek, or Creek Mary.

Mary had learned to speak English from missionaries before her people crossed the Savannah River and entered Georgia. She sincerely believed at first that the Indians and the pioneers could live together in peace. Her son, Opothle, fathered by a white man, was living proof of this.

She changed her mind the day she came upon an Englishman whipping one of her people, claiming the government had given him the Indian's lands. After helping the Indian escape, Mary returned to her home, furious. She had a violent argument with her husband. Like most men of his race, he intended to be the head of the family, and he thought it was only natural that the whites should exploit the Indians. This was too much for the majestic Amayi. She took half of their blanket — a gesture that, according to the custom of her people, meant she was free — and left Kingsley to his laws.

The Creek nation's finest warriors responded to Amayi's cry for war. They attacked Savannah, thinking they had the advantage of surprise. But

Amayi, a Creek Indian, was married to an Englishman, but left him and later wed a Cherokee warrior.
A Creek Marriage, engraving ca. 1811.

Mary Creek declared: "Not another inch of land for the whites!" Yet she was forced to follow the "Trail of Tears" that led the Cherokees to the West. *Interior of a Creek Indian Tent*, drawing from the beginning of the 19th century.

the English had been warned and were prepared for the attack; Mary suspected that her husband had betrayed them. She went to her home in the middle of the night to fetch her son, then set off to join the Creek warriors but lost her way.

A Cherokee brave, Long Warrior, found her and led her to Okelogee, his village. He asked her to stay with him to replace the wife he had just lost. Amayi turned him down, saying that her place was with her people, the Creeks. The warrior accompanied her part of the way so that she wouldn't become lost again. They parted. That night, when Amayi stopped to nurse her child and then prepare for sleep, Long Warrior reappeared. He had followed to watch over her. He made a fire for her and gave her a superb bearskin. Amayi wrapped herself in the bearskin and invited him to join her. The next day, they returned together to Okelogee.

During the American War of Independence the pioneers expanded their territory. Okelogee was attacked and everyone fled. Amayi saved only her bearskin and her two children, Opothle and Talasi, her son by Long Warrior. She traveled north with the Cherokees and the Creeks, who had answered her call to help her adopted tribe. The men went to fight the colonists.

After a long wait, Amayi was told that Long Warrior had been killed in the frontier war. But one spring day he returned — and found her busy building a house for her family with a Scot, Hugh Crawford. That night she went to Long Warrior, bearskin in hand, and said: "My soul is come to rest with your body and will never leave you."

In the War of 1812, the Creeks sided with the British while the Cherokees placed their confidence in the Americans, who had promised to recognize them as a nation. Amayi desperately tried to prevent the split between the nations, appearing before the council with her son Talasi, born of her love for a Cherokee. But her plea was in vain.

In the Creek War that followed, the Cherokees fought at General Andrew Jackson's side, notably in the Battle of Horseshoe Bend in 1814. Long Warrior was killed. He had just become a grandfather. His grandson, Dane, was the first of Amayi's grandchildren to be wholly Indian by blood. It was Dane who, many years later, told his grandmother's story to the American writer Dee Brown.

Mary Creek told all who would listen: "Not another inch of land for the whites." These words became the Cherokees' slogan. But in 1830 the Indian Removal Act empowered President Andrew Jackson to send the southeastern tribes west. The Chocktaws and Creeks were deported. In 1835 the Cherokees were forced to sign a treaty in which they surrendered all their territory east of the Mississippi. Side by side with her chief, John Ross, Mary Creek tried to convince her brethren to denounce this unjust treaty, but it was ratified and went into effect. The Cherokees then appealed, and Judge John Marshall ruled that the tribe constituted an independent nation and could not legally be expelled from its lands. Jackson overruled this decision.

Beginning in 1838, Amayi and the Cherokees became the last of the "Five Civilized Tribes" of the southeast — with the Chocktaw, Chickasaw, Creek, and Seminole — to be led by force on what became known as the "Trail of Tears" to the Indian Territory, now Oklahoma.

Mary Creek must have been about ninety-five when she died after giving her "medicine" — a Danish coin, which she wore on a chain — to her grandson, Dane. He told Dee Brown that Mary's descendants, members of the Cherokee, Cheyenne and Sioux nations, would "live forever, like the coyotes."

Mary's descendants are members of the Cherokee, Cheyenne and Sioux tribes. *Indian Woman*, engraving, 1881.

FLORA TRISTAN
FRANCE — 1803-1844

My grandmother was a funny, good-natured woman. . . . Proudhon (the father of anarchism) said of her that she had genius. . . . It is probable that she never knew how to cook. A blue-stocking socialist, an anarchist . . .

Paul Gauguin

During her lifetime Flora Tristan made a reputation in literary circles, with the socialist movement and workers, and with defenders of communal utopias. Her name was evoked at the European revolution of 1848 and she was rediscovered by the social and cultural movements that excited the youth of the 1970s. But between these two eras she fell into obscurity; the only thing she was remembered for was being the grandmother of the painter Paul Gauguin.

Born and raised in Paris, Flora Tristan was the daughter of a Frenchwoman and a Peruvian. At the age of seventeen she took a job in an engraving workshop. A year later she married her boss, but she did not love him, and quickly found his mundane life unbearable.

She left their home to spend the next five years discovering Europe, which was in the throes of the Industrial Revolution. Colossal fortunes were being made at incredible speed while country people crowded into towns ill-prepared for the influx. Initially full of hope, the newcomers soon found themselves working sixteen- or eighteen-hour days for miserable wages. Flora was deeply shocked by this situation.

In 1833 she traveled to Peru to claim the inheritance left by her father. But her parents' marriage was not recognized in Peru, and Flora was regarded there as illegitimate. She wrote about her personal disappointments and the frightening contrasts of Peru, its riches and its poverty, its social struggles, and its civil wars. Her account, *Peregrinations of a Pariah*, was published in Paris in 1838, the same year as her novel *Mephis*.

Flora became politically active; she defended divorce, free love, and the abolition of the death penalty. She also entered into a relationship with Charles Fourier, promoter of a humanitarian kind of socialism that encompassed the emancipation

Flora Tristan, best-known for being Paul Gaugin's grandmother, was a "founding mother" of feminism.

Influenced by a concept of woman as Mother and Redeemer, Flora Tristan wanted women to participate in societal evolution. Lithograph by B. N. Est.

funds. On July 1, 1843, the first edition rolled off the presses.

Flora started on a tour of France to publicize her ideas. But she died along the way, in 1844. Her account of the journey was published in 1975, after she had been rediscovered.

Her premature death ended the intellectual and political adventure she had made of her life. In many respects, Flora Tristan's attitudes and goals were far more advanced than those of the men of her day, far beyond 19th century working

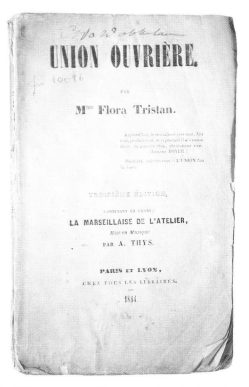

In *L'Union Ouvrière,* Flora pleaded for the inclusion of women in the workers' struggle.

of women. Flora's husband had no part in this open and creative intellectual environment. The couple's relationship deteriorated further, until he took their daughter away from Flora and eventually tried to kill his wife. She escaped with a wound.

Flora took up her pilgrim's staff again, this time heading for England, then the ideal place for exploring the evolution of industrial society and predicting the future of Europe. About ten years before her arrival, English workers had created their first trade union, and they had just joined in the Chartist movement. Flora wrote a social portrait of England, covering every rung on the socioeconomic ladder.

"She wanted to know everything, observe everything, and she saw everything that this nation contains in the way of deep and hideous wounds," wrote Eléonore Blanc, her first biographer. Outcasts, prostitutes, Chartists — she met everyone,

and took care to paint an accurate picture. She wrote with a great deal of sensitivity and emotion — sometimes too much, by modern standards. *Walks in London* appeared simultaneously in Paris and London in 1840 and was reprinted three times in two years. Flora owed this quick success to the literary and socialist movements and to the workers, to whom she dedicated her book.

By the time *Walks in London* was in print, Flora was entertaining the idea of publishing a news sheet or series of pamphlets, *L'Union Ouvrière* (The Worker's Union), to disseminate her ideas. In the series she pleaded for the creation of an international cooperative and for the inclusion of women in this struggle.

She had difficulty financing the publication at first, for she sought support from the working class in vain. But recourse to the intellectuals proved fruitful: George Sand, among others in literary and political circles, raised the necessary

class aspirations. Influenced by a concept of woman as Mother and Redeemer, she wanted women to participate fully in the evolution of society. She sought for women's rights to be recognized and she believed women should form unions just like male workers. She was convinced that women as educators had an essential role to play in the future of humankind.

ROSA LUXEMBURG

POLAND 1871 — GERMANY 1919

Rosa Luxemburg exhorting the crowd after the 1907 Socialist International congress in Stuttgart. At her side is her friend Clara Zetkin.

"Freedom is always the freedom of those who think differently," said Bloody Rosa. Presented as a dangerous shrew by her enemies, this revolutionary was in fact a gentle, sensitive, often lonely woman.

Daughter of a Jewish merchant, Rosa Luxemburg was born in Zamosc, Poland, but her family settled in Warsaw when she was three. A year or so later, a problem with her hip obliged her to remain in bed for a year; the little girl used this time to teach herself to read and write. Her illness left her with a malformed hip. She walked with a limp all her life.

Precociously gifted, Rosa was already translating German literature into Polish at the age of nine. Her political activism and rebellion against authority began in high school. She became a member of the revolutionary Proletariat party, risking arrest and imprisonment. Like many other radicals of the Russian Empire, she left secretly for Zurich, in 1889. There she took university courses in mathematics and natural sciences, then branched out into law and social sciences. She obtained a doctorate in political science in 1898.

From then on, the growing list of Rosa's friends and colleagues reads like a Who's Who of the history of Communism. By 1898 she had already met Leo Jogiches, who was her lover for many years and remained a lifelong friend. At odds with the Polish Socialist Party, the pair founded the Social Democratic Party, which eventually became the Communist Party. Rosa believed in socialist internationalism, a point of view that would later put her in conflict with Lenin, who favored national self-determination.

Having obtained German nationality through a marriage of convenience, Rosa settled in Berlin, where she plunged into a whirlwind of activity. Upon her arrival she had joined the Social Democrats, the largest party of the Second International, and had become an expert in Polish affairs. She vehemently criticized Eduard Bernstein's anti-Marxist revisionism; Rosa defended Marxist orthodoxy and the need for revolution in *Sozialreform oder Revolution* (Reform or Revolution). Karl Kautsky, the Second International's great theoretician, sided with her, and Bernstein's ideas were dismissed as deviant. Rosa's prestige was at its peak. She wrote prolifically and spoke often, demonstrating force of argument and a deep capacity for analysis. Also at this time she became friends with Clara Zetkin, who fought for women's rights as well as for socialism.

Rosa appeared in a group photograph taken at the International Congress in Amsterdam in 1904: the only woman among many old men. As soon as she returned from Amsterdam to Berlin she was thrown in jail for having insulted Emperor Wilhelm II. That was her first imprisonment. She was jailed again in 1906, this time in Warsaw, where she had gone to take part in the budding Russian revolution; it became the most important experience in her life, for before she had believed that it was in Germany that all the necessary preconditions for world revolution were found.

In prison, she made friends with her cellmates and her warders, rediscovered poetry, literature, and botany, and wrote numerous letters. "The world is beautiful, despite all its horrors!" she said.

Journalist, political leader, and pacifist, she was nicknamed "Rosa the Red" and "Bloody Rosa."

Even in prison, Rosa never lost her femininity. She was not pretty, describing herself as a "pile of tinsel," but she dressed with care, in a simple, sophisticated fashion.

Rosa continued to defend the theory of revolutionary mass action — the mass strike, which she considered the principal tool of the proletariat. In contrast to Lenin, Rosa believed that the development of the party would evolve naturally from the struggle of the rank and file. On returning in 1907 to Berlin, where she taught for seven years at the school of the Social Democratic Party, she quarreled with the party leaders, Karl Kautsky and August Bebel. She was already angry with Leo Jogiches, who had been unfaithful to her after his escape from the Warsaw prison. Rosa, then in her early 40s, took another lover, 22-year-old Konstantin Zetkin, son of her friend Clara.

In 1913, in Frankfurt, Rosa spoke publicly against military aggression and in favor of peace. For this, she was sentenced to a year in prison. Along with fellow activist Karl Liebknecht, she firmly opposed war just when the Social Democratic Party was supporting the government's intent to go to war. During her imprisonment, Rosa sharply criticized the Social Democrats' position in a pamphlet, *Die Krise der Sozialdemokratie* (The

Crisis in German Social Democracy), which appeared under the pseudonym Junius.

As soon as she was released from prison, she joined the struggles of pacifists such as Clara Zetkin, and with Liebknecht founded the Spartacus League. Liebknecht and Luxemburg were jailed again, and remained in custody until the end of World War I and the German revolution of November 1918.

Freed, the pair arrived in Berlin just in time to collaborate in the creation of the German Communist Party in December 1918. Rosa tried to limit the Bolshevik influence on the party, for she did not appreciate Lenin's dictatorialism. Their party's inspiring slogans had considerable influence, and engendered an attempt at revolution in the Commune of Berlin in January 1919. For their part in the hostile confrontation, Rosa and Liebknecht were arrested by reactionary troops and taken to a hotel. There Liebknecht was murdered, and Rosa was beaten black and blue before being killed and thrown into a canal.

Rosa as portrayed by Barbara Sukowa, in the film directed by Margarethe von Trotta, who said Luxemburg was "worth devoting one's life to."

MARGARET SANGER

UNITED STATES — 1883-1966

Margaret Sanger's motto could have been "Love and Liberty for Women." Her life was one long struggle to obtain for all women the right to love without giving birth.

Her father, Michael Higgins, was a free-thinking Irish stonemason in Corning, New York. Her mother, Anne, was a devout Catholic who had eleven children and seven miscarriages before dying at age forty-eight, exhausted by tuberculosis and worn out by childbirth. Margaret, who was sixteen when Anne died, had stood by helplessly and observed her mother's fate, which affected her thinking and influenced her destiny. She later worked as a nurse in a maternity ward in New York City, where she saw many women die from self-induced abortions amid an atmosphere of general indifference. Then there was the coarseness of the doctors, who refused to give information about contraception to women, suggesting instead that they make their husbands sleep elsewhere if they didn't want to have children.

It is thus not surprising that this courageous young woman took up the cause for which she would fight all her life: the right for a woman to love freely and control her own body. She undertook an arduous campaign to persuade doctors to provide information about "birth control," a term she coined in her magazine, *Woman Rebel.* In the face of solid opposition and even direct attacks from the opposite sex, she broadened her activities to include the legal system, challenging the laws against sending birth control information and contraceptive devices through the mails and against opening family planning clinics.

Ultimately she succeeded in changing the laws. She founded what would become the Planned Parenthood Federation, helped to popularize the use of diaphragms, and in her seventies was instrumental in forcing the medical establishment to develop oral contraceptives — a principal that had been known for decades but never acted upon.

Faithful to her convictions, this fearless redhead put her theories into practice in her private

Margaret Sanger fought for a woman's right
to love freely and control her own body.

life. She announced to her first husband, an architect named William Sanger, that she could never find fulfilment in marriage unless she was free to have other sexual relationships. On the nights when she was separated from him, fighting for her cause, sex was the one thing that permitted her to sleep. Given her husband's traditional upbringing, their marriage was doomed to fail. They divorced and Margaret obtained custody of their three children. She continued to fight for what she believed was right, taking and leaving lovers at an astonishing rate. She also kept up an intimate friendship, which lasted nearly all of her life, with the sexologist Havelock Ellis.

At the Fifth International Birth Control Conference, held in Tokyo in 1955, Margaret disclosed the development of the Pill.

Margaret Sanger pleaded the cause of birth control before a Senate committee in 1931

In 1922 Margaret remarried. Her second husband, J. Noah H. Slee, was a South African tycoon of Dutch origin. He was sixty-four and she was thirty-nine. The marriage was a success. Margaret could continue to have outside relationships, since her extraordinary emancipation excited and fascinated her husband. He accepted her occasional affairs as chapters in what he termed "the story of her life."

To simply teach by example was not sufficient for Margaret. She wrote a number of books on sexuality and birth control methods, including *What Every Mother Should Know*, published in 1917, and *My Fight For Birth Control* in 1931. Because of her influence, her British counterpart, Marie Stopes, added a chapter on birth control to her celebrated manual, *Married Love*. Sanger also wrote an autobiography, published in 1938. In her old age she was pleased to be able to say to her adolescent granddaughter that she had never given a kiss that wasn't sincere.

In reflecting on Margaret Sanger's life, we must remember what woman's lot was like at the time. Women were subjected to contempt and to a strict moral code, defined by religion and defended by the law. Working women were treated with amused condescension at best. Free-thinking women were obviously "sinners." But Margaret managed to lead both a social and personal battle without losing her zest for life, her sensuality, and her enthusiasm. She exemplified an almost masculine attitude toward sex, based on equality. Today, women seek their right to be different. But the progress that has been made, the abolition of taboos, and the freedoms achieved are due to people like Margaret Sanger.

Conquering blindness and deafness, Helen Keller used her other senses to experience life fully. Here, she examines an Egyptian monument in Cairo's Antiquities Museum.

HELEN KELLER

UNITED STATES —1880-1968

acquire knowledge, she achieved what may without exaggeration be called a miracle. To speak of Helen Keller is also to speak of her teacher and friend, Anne Sullivan, whose sensitivity and patience helped Helen discover herself and communicate with the world that surrounded her, a world of which she knew so little.

Helen was born near Tuscumbia, Alabama, in 1880. At the age of 19 months she was struck by a severe illness, probably scarlet fever, which left her deprived of sight and sound, and thus of speech. It is terrible to think of the years the child spent in solitude and ignorance before her parents sought help from Alexander Graham Bell when Helen was almost seven. The great inventor and champion of education for the disabled sent them to an institute for the blind in Boston. The Kellers were ready to undertake anything that could help them break into little Helen's silent world.

Anne Mansfield Sullivan, a twenty-year-old graduate of the institute, agreed to teach the little girl. Anne was partially blind, a fact that created an immediate bond of friendship between the two. Her task was daunting but she persevered, determined to at least teach the child the rudiments of language. She soon discovered that behind Helen's wall of silence was an intelligent girl who desperately needed love and wanted to communicate. What began as an initiation through touch to the language of the deaf evolved in stages to the written word and then, in 1890, to the spoken word.

Having overcome tremendous obstacles, capable now of learning and communicating in a systematic fashion, Helen threw herself into an incredible search for knowledge. In addition to her mother tongue, English, she learned to speak French and German and studied the Classics. She was graduated cum laude with a bachelor of arts degree from Radcliffe in 1904.

Helen Keller's story is an outstanding example of what a person can accomplish in the face of total adversity. At the age of one and a half, before she had a chance to absorb the sights and sounds that could have helped guide her in her isolated world, she was struck by illness and became blind, deaf, and hence mute. But thanks to her great courage and her desire to live and to

She began to publish at age twenty-two, starting her works at a point where many others finish, with her autobiography, *The Story of My Life*. What might have seemed overdone in a novel was appropriate here, for the book tells of her personal tragedy, of her courage, and of the methods her teacher, Anne, employed to build a bond with her. The following year, she published an essay, *Optimism*, a hymn to hope and the beauty of life. Over the years her works included *The World I Live In* (1908), *Song of the Stone Wall* (1910), *Out of the Dark* (1913), *Helen Keller's Journal* (1938), and *Teacher* (1956). The last two dealt largely with Anne Sullivan, who even after

Here, Helen converses with Eleanor Roosevelt by reading her lips during a meeting in 1955.

Helen was graduated with honors from Radcliffe College in 1904; she was already an established author.

her marriage to John Macy remained Helen's helper and companion until her death in 1936.

Helen Keller was a tall, thin, elegant woman; the only visible evidence of her handicaps was her fixed, vague gaze. Her story became known and admired throughout the world, giving momentum to the movement for education for the disabled. She was proof of what could be achieved in an apparently hopeless case. Not only did she serve as an example, inspiring governments and educators to pursue more energetically programs for the rehabilitation and education of the blind and deaf, she also campaigned actively around the world, raising funds to improve living conditions for the sensorily disabled. In addition she was an active journalist and a spokeswoman for radical social and political reforms. An ardent socialist, she enthusiastically campaigned for women's right to vote, the abolition of the death penalty, the prohibition of child labor, and women's right to birth control as advocated by Margaret Sanger.

Helen Keller died in 1968, just a few weeks short of her eighty-eighth birthday. Although we can admire her personal courage, read her books, and learn something of her long life, those of us who possess all five senses are exasperatingly incapable of understanding the experience of such a woman. The world she knew differed dramatically from ours. It is thanks to Helen Keller that we know such a world exists and can learn to respect those who live in it.

DOLORES IBARRURI

SPAIN — 1899-1989

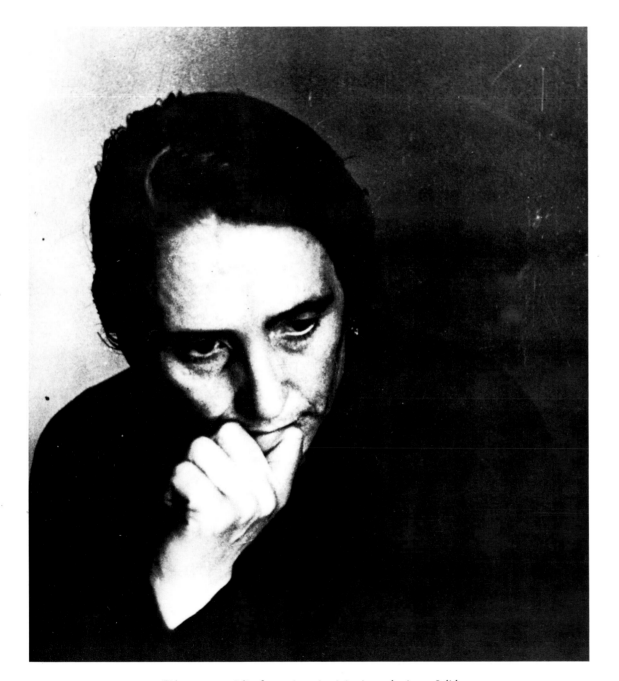

"I became a socialist from witnessing injustice and misery. I did
not need to look at myself in a mirror to see how much other women suffered,"
La Pasionaria said, recalling her youth as the daughter of a miner.

"No pasarán!" They shall not pass, they will
not overcome! Dolores Ibarruri's appeal to struggle
against the fascists fast taking hold of Spain became
the Republican battle cry, and the woman called
La Pasionaria went down in history.

In her own words, Dolores Ibarruri had little
to look forward to in "a gray life, the life of a
slave." The eighth in a family of eleven children,
she was born in Gallarta, a Basque village whose
residents had been miners for generations. Each
morning she watched her father depart for the
nearby mine, and every evening she listened to
him and his friends lament the loss of people whose
lives had been claimed by the mine. "I became a
socialist from witnessing injustice and misery. I
did not need to look at myself in a mirror to see
how much other women suffered," she said later.

It was nearly impossible for a worker's
daughter to escape the fate that went with her
station. Dolores dreamed of becoming a teacher,
but was forced to leave school to work, first as a
seamstress, then in the kitchens of wealthy families.

She met and married a young socialist miner,
Julián Ruiz Gabina, and they settled in
Somorrostro, not far from Gallarta. Her profoundly Catholic family objected to this revolutionary, but Dolores was already reading Karl Marx
and shared the "subversive ideas" that would
eventually land her husband in prison.

During the general strike of 1917 Dolores
committed her first militant act, delivering arms
to the workers. After the strike, with her husband
in prison, she joined the local socialist organization in Somorrostro. The following year, encouraged by the success of the Bolshevik revolution, she began writing of her beliefs, and published
her first article in a newspaper called *El Minero
Vizcaino* (The Biscay Miner). She signed the piece
"Pasionaria," Passion Flower, creating the name
the world would come to know her by.

The Spanish Communist Party was formed
in 1920. Elected a member of the Biscay regional
committee, Dolores participated in her first political conference, much to the dismay of the
proper matrons of Somorrostro. One of them, a

To cries of *"No pasarán!"* Dolores Ibarruri fought against the fascist Falangists during the Spanish Civil War, but Franco's supporters won and she went into exile in the Soviet Union.

mine owner's wife, tried to tempt Dolorès to drop her political activity by promising a nice house and a good job for her husband. Despite her poverty, the recent deaths of two of her daughters, and the continued imprisonment of her husband, Dolores had lost none of her determination, and refused the offer.

Suffering from the stage fright that she would never completely lose, La Pasionaria delivered her first major speech in Bilbao on May 1, 1931. On the streets, this woman — always dressed in traditional black and white — was recognized as a member of the Communist Party Central Committee. Her popularity became embarrassing to the government; in Madrid, where she collaborated on the *Worker's World*, she was arrested and jailed. The first thing Dolores did upon her release was to bring her two children to live with her in Madrid. But, separated from her husband by then, increasingly busy, and often traveling, she finally resolved to send them to the Soviet Union to attend school.

In 1936, with the Popular Front election victory, Dolores Ibarruri became the parliamentary representative from Asturias. She immediately left for Oviedo, where many political prisoners were jailed, to lead a demonstration for their release. Dolores ignored the prison director's machine guns, and after negotiating for several hours achieved her aim. But her success was short-lived. On the night of July 18, a voice signaled the start of the fascist Falangist rebellion with the words, "A serene sky is over Spain." General Francisco Franco had launched an insurrection against the republic.

The next day, in a celebrated radio speech, Dolores exhorted the Spaniards to defend themselves. "Arise!" she said, "fascism will not succeed!" *No pasarán!* The watchwords of the Spanish Civil War were born, and La Pasionaria became its fervent symbol. She appealed for aid throughout the world. "It is better to die on one's feet than to live on one's knees," proclaimed La Pasionaria.

Back in Madrid, she dug trenches, welcomed the international brigades of volunteers who came to join the struggle, and fought relentlessly. But the German army, in aid of Franco's supporters,

forced the opposition to retreat. A Communist witch-hunt was launched, with La Pasionaria especially targeted by the fascists. Her party decided that she had to leave Spain for her own safety. She left on March 6, 1939, and would not return until nearly forty years later.

La Pasionaria sought refuge in the Soviet Union, and for many years headed the Spanish Communist Party from her exile. Constantly informed of events in Spain, she commented on

Leader of the Spanish Communist Party from her exile, La Pasionaria returned at age eighty-one to her native country, where she continued to play a symbolic role.

them for her followers via Radio Independent Spain until 1977. That year La Pasionaria, still considered a living symbol of the Communist movement, was finally allowed to return home.

In 1986, Dolores Ibarrui, gazing up at the stars one night in the village where she was born, declared that she would die there. And when she did three years later, all Spain raised its voice to pay homage to her.

DJAMILA

ALGERIA — 20TH CENTURY

Such a sweet name, yet synonymous with the sufferings the Algerian people underwent in their war for freedom from French colonial rule. The name Djamila encompasses all the Algerian women who fought for their country's independence, both openly and in secret. There were many Djamilas, but two women are particularly well-known because of the publicity they were given by the press in France and Algeria — Djamila Bouhired and Djamila Boupacha.

A young militant in the National Liberation Front, Djamila Bouhired was charged with two bombings during the Algerian War of Independence.

Djamila Bouhired, at the age of twenty-two, gave everything up to follow "the tradition of Abdel-Kader," the 19th century emir who was one of the first to resist French rule. In mid-November 1956 she was entrusted with the care of Yacef Saadi, Ali la Pointe, and Alilou, three guerrillas from the National Liberation Front who were hiding in the home of her uncle. She won the trust of Yacef, the guerrilla leader known as the "Captain of Algiers," and became the best of his liaison agents.

Djamila Bouhired declared to the judges who sentenced her to death: "You will not prevent Algeria from becoming independent."

On April 9, 1957, a group from the Front was changing its headquarters when it ran into a patrol squad in Algiers' labyrinthine old Casbah quarter. Djamila stepped forward, making herself a target to cover her companions' flight. She was shot in the shoulder and arrested. Important documents meant for Yacef and Ali were found on her. The nightmare began.

"From the 9th to the 26th of April, I was interrogated and tortured without interruption," she later recalled. She was submitted to electric shocks and her shoulder wound was reopened by repeated beatings. They wanted her to reveal Yacef's address and confess to participating in bomb attacks in Algiers, but she refused. At her trial, a false confession was presented. Djamila brought charges of torture and her lawyer asked that these be added to the record; the court refused. She was convicted and sentenced to death on charges of having planted two bombs: one on September 30, 1956, the other on January 26, 1957. (At the time of the first attack she had not even joined the Front yet.)

She burst out laughing when the judge passed sentence. Then she made a speech to the court, which ended with these words: "In killing us . . . you will not prevent Algeria from becoming independent. *Insh'Allah.*"

The death sentence was later commuted to life imprisonment. Djamila was freed when Algeria gained its independence in 1962. Today she lives in Algiers.

* * * * *

Djamila Boupacha started by stealing medical supplies and taking them to wounded guerrillas. Later she did liaison work, gathered information, and sheltered agents of the Front. She was arrested at her parents' home near Algiers on February 10, 1960, and taken to a so-called "sorting center." Djamila, who was barely eighteen years old, was brutally interrogated. Her father, sister, and brother-in-law were also tortured. At the end of thirty-three days of horror, Djamila was ready to sign any confession presented to her.

Her brother, also incarcerated, sent a plea for help to Gisèle Halimi, a Tunisian-born Paris lawyer, who accepted Djamila's case without knowing any of the details. During her first visit to the prison where Djamila was held, Halimi noticed that Djamila's moods "shifted sharply from extreme depression, when she seemed indifferent to her fate, to profound and almost mystical enthusiasm about being a young Algerian militant."

Djamila revealed to her horrified lawyer everything she had endured: electric shocks, cigarette burns, defloration with the neck of a bottle. The two women strove to bring these incidents to the

The Casbah of Algiers, a labyrinth of small streets where the Front's guerrillas could lose themselves in crowds and alleyways.

Arrested, imprisoned and tortured, Djamila Boupacha worked tirelessly to prove that her confessions had been obtained under torture. She was released shortly before Algeria obtained the independence for which she had fought. Here she presides over a meeting four days before the referendum for self-determination on June 28, 1962.

authorities' attention, but a doctor who examined Djamila at her own request refuted her accusations.

The general silence surrounding the villas called "sorting centers" had to be broken. It was common knowledge that they were torture centers where atrocities were committed with total impunity. Djamila was prepared to fight to prove that her confessions had been obtained under torture. Her lawyer obtained a postponement of the trial and returned to Paris, where she wrote to President Charles de Gaulle and stirred up interest about the case in Parisian intellectual circles. Many people responded to her call. Simone de

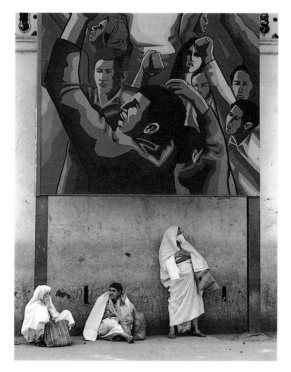

Algerian women enthusiastically participated in the fight for independence, but after it was won, many returned to their former status.

Beauvoir published an appeal on Djamila's behalf in the influential *Le Monde* newspaper on June 3, 1960. Several days later the magazine *L'Express* ran an article on the case by Françoise Sagan. Letters flowed in from around the world. A pressure group was formed. Djamila began to feel there was hope for her.

On June 17 a second postponement of the trial was obtained. Ultimately the case was transferred from Algeria to France. It eventually came to nothing because of lack of proof. Djamila was examined by another doctor but time had erased the traces on her body. She could have identified her torturers had she received photographs of the soldiers and paratroopers who had "taken care" of her. But French military officials in Algeria refused to send photos unless she identified the men by name — as if they had introduced themselves before beating her. This maneuver to protect the men responsible was excused as necessary to preserve army morale.

Djamila Boupacha was freed in 1962, shortly before the referendum for self-determination that ended French colonialism in Algeria.

ANGELA DAVIS

UNITED STATES — 1944-

A woman, a black, and a Communist, Angela Davis rose to the head of the 1960s civil rights movement in America. She remains one of its living symbols.

Great-granddaughter of a slave and daughter of Alabama schoolteachers, the young Angela used to spend her vacations with her grandmother, who lived in a cabin on a cotton farm. There Angela discovered her roots and her identity as someone who would fight racial and economic injustice with whatever means were available. At school she was upset by the hunger of her classmates, and stole money from her father to buy them food.

Angela realized that her family was relatively well-to-do: her father had managed to save enough money to buy a gas station and a house. The family had left subsidized housing in Birmingham in 1948, when Angela was four, to move into a single-family house. Angela's awareness of racial differences increased the following year when a house nearby exploded; a black family had been punished for daring to move onto a white street.

She visited New York while still young, and soon noticed that there she could play normally, ride in the front of a city bus, and go to the same movies, parks, and restaurants as white people. New York still had progress to make: mixed couples suffered harassment, the Communist witch-hunt was in full swing. But Angela far preferred the freedom of this city to Birmingham.

In her memoirs, she relates that one day she and her sister Fannie entered a Birmingham shoe store, put on French accents, and pretended to be from Martinique. They were dealt with pleasantly, until Angela revealed the deception and said that

In a United States shattered by racial conflict and the Vietnam War, Angela Davis fought for black rights and joined the Communist Party. Her support for the imprisoned "Soledad Brothers" led to her being accused of complicity in a murder, and she was arrested.

LIBERTAD PARA ANGELA DAVIS

ANGELA DAVIS POSTER
BY N.Y. COMM.-TO FREE ANGELA DAVIS
E. SUITE 425. N.Y. N.Y. 10011

all blacks had to do to be treated with respect was pass themselves off as foreigners.

In 1955, Martin Luther King appealed for a boycott of Montgomery's segregated bus service. A rise in violent racial incidents followed this plea, and in 1959 King launched the black passive resistance movement against racial discrimination. Angela joined the movement, adding her voice to the demonstrations in New York in 1960.

The movement spread, organizations multiplied, sit-ins grew common. "Freedom Now," the Student Non-Violent Coordinating Committee proclaimed, inspired by the tactics of Gandhi. This was a time of study, travel, and growing involvement for Angela. She won a scholarship to Brandeis University in Massachusetts in 1961. The next year Angela attended a Young Communist Congress in Helsinki, then traveled home by way of Paris, where she was intensely moved by the aftermath of the war in Algeria. In 1965 Angela traveled again to Paris, then returned home long enough to witness race riots breaking out in American ghettos. She spent the next two years in Germany, working on her dissertation in philosophy.

When Angela returned from her studies in Europe, Black Power had supplanted non-violence, and the Black Panthers were born. She enrolled at the University of California at San Diego to complete her dissertation under the Marxist professor Herbert Marcuse, and organized the black movement there. It was not easy — her companions accused her of trying to do "a man's job," while police repression was supported by Governor Ronald Reagan, who called the ghetto rioters "mad dogs." Convinced that the civil rights struggle could not be limited to the question of skin color, Angela Davis "after lengthy reflection" joined the Communist Party in July 1968. The following year, she visited Cuba.

She was appointed an assistant professor of philosophy at the University of California at Los Angeles, but regulations dating from 1949 barred Communists from working for the university. At Reagan's behest, she was summoned for questioning. "Are you a Communist?" she was asked.

With her name on the FBI's "most wanted" list, Angela was arrested in New York.

Posters and banners expressed support for Angela.

Instead of invoking her Fifth Amendment right not to incriminate herself, Angela replied that she was. She was fired in 1969. The entire campus mobilized to defend her, and the courts declared the firing unconstitutional. At her first lecture afterward, fifteen hundred students and teachers stood up to cheer.

In mid-February 1970, Angela saw on the front page of the *Los Angeles Times* a photo that would ultimately bring her a prison sentence. It showed three black men; despite the chains that bound them, they exuded a strength that moved her. Prisoners in the Soledad penitentiary, the men were accused of killing a guard. Their supporters claimed the prison authorities had cooked up the story to get rid of George Jackson and his two fellow prisoners, who were seen as troublemakers. Angela came to the defense of the "Soledad Brothers," wrote to George Jackson, and organized a solidarity meeting.

On June 19, the day of the rally, the university voted not to renew her contract. Then, on

Crusading again, in 1984.

August 7, George Jackson's brother, Jonathan, tried to free a black prisoner during a trial. Jonathan, the judge, and two other people were killed in the ensuing shootout. One of Jonathan's guns, it proved, was registered under the name of Angela Davis. It was not a crime to carry a gun, and there was no other proof of complicity by Angela, but she was placed on the FBI's "most wanted" list nonetheless. She was arrested and spent sixteen months in jail. While she was there, George Jackson was killed trying to escape.

Angela Davis was finally released on bail, and on June 4, 1972, an all-white jury acquitted her. Since then, she has written her autobiography, run for U.S. vice president on the Communist ticket, and divided her time between teaching and activism.

FLORENCE NIGHTINGALE

ITALY 1820 — ENGLAND 1910

At Scutari during the Crimean War, Florence Nightingale never rested
in her efforts to save and heal wounded British soldiers.

In 1820, in the golden splendor of Florence, a daughter was born to a couple whose marriage had been arranged in the manner customary to British gentry. Belonging to this social class in the early 19th century, and being born female, subjected one to many restrictions on personal development. But certain women managed to find enough freedom in this way of life to follow their own calling. Florence Nightingale, named for the city of her birth, was one such woman. Her calling was to care for the sick and injured.

Florence traveled widely in her youth, crisscrossing Europe and Egypt. Discovering early in life a fascination with the arts of healing, she took advantage of her travels to study hospital systems wherever she visited. The first battle she had to fight was in convincing her parents to let her study medicine and surgery at the nursing school in Kaiserwerth on the Rhine in Germany.

After completing her studies in Paris, she settled in London and soon was using her own money to help run a hospital. When the Crimean War broke out shortly thereafter, the dreadful battle contions, inadequate medical care, and ravages of a cholera epidemic among the British troops inspired Florence to go with thirty-eight other female volunteers to the front in Constantinople. This was the first such action, some years before the formation of the Red Cross.

Untiring work, the creation of two blood banks in Scutari and Balaklava, and ceaseless vigilance over the wounded by her and her companions enabled Florence to lower the military mortality rate dramatically. She had succeeded in proving that quick medical intervention could save lives, even if the available surgical techniques

Florence's unrelenting campaigns convinced the British government to educate women in the field of nursing.

Hospital reformer, educator, writer . . .
Florence in 1873.

were rudimentary and anesthesia non-existent. Her own health became fragile, but this did not keep her from working.

The accomplishments of the volunteer medical team and unrelenting pressure by Florence convinced the British government of the need to educate women in the field of nursing. The public contributed some £50,000 in her name to start a nursing school at Saint Thomas's Hospital, the first modern school of its kind. Florence Night-

ingale did not limit her role to education. She turned her attention to the health and housing of the British troops stationed in India and was thus led to study the country itself. She described its miserable living conditions in books and articles, and also published several works on nursing and medical care in general.

Hospital organizer, educator, and writer, Florence Nightingale defended to her death the idea that the health system of her time needed radical reformation. She died at the age of ninety, having become the first woman to receive the Order of Merit.

But who was she, behind that determined facade? No one really knows. Her true personality is hidden behind the icon that books and popular culture have made of her. Behind the images painted in literature, art, even poetry (Longfellow dedicated his "Santa Filomena" to her) there must have been temperament and passion. We know Florence Nightingale as the woman who never slept because she was too busy ensuring the com-

fort of her patients. Yet she spent the last decades of her life virtually bedfast, an invalid, carrying on a voluminous correspondence but never seen in public. The physical basis for her infirmity — if there was one — was never known. Some have even suggested that she chose to live as an invalid in order to devote all her energy to promoting the causes that consumed her.

She is shown in art at the bedsides of the stricken, her hand supporting a head or offering a warm drink, her face eternally lit with a small smile: the incarnation of goodness. The view of her in Longfellow's poem is typical:

A Lady with a Lamp shall stand
In the great history of the land,
A noble type of good
Heroic womanhood.

In fact she hated this image and objected to being typed. But the "real" Florence Nightingale, certainly much deeper and more complex than the image, was an enigma.

MOTHER TERESA

YUGOSLAVIA — 1910-

Nobel Peace Prize winner in 1979, this fragile, wrinkled little woman has dedicated herself to the poorest of the poor with fierce will and independence. Day after day for decades, the "Saint of Calcutta" walked with death and tamed it. At eighty, nearly at the end of her strength, Mother Teresa retired — only to retract her decision after being re-elected as head of her order.

She was born Agnes Gonxha Bojaxhiu in Skopje, Yugoslavia, in 1910; her parents were Albanian. At the age of eighteen she became a novice nun with the Sisters of Loreto in Darjeeling, India, abandoning her given name to become Teresa. Once her novitiate was finished, she was sent to Calcutta to teach geography in a school for Brahmin girls, a post she occupied until an autumn day in 1946 when she felt called by God to dedicate her life and work to her privileged students' socioeconomic opposites, "the most outcast beings in the world."

Her sense of compassion and justice and her desire to dedicate herself to works of piety developed in Calcutta, a true hell where extreme misery coexists with aggressive government promotion of scientific progress. Teresa concentrated her efforts on the lowest rung of the socioeconomic ladder, trying to lessen the awful hunger and despair by taking the fatally ill off the streets and giving them a sanctuary where they could be cared for until their deaths.

In 1948 she founded the Order of the Missionaries of Charity, which was distinguished by a rapid rise in church approval: it received canonical sanction from the pope in 1950 and became a pontifical congregation — answerable only to the pope — in 1965. Mother Teresa, who took Indian citizenship and adopted the sari as the habit of her order, has sometimes told of how she had only five rupees in her pocket when she began this enormous undertaking. She founded an open-air school for poor children, a hospice for the dying

The "Saint of Calcutta" had only five rupees in her pocket when she founded the Order of the Missionaries of Charity and began building its network of hospitals, orphanages, and schools.

near a temple of the dark goddess Kali, maternity hospitals, welfare centers, leper hospitals — obstacles seemed to dissolve before her determination and energy. Gradually, the activities of her order spread over five continents; there are hundreds of Missionaries of Charity houses throughout the world. Within their walls, the only objective is to give love without ideological or religious restriction. The sisters of the order dedicate themselves to helping those in need, giving them care and counsel.

The campaign for family planning in India

With no training or administrative experience, Mother Teresa has built an international network of institutions — yet her face still reflects such serenity.

found a determined foe in Mother Teresa, for she believes that only love can relieve misery, and with her own love has proved what is possible. At night, desperate Indian women abandon children they

cannot care for in garbage cans; each morning a sister from the order seeks out and gathers up the babies to take them to the home created by Mother Teresa. "If you don't want your children, give them to me," she has said.

At the same time, Mother Teresa aggressively promoted instruction in natural contraception, and fiercely opposed the sterilization of lepers, because she believes that nobody knows where or in what circumstances the spirit of God reigns. Nothing has shaken her faith in life, not overpopulation, nor the miserable conditions that prevent many Indian children from surviving to adulthood. "I take people one by one," she retorts, affirming her confidence in the individual and her conviction that we must accept the mystery of creation, respecting each part of the world and each of its infinite possibilities.

At the end of the 1980s, the political opening of the Soviet Union encouraged Mother Teresa to help Armenian earthquake victims and Red Army soldiers wounded in Afghanistan. Soon afterward, a hospice in Moscow was named for her. The

Soviet Union now has five houses belonging to the Order of the Missionaries of Charity.

No degradation or misfortune left her indifferent; despite her rejection of homosexuality, Mother Teresa opened a hospice for AIDS sufferers in New York City. And she has never limited her involvement to administration. After receiving the Nobel Prize she continued to travel the world, speaking out for the poor, visiting with kings and queens, receiving the special benediction of the pope. Not even old age has stopped her; she has pursued the objective she had set for herself: to relieve the suffering of the sick and dying, to give her love until the last breath.

Mother Teresa approached sanctity in the humble work she ceaselessly performed; she has lived an extraordinary, transcendant life, far from passive contemplation. The assurance with which this often clearly exhausted woman toiled throughout her sixties and seventies shows that she drew on resources inaccessible to most of us. If there is a person in the world today who can aspire to saintliness, it is Mother Teresa.

Mother Teresa has dedicated her life to caring for "the most outcast beings in the world," like these migrants living in the streets of Calcutta.

147

SAPPHO

GREECE — 7TH-6TH CENTURIES BC

A brilliant poet, Sappho scandalized ancient Greece: her verses sang of women,
but, more importantly, they were written by one.

Beauty I served;
Indeed, was there for me
Anything greater?

The words are from Sappho, the "female Homer," whose sensuous verses caused as much scandal as admiration because she dared to express her genius by singing of love and of young girls.

According to myth, the sea brought the lyre of Orpheus to the shores of Lesbos. Sappho, the mother of Greek poetry, was born on this island. Lesbos, a rival of Athens, was strongly influenced by the Orient. In Athens, women knew their place. In Lesbos, women were free, the equals of men.

Sappho's family, more Oriental than Hellenic, came from Asia Minor. She was said to descend from Pentilo, son of Orestes and grandson of Agamemnon. She belonged to the aristocracy; she had a grandmother named Cleis and two brothers, one of them beloved and the other detested; and according to Ovid, her father died when she was six. Nothing else is known about her origins.

Socrates called her "the beauteous Sappho" but was probably referring more to her verse than to her looks. She was far from a classic Greek beauty. There are many portraits of her — only Homer was portrayed more often — but the artists never saw her; they portrayed her according to the standards of their times. The poet Alceaus, who was her friend and may have been in love with her, briefly described the mysterious Sappho as "violet-decked, virtuous, honey-sweet smiling Sappho."

More accurate, perhaps, are the descriptions by the unknown early biographer who called her "ugly, brown, very small" and by a commentator on the much later satirist Lucian: "She was very badly proportioned, tiny and brown, like the nightingale whose tiny body is covered with unbecoming feathers." Baudelaire, then, must have let his pen run away with him when he wrote of "the male Sappho, the Poet and the Lover/ Fairer than Venus in her pallid pleasures."

But he was right to continue:
Azure is vanquished by the spots that cover
The tenebrous circle traced by the mad measures
Of the male Sappho, the Poet and the Lover.

Whatever her looks, Sappho wrote beautiful verse. With infinitely tender words, she glorifies love. Her lines depict the beauty, grace, and sensuality of women and tell of desire, jealousy, and solitude. Sappho created erotic lyricism, invented the Sapphic strophe utilized by Latin poets, and still influences poetry today. It is a great loss that, of her nine volumes of lyric poems, only the "Ode to Aphrodite" survives in its entirety.

Sappho began to write when she was about seventeen. By the time she was twenty, her fame already equaled that of the poet Alcaeus. Praised by some, ridiculed by others, she angered Pittacus, tyrant of Lesbos, by supporting the aristocracy

Sappho taught music, dancing, and singing to young girls who sometimes made her heart beat faster.

instead of his democracy. She spent some five years of exile at Syracuse, in Sicily, as a result.

When she returned to Mytilene, Sappho, who was also a choir mistress, founded a salon where she taught music, dance, and singing to noble young girls. She chose tender adolescents in order to more easily inculcate her ideas. Touched by their bodies and their voices, Sappho fell in love with Gongyla, Anactoria, and Atthis.

I loved you, Atthis, long ago . . . and you
A small ungainly girl, I thought.

Plato made her the "tenth Muse."

The beloved young student soon let herself be courted by boys, however, and Sappho discovered jealousy. Then Atthis left her for Andromeda, a woman who directed another salon, and Sappho learned despair.

The shameless poet was attacked on all sides. Like Aspasia, the consort of Pericles, she was regarded as a foreigner. Shocked conservatives did not want to know this woman from debauched Asia who dedicated a fervent cult to the goddess Aphrodite, herself of Asian origin. At a time when Athenian women were wistfully thinking of emancipation, critics derided the dangerous Sappho and her feminine loves, and spoke of the women of Lesbos, the Lesbians. Nevertheless, in her time Sappho was more reproached for being a woman — the first to raise her voice and show her genius in the world of antiquity — than for loving women.

Hence, having been recognized as a great poet, it was as if she could no longer be recognized as a woman. Plato, a warm admirer of Sappho, made her a daughter of Zeus.

There are nine Muses, they say — how foolish!
For here in addition is Sappho of Lesbos, the tenth.

This was a convenient way to honor the immortal

poet without acknowledging the mortal woman. Then there was legend of the second Sappho, who was blackened with all the vices of the real woman, thus allowing the poet Sappho to come forth in all her splendor as the tenth muse. Plutarch, who also greatly admired her, found still another way: he made her an intermediary between the gods

CHOCOLAT GUÉRIN-BOUTRON

GOUNOD 1818-1893

SAPHO

Though long decried by the prudish, Sappho was never forgotten thanks to the poets who, down the centuries, continued to evoke her name.

and humankind and compared her "transports" to those of the Pythia.

It is said that at the end of her life, Sappho fell in love with a young sailor named Phaon, and that her desperate love drove her to suicide. But if, as Ovid tells us, she really did throw herself off a cliff into the sea, perhaps it was not for love but simply to join the gods — for Sappho believed in her immortality as a poet.

MURASAKI SHIKIBU

JAPAN — 10TH-11TH CENTURIES

An imperial lady-in-waiting of the mid-Heian period (794-1185), Murasaki Shikibu wrote the
world's first novel, as well as verse and a detailed diary.

Murasaki Shikibu's *Genji-monogatari* (The Tale of Genji) is not only a mainstay of Japanese literature, it is also considered the world's first novel. And thanks to its writer's diary, we know many details of her life — almost everything, except her real name.

If women figured at all in medieval Japanese records, they were left anonymous. "Murasaki," which means "violet" or "mauve," is open to differing interpretations. We know that she was of the Fujiwara family, and since "fuji" means "wisteria," she was perhaps given the flower's color as a pen name. Others say that she is simply known by the name of her principle heroine, Murasaki-no Ué.

Murasaki Shikibu lived in the middle of the Heian era, almost four centuries of peace and cultural expansion during which the arts and the cult of beauty flourished. The nobles — useless and lazy, but cultivated — spent much of their time communicating through poetry. The best way to gain influence at the imperial court was to introduce one's daughters as ladies-in-waiting to the empress or other royal ladies. The literary education of girls was emphasized so that they might catch the emperor's eye.

The future novelist and diarist had the luck to be born into a family of well-known poets and was raised in literary circles. Her father, a provincial governor, watched closely over his children's education, especially his son's. However, his daughter received the greater benefit from her brother's lessons, which she attended, often in hiding. Passionately fond of learning, she memorized whole passages of Chinese classics that were considered improper for females. Later she wrote in a celebrated passage in her diary: "When my father came to recite Chinese lessons with my brother, I whispered the answers to him." Such scholarship made her father regret that Murasaki was not his son and heir.

She lived at home in Kyoto until about age twenty-seven, when she finally consented to marry. Her suitor was a distant cousin named Fujiwara Nobutaka, a lieutenant of the Imperial Guard

Her best-known work is *The Tale of Genji*, which covers three-quarters of a century and more than a thousand pages. Scene from *Genji-monogatari* on a scroll.

who was twenty years her senior and who already had a number of wives, concubines, and children. He had become insistent — in verses that she wrote years later she had him say:

Spring will arrive
And I wish you to know
That the snow will end by melting.

She answers:

Certainly, springtime approaches;
The snow of the white mountain accumulates,
But none can say when the snow will melt.

This undistinguished but very vain man took advantage of his wife's literary talent, going so far as to read her letters to him aloud in public. Three years after their wedding, Nobutaka died, leaving his last wife with a daughter to whom she would

devote all her love and who would follow in her steps to become a poet.

Although courted, the widow declined all offers so as to dedicate herself to literature. She was at the center of a feminine literary circle that included the most eminent women authors of the day, such as Sei Shonagon, creator of *The Pillow Book*, who was famous for the irony with which she depicted her characters; and Izumi Shikibu, writer of passionate love poetry.

Murasaki Shikibu had became a member of the imperial court as a lady-in-waiting — a great honor, but one now becoming controversial because of the loose morals of the court. If she was criticized by her friends for staying, however, at least the debauchery and backstairs intrigues served as inspiration. At about age thirty-five she began to write *The Tale of Genji*, which was originally meant to be read aloud. The work focuses on the adventures of Prince Genji, but covers three-quarters of a century, three generations, fifty-four chapters, and over a thousand pages.

Reactions were mixed. Some Buddhist priests found the work provocative, with too great an emphasis on sex. In their view, Murasaki Shikibu was a lost soul, so even her supporters, while praising the book, took the precaution of reciting a prayer for the author's salvation.

Yet others found the tale a highly moral work in which the wicked were punished and the good rewarded. These partisans went so far as to assert that the novel was written at the command of Princess Senshi, who was dying of boredom, and that after Murasaki Shikibu went to the Ishimaya temple and prayed for inspiration, the story came to her.

In time, Murasaki Shikibu entered legend. Her novel serves as a theme and inspiration for Japanese painting and decorative arts, and is still read not only as a major literary work but also as a historical document on the cultivated aristocracy of the Heian period. Murasaki surely did not guess this when she wrote:

In this world,
All that was written will disappear.

MARIANA ALCOFORADO

PORTUGAL — 1640-1723

Mysterious Mariana, abandoned by a faithless lover. . . . Was it really she, the Portuguese nun, who wrote the five letters famous for their magnificence and passion? Or is the heroine of *Lettres Portugaises* purely imaginary?

"Consider, my love, how excessively shortsighted you were." Thus begins the first letter from the betrayed nun to her false beloved. The series of five letters, written over the course of six months, forms one of the most beautiful monologues on love in Western literature. Mariana's words flow like tears and reveal her despair: "Adieu; love me forever; and make me suffer more." The French officer who seduced her has returned to his country, and she entreats him to come back, knowing all the while that he will not even answer her letters. "I write more for myself than for you; I am only trying to console myself." Mariana knows that her love is infinitely greater than her lover's; she does not even try to raise his passion to the level of her own. Resigned, she finally loves only her love for him.

When the letters were first published, on January 4, 1669, in Paris, their enigmatic quality immediately captured the public's imagination. The original edition included a note from the publisher, which began: "After a great deal of effort, I was able to procure an accurate copy of five Portuguese letters that were written to a gentleman of quality, who had done his military service in Portugal." Their publication raised many questions, and provoked counterfeit "replies."

Since the faraway author of the letters could not be identified, an attempt was made to find the man to whom they were addressed. Handwritten notes on copies of the originals mentioned the Chevalier de Chamilly, though as the Duc de Saint-Simon noted, "To see him and hear him, one would never have believed that he could have inspired such an immoderate passion as the one that is the soul of these famous Portuguese letters." Yet Chamilly could indeed have been the nun's lover, since he had been sent by Louis XIV to fight in the Portuguese campaign with Maréchal Schomberg's regiment.

Mariana's destiny: a life dedicated to the love of God.
An anonymous 17th century portrait of a "nun of Monza."

152

The author of the Portuguese letters lived much of her life in a convent.

increasing fervence of his pleas, the nun resisted the temptations of her flesh, though she had already pledged her soul to the young officer. He left for Andalusia with his regiment in February 1666, and she came to regret her reluctance. Long months of separation only increased her passion and desire, and as soon as he returned she became his mistress. Chamilly's brand of love was nothing like Mariana's great tragic passion. Fickle and afraid of scandal, he fled Mariana, returning to France as soon as the war ended.

Drawing from a 1926 French edition of
Lettres Portugaises.

When the letters first came to light, no one questioned their authenticity as documents expressing the love of a real woman for a real man. But nearly a century after their publication, a storm of controversy arose. "I would wager anything that the Portuguese letters were written by a man," the philosopher Jean-Jacques Rousseau declared. Indeed, many thought that a text of such strength and literary quality could have been produced only by a French writer. The dramatists Molière, Racine, and Corneille, the moralist La Rochefoucauld, and even a woman, the Comtesse de La Fayette, were suspected of authorship. A court secretary, the Comte Lavergne de Guilleragues, was scrutinized; he certainly wrote, but nothing important enough to leave such a mark on history. Yet he was credited in some foreign editions of the work, first in Cologne, Germany, as its translator, then in the Netherlands as its author.

In 1810, a Frenchman named Boissonade confirmed the belief of those who considered the letters the authentic work of an impassioned woman. He claimed to reveal her true identity, found in a handwritten note in his copy of the work. The Portuguese nun, he said, was Mariana Alcoforado, and her lover was indeed Noël Bouton de Chamilly, who in his vanity had had the letters read to his entourage.

The daughter of Francisco Alcoforado, an officer and royal official, Mariana had taken her vows at age sixteen, not because she had a religious calling, but for her family's convenience. When her mother died, Mariana was entrusted with the care of her three-year-old sister, Peregrina, and they set up house together in an apartment near the convent. Mariana lived peacefully until Maréchal Schomberg's troops arrived in Beja in the 1660s. Her brother, Lieutenant Balthazar Alcoforado, belonged to the regiment, and introduced his sister to Captain Chamilly, whom she had already noticed during the troop's parades.

Chamilly began to visit her secretly in her apartment, trying hard to seduce her. Despite the

Mariana never repented the violation of her religious vows, but lived the rest of her life scrupulously fulfilling a nun's duties. She died at the age of eighty-three. She had given the world a beautiful expression of passionate love. Declared the French novelist Stendahl, "One should love like the Portuguese nun, with a soul on fire."

THE BRONTE SISTERS

EMILY (1818-1848) AND CHARLOTTE (1816-1855)
ENGLAND

While the Brontë sisters' genius was for writing, their brother Branwell's talent lay in art.
Here, his portrait of Anne, Emily, and Charlotte.

The lonely wilderness of the Yorkshire moors is the backdrop against which we view the enigmatic Brontë sisters. Who were these women, whose gift for fiction grew and flourished within the limits of rural, secluded family life? Charlotte and Emily lived only briefly, their days dominated by toil, their evenings spent quietly by the fire as rain beat on the windows.

Their father was Irish in origin — Patrick Brontë (born Brunty, a name he changed because it sounded common). An Anglican priest, he moved into Haworth vicarage with his family in 1820. A year later his wife, Maria, died of cancer, leaving Patrick to raise their six children: Maria, Elizabeth, Charlotte, Patrick Branwell, Emily, and Anne. The children's Aunt Elizabeth Branwell moved in with the family to care for them, and remained until the end of her life. She instilled in them the importance of charity, dressed them in old-fashioned clothing, and taught them to cook, iron, and perform other domestic chores. But when evening came Aunt Elizabeth's regime ended: oblivious to her wishes, the children threw themselves into reading books, magazines, and newspapers. Without other children to play with in their isolated village, they became adept at imagining fantastic worlds peopled with heroes. And to the company of their aunt they preferred that of the maid Tabitha, who regaled them with tales of local superstition while she baked them cakes.

In 1824, the girls entered Cowan Bridge, a boarding school in Lancashire for the children of poor clergymen. The harsh discipline and difficult living conditions left Charlotte with painful memories that she shared with the world in *Jane Eyre*. A year after starting school, Maria and Elizabeth fell ill with typhoid, and all the sisters returned home. After the deaths of her two older sisters, Charlotte found herself acting as mother to the younger children.

Back at the Haworth vicarage, the children resumed their story-telling and their fantasy worlds — the best reality available to them. They collaborated in their imaginings, sharing the worlds they created, integrating their fictional selves into their daily activities. And they began to write down their creations. Using minuscule script, they called their works "miniature novels," integrating history, literature, legends, religion, and politics into an enormous body of work. Today, five thousand pages remain of the children's brilliant day-dreaming; most of it was created by Charlotte and the unstable young Branwell, their sisters' writings having largely disappeared.

At fifteen, a quiet and thoughtful Charlotte was sent to boarding school in Roe Head, where she spent a year. Too shy to join in the games, she preferred to sit under a tree and read. But at night, her ability to entertain the other girls with ghost stories won her several close friendships. With one fellow student, Ellen Nussey, she would cor-

could not adapt to adult realities: addicted to alcohol and opium, he died at the age of twenty-seven.

Emily left Roe Head to return to her family. Solitary and secretive, she left the house only to go to church or to walk on the moors. When Charlotte, homesick herself, returned to Haworth, the three sisters considered opening a school so they could earn a living without leaving home.

In 1844 the Brontë sisters attempted to realize their dream of starting a school, yet in remote Haworth it did not attract students. Then one day Charlotte stumbled across some poems of Emily's and was surprised by their quality; this inspired the three sisters to publish the verses that, unbeknownst to one another, all had been writing. They paid for it themselves and used the pseudonyms Currer (Charlotte), Ellis (Emily) and Acton (Anne) Bell. Only two copies were sold, but they did not let that discourage them. Each was at work on a novel.

All three of these first novels were published in 1847. Charlotte's *Jane Eyre* was an immediate success. Anne published *Agnes Grey*, and Emily, *Wuthering Heights*. Emily's novel, which unlike the other two does not rely on autobiographical events, reflects her violent imagination and was initially judged savage and bestial by the unappreciative critics. Many years passed before it came to be recognized as one of the greatest of English novels. Emily had no intimations of that, for little more than a year after *Wuthering Heights'* publication she died of tuberculosis, having refused to take care of herself after her beloved Branwell's death.

Soon Anne died too, also of tuberculosis. Charlotte had lost her three siblings within months. She found herself alone with her father at the vicarage. She wrote *Shirley* and *Villette*, which increased the popularity of "Currer Bell," and became friends with her editor and his wife. But her daily life remained monotonously lonely without her brother and sisters. Finally, after rejecting three offers of marriage, she accepted the proposal of her father's curate, Arthur Bell Nicholls.

Their marriage was short. Charlotte was pregnant when she fell ill and died in 1855. Thus the curtain dropped on the brief history of the Brontë sisters. Only their few books pass down the heritage of their genius.

Portrait of Charlotte by George Richmond. While her *Jane Eyre* found immediate success. . .

Emily's *Wuthering Heights,* deemed savage by critics, was not appreciated until long after her death.

respond until her death; these letters provide much insight into Charlotte's life and feelings.

On returning to Haworth, Charlotte took charge of her sisters' education for three years, then left again for Roe Head, this time to teach. Emily accompanied her as a student. Charlotte had to earn a living to help provide for her family, and in particular to sustain Branwell's efforts to establish himself as an artist. But the brother who had led the childhood journey into fantasy

This would require that they perfect their knowledge of French and acquire a basic understanding of German. Charlotte and Emily left for Brussels in 1842 to live and study languages at the Héger boarding school. Emily returned to Haworth for good upon the death of Aunt Elizabeth, while Charlotte continued to study abroad. She became devoted to the brilliant and witty Constantin Héger. Was it amorous devotion? Certainly Madame Héger disapproved of the relationship.

GEORGE SAND

FRANCE — 1804-1876

Novels, plays, essays, diaries . . . George Sand was nothing if not prolific.
1838 portrait by Auguste Charpentier.

Her practice of dressing like a man and smoking cigars drove her admirers and detractors to opposite extremes. Those who did not appreciate the challenges she posed to society criticized her brusque, masculine demeanor, while those who loved her did their best to find her feminine despite the scant encouragement she gave them. For George Sand, née Aurore Dupin, was neither beautiful nor charming — but she was a writer.

"You have to have known her as I knew her to know all that was feminine in this great 'man,' the immensity of tenderness to be found in this genius," wrote Gustave Flaubert on Sand's death. Many have spoken or written of the dual-edged personality of the writer, who aroused comment because of both her revolutionary attitudes and her noticeably active love life.

Aurore Dupin's father was a military officer. Her grandmother, with whom she and her mother lived after her father's death in 1808, descended from German and Polish nobility. Four-year-old Aurore was taken down a peg upon arriving at her grandmother's residence, Nohant: "You weren't to roll on the ground, laugh noisily, speak like a native of Berry. . . . You had to speak to her in the third person: 'Would my Granny allow me to go into the garden?'" The little girl suffered from this rigid upbringing, but even more from the climate of tension between her mother and grandmother.

So it was with relief that Aurore went to board in a Parisian convent at the age of about thirteen. She distinguished herself first as the uncontested leader of the "little devils," then, intrigued by the mysteries of religion, talked of becoming a nun. Her grandmother, who believed in God but not much else, was alarmed enough to remove Aurore from the convent.

On the death of Madame Dupin soon afterward, Aurore spent a year in the country, then settled at Nohant, which her grandmother had left to her. Aurore was then seventeen years old and had already met Casimir Dudevant, her future husband. She threw herself eagerly into reading, discovering a multitude of authors, and was exceptionally impressed by the philosopher

Sand with the pianists Franz Liszt and Frédéric Chopin,
on a fan painted by Sand and Charpentier.

Jean-Jacques Rousseau. After marrying Baron Dudevant, she gave birth first to a son, Maurice, to whom she remained close throughout her life, and then to a daughter, Solange, who was probably the result of an adulterous liaison. The marriage was unsuccessful, and the two led their own lives. In the meantime, Aurore had begun to write.

In 1830, she met Jules Sandeau, seven years her junior, and after a year left Nohant to live with him in Paris. Aurore discovered there the intellectual and artistic bohemia, and wanted to be part of it, not necessarily as a man, but as a writer. She dressed like her male friends to be indistinguishable from them, and then, as she herself said, "to be able to be alone in the street." At the same time, she adopted a masculine pseudonym because she was working in tandem with Jules Sandeau: together they wrote a novel, *Rose et Blanche*, under the name Jules Sand. Aurore had also begun to write reports and news for the newspaper *Le Figaro*. She distanced herself professionally from her lover by publishing *Indiana* under the name George Sand in 1832. The novel

sold briskly, and was a critical success as well: "*Indiana* is a declaration of war against the Napoleonic Code," wrote a critic. "It brings tears to your eyes and enriches the intellect."

She worked very hard and had a series of amorous adventures, but also developed great friendships with writers, theater people, and philosophers. In 1833, Sand published *Lélia*, a novel of memories and symbols that dealt with the problem of women's lack of position in society. It was simultaneously a triumph and a scandal. Gustave Planche, a literary critic who was in love with Sand, was so angered by an attack on the book that he challenged the attacker to a duel.

At this time she met the young poet Alfred de Musset. Their liaison was stormy, with Sand playing lover, mother, and nurse to him, all at the same time. They spent two tumultuous years together, each taking turns breaking off the relationship. After one such rupture, Sand cut off her long black curls and sent them to Musset, moving him so that he returned to her. Finally she put an end to the union.

In 1838, Sand began a quiet affair with Frédéric Chopin that was to last almost ten years. During this decade, she continued to read and write. In 1841, she founded the *Revue Indépendante* with Pierre Leroux; she was impassioned by the 1848 revolution, but when it failed she returned, disillusioned, to Nohant, in her beloved Berry region. There she continued to use her influence to defend the condemned republicans. She still wrote prolifically: the so-called rustic novels, which were very successful, and memoirs and plays. She formed more prudent liaisons, first with her secretary, Alexandre Manceau, who died

She wore men's clothes, smoked cigars, took famous
lovers — outrageous!

when she was sixty; then with Charles Marchal, twenty years her junior.

George Sand became "the good lady of Nohant," an exemplary grandmother who wrote children's stories. By the time she died, Sand had completed some seventy novels and narratives, two dozen plays, numerous essays, and intimate journals. And if with time her works have not stood up to the competition of Stendahl, Flaubert, Honoré de Balzac, or Emile Zola, who used their pens in a more original fashion, Sand still found her own way of putting art into her life.

VIRGINIA WOOLF

ENGLAND — 1882-1941

Virginia Woolf was plagued by mental illness throughout her life.
A 1912 portrait by her sister, Vanessa Bell, in the National Portrait Gallery, London.

She was a great writer, a woman of haunting beauty whose private life was tortured but whose sense of humor never failed. Virginia Woolf is one of the 20th century's most alluring writers, at once a myth and misunderstood.

Virginia was born in London into a large family, both her parents having offspring from previous marriages. The children got along well and Virginia's early years were happy and creative. Her father, Sir Leslie Stephen, was a scholarly figure, an eminent Victorian who entertained the old social and literary generation at Hyde Park Gate, their home. Her sweet and affectionate mother, Julia, who was at times confused and lost in her own thoughts, acted as an intermediary between the children's world and the more somber and inflexible world of Leslie Stephen. Virginia later took her mother as a model for Mrs. Ramsey, a complex character in her 1927 novel, *To the Lighthouse*. According to her brothers and sisters, the portrait was astonishingly accurate.

The first upheaval in the life of the family came with the death of Julia when Virginia was thirteen. Her father plunged into neurotic melancholia, and Virginia experienced the first of many mental breakdowns, the "madness" that plagued her for the rest of her life.

Just when the family was rediscovering happiness and stability two years later, her eldest sister, Stella, who had taken charge of the household, died of peritonitis after returning from her honeymoon. Within two years, just when Virginia was entering adolescence, she had lost the two women she loved most. On top of this, starting at age eleven and for some years following, she was subjected to sexual abuse by her half-brother Gerald and said nothing. This irreparably perturbed her outlook toward love and sex.

Virginia's enormous capacity for affection was directed toward females from an early age. She had what were called "romantic friendships" with a number of women. In 1912 she married Leonard Woolf, a colonial civil servant who gave up his career in India for her. They formed the core of the Bloomsbury group, which included some of the leading cultural figures of the time, such as E.M. Forster, John Maynard Keynes, and Clive Bell. Bell married Virginia's sister, Vanessa, a talented painter. The almost daily correspondence the sisters exchanged throughout their lives reflects an antagonistic yet intimate relationship, a mixture of love, admiration, and jealousy.

The members of the Bloomsbury group were talented, creative, and outrageous. In opposition to the prim and stuffy moral attitude of the Victorian era, they insisted upon plain language in everything relating to their love lives. Before marrying Leonard, Virginia even had a relation-

Virginia and Leonard Woolf, and their literary and artistic friends formed the core of the Bloomsbury group.

ship with Lytton Strachey, a gifted and unself-conscious homosexual. They briefly considered marriage, but, as he confessed, he was afraid she might kiss him.

Virginia published her first novel, *The Voyage Out*, in 1916. The many works that followed included *Night and Day, Mrs. Dalloway, Orlando, The Waves*, and *The Years*, in addition to her

prolific correspondence, articles of literary criticism, and work for the Hogarth Press, founded by the Woolfs to publish writings by members of the Bloomsbury group. Virginia now seems a tireless worker, but she thought of herself as a beautiful, old-fashioned semi-invalid writing in the seclusion of her summerhouse in the garden.

At the beginning of World War II, the Woolfs moved to Monk's House, in Sussex, which they rented because Virginia's mental instability made living in London difficult. On February 26, 1941, she finished writing her last novel, *Between the Acts*. The period after the completion of a novel was always dangerous for her. In addition, Britain was undergoing the most severe bombings of the war, the prospect of a German invasion seemed imminent, and her husband was Jewish. Virginia

had borne the ever-present threat of her precarious mental state for many years with courage and even a certain kind of humor, but she could not face the prospect of another breakdown.

On the morning of March 28, Virginia wrote two letters, which she put on the dining-room mantlepiece. One was for Vanessa, the other for Leonard. Then she set out for the River Ouse and never came back. She wrote in the last sentence of her letter to Leonard that two people could not have been happier than they had been. Thus closed a life distinguished by a love of words and by sexual failure. Her frustrated desires and her capacity to give and receive love produced rich works in which longing for normality is always present. Literature could not be the same in the 20th century after Virginia Woolf.

Virginia with her father, Sir Leslie Stephen, a scholarly figure who entertained Thomas Hardy, Henry James, and other literary lights at Hyde Park Gate, the Stephens' home.

KAREN BLIXEN

DENMARK — 1885-1962

The woman called "Baroness" in her native Denmark and she whom the Kikuyu tribespeople called "our mother" were one and the same. And whether she called herself Isak Dinesen or Karen Blixen, she was, in her own words, "not a writer, but a storyteller; not a page in a book, but a voice."

All her life Karen was torn by the conflicting values she absorbed from the two vastly different sides of her family. Her mother came from a bourgeois family in which the women aired feminist views, while her father descended from affable country nobles whose women aspired only to decorate their surroundings. Of his five children, Karen's father favored her the most; he gave her his passion for nature, taught her to dream, and talked to her of life. The little girl saw her own life as "a sea crossing" and took as her motto a phrase of Pompey's: "It is necessary to navigate; it is not necessary to live." While Karen was still very young, her father committed suicide. "It was as if a part of myself were dead, too," wrote Karen.

At the age of fourteen, she left for Lausanne, Switzerland, with her mother and two sisters; there she studied French, drawing, and painting. She was so enamored of these last two pursuits that, despite her family's reluctance, she enrolled in the Academy of Fine Arts in Copenhagen in 1903. She was painfully conscious of the difference in social station between herself and her noble cousins, whom she saw frequently, and she tried to overcome her inferiority by seeming intellectual. She became even more frustrated by her social inferiority when she fell madly in love with one of her cousins, Hans Blixen, a brilliant boy from a great family, who paid her no notice. Depressed, she left for France in 1910 to pursue her art studies; two years later, she went to Italy.

Karen Blixen was permanently marked by her stay in Africa, where she tried to make a life for herself. Having failed, she left her farm and threw herself into writing

160

Each time she returned home from a trip, Karen sank into a depression; this continued throughout her life. On her return from Italy, she accepted a proposal of marriage from Bror Blixen, Hans's brother. The whimsical artist was very different from her young, noble, extroverted fiancé, but "between us," noted Bror, "we built up in our imagination a future where everything, save the impossible, had its place." On the advice of an uncle, Bror decided to settle in Kenya. Karen would follow him there, and they would marry the day she arrived in Mombassa.

Karen joined her fiancé in Africa in January 1914. She became Baroness Blixen-Finecke, and with her husband explored his new land, about twelve miles from Nairobi. Bror thought the estate ideal for growing coffee — even if his original idea had been to raise cattle. He proved wrong.

Later, Karen would write: "I realize how much I have been favored to have been able to lead a free and humane life in a peaceful land, after having known the noise and worry of the world." She immediately liked this immense continent and its inhabitants. She felt that she had established with them a rapport like the one she had shared with her father. A Somali, Farah Aden, helped her settle in, looked after the house, became her confidant; she called the deep relationship, which lasted eighteen years, "creative unity." She made friends with the Kikuyus who worked the land and with their chief. But her relations with the other colonials remained cold.

Bror often left her alone at the farm, but she never showed him how jealous this made her. Even when she became seriously ill with syphilis, which she caught from him, and which he had probably contracted from a Masai tribeswoman, she did not consider leaving him. It was he who successfully sued for divorce some years later.

For Karen had met someone else: Denys Finch Hatton, a cultured man passionate about Africa. She loved him deeply, awaited his visits eagerly, and sank into a depression when he departed. During the long periods when he was absent on safari or in Europe, she would become mired in

"To dream, that is the suicide which well-bred people can allow themselves," she wrote as Isak Dinesen.

the troubles of the farm, which was rapidly losing money. And then he would suddenly reappear, and spend long evenings with her, listening to Schubert or to the stories she told so well.

With her divorce, the world that Karen had built for herself in Africa by sheer strength of will began to collapse around her. Though she managed the farm alone for ten years, she was ultimately forced to sell it. And as she was sadly arranging the future of the Kikuyus living on her land, Denys was killed in a plane crash. At the age of forty-six she returned to Denmark — financially ruined, still ill, and alone.

"To dream, that is the suicide which well-brought-up people can allow themselves," Isak Dinesen said in the voice of the heroine of her *Seven Gothic Tales*. Under this pseudonym Karen had started to write seriously, and published this first work in the United States in 1934. Then

came *Out of Africa*, in which she told her own story so well, relating her "real terror of abandoning life and soul for something which can be lost again," a fear that never left her. By the end of World War II, after publishing *Winter's Tales*, Isak Dinesen was a well-known writer. She surrounded herself with young people who venerated her and gave in to her every whim.

From Dinesen's memoir *Out of Africa*, Sydney Pollack made a film in which Meryl Streep played the baroness.

Twice Karen Blixen was nominated for a Nobel prize; both times another won it. But she was welcomed with great honor when she visited the United States for a few months toward the end of her life. She retained her vitality even as a sick old woman who consumed only grapes, oysters, and champagne because she had always wanted to be "the thinnest woman in the world." Fleshless, with her big black eyes, she looked like a bird. She died of malnutrition in 1962.

AGATHA CHRISTIE

ENGLAND — 1890-1976

Agatha Christie was a very Victorian old lady
who never gave the impression that she was working.

She was an Everywoman from the English middle class, very Victorian, a bit of a snob. As the "First Lady of Crime", Agatha Christie created two alter egos whose adventures were as unbelievable as they were thrilling: Hercule Poirot and Miss Marple.

"One of the greatest pieces of luck you can have in life is to have a happy childhood. I had a very happy childhood." Agatha Miller was born into a close family; her sister, brother, and parents got along marvelously in their home in Torquay, Devon. Their American father spent his days at his club, while their mother remained at home with the children. The children's care was primarily the responsibility of their Nursie. Agatha was fascinated by the world of servants and its rules, and described them in detail, with typical detached British humor, in her autobiography.

Her parents, who enjoyed the frequent company of intellectuals, refused to send her to school. Clarissa Miller decided that her daughter should not learn to read before she was eight, but at five little Agatha, who loved fairy tales, figured things out well enough by herself to read something called "The Angel of Love." "Madame, I am afraid Miss Agatha knows how to read," Nursie confessed the next morning. From then on, the child spent as much time reading as in playing outside. She soon wrote her first story, a short melodrama that she staged for her sister, Madge. The plot revolved around the inheritance of a castle and included two heroines, the Kind One and the Bloody One.

Madge used to enjoy frightening her sister by talking in a hollow voice, turning herself into the imaginary "older sister" who lived in a cave. Even many years later, confided Agatha in her autobiography, all Madge had to do was speak to her in the voice of "the older sister" to give Agatha the shivers. Why, she wondered, did she love being frightened? And she asked herself: what instinctive need is satisfied by terror?

Agatha's father died when she was fourteen years old, and the family's pleasant life suffered. Agatha was then becoming a young lady, enjoying horseback riding, dances, and other frivolous pastimes. A girl didn't worry about what she would be; she waited for a man to come along, Agatha noted, entranced by this notion. She spent two years in a French boarding school, studying music and singing, then accompanied her mother to Egypt, where she flirted with appropriate young men. She resumed this occupation on her return to Torquay, for it was time to find a husband. Colonel Archibald Christie, a Royal Flying Corps pilot, won out over the other suitors. They were married on Christmas Eve, 1914, before Archie left for the front.

During the war, Agatha worked as a volunteer at the Torquay hospital, where she became fascinated by poisons. From this interest came the idea for her first novel, *The Mysterious Affair at Styles*, whose hero was the Belgian former police inspector destined for fame: Hercule Poirot. Writing made Agatha "tired and bad-tempered," but she finished the book quickly. It took four years, though, to find a publisher, and then she was persuaded to sign a contract that gave her very little money. Like many novices, she was so anxious to publish that she was easily taken advantage of. "I would have signed anything," she said. She later hired an agent, Edmund Cork, who managed her business matters and was a loyal friend until she died.

After the war, the Christies moved to London, had a daughter named Rosalind, and found a country house where Agatha lived her dream life of wife and mother while also completing a series of highly successful mystery novels. The shadow of adultery darkened this idyllic scene: Archie took a mistress. The self-possessed young Agatha reacted in a fashion worthy of a mystery writer. On December 4, 1926, her car was discovered near a pond; there were papers and a fur coat, but no Agatha. The bottom of the pond was dragged in vain, the search continued for a week and Agatha was finally found in a Yorkshire hotel, registered under the name Neele — the name of her husband's mistress. Oddly enough, Agatha "forgot" to include this episode in her memoirs.

Amidst her bric-a-brac, Agatha Christie at her desk.

After her divorce, Agatha came to the realization that she was a professional author, but still clung to the idea that writing books was, as she put it, merely the logical follow-up to petit-point embroidery. She took the Orient Express to Baghdad, where she stayed with some archaeologist friends. Returning there the following winter, she met a timid, twenty-four-year-old archaeologist named Max Mallowan. The fifteen-year difference in their ages did not stop them from falling in love, and they were married.

Agatha now combined writing with participation in her husband's digs. While she found "ordinary life" amusing enough, she had enough energy left over to throw herself into the theater and to create a new character: the wickedly Victorian, ineffable Miss Marple. She also began her autobiography, describing her troubles with Rosalind's governess and with bedbugs during her travels, as well as her weaknesses for the color purple, apples, and traveling (despite the bedbugs!), and her immoderate passion for houses. There, too, she relates that one of the most memorable events in her life was the acquisition of her first car — the other being dining with the queen in Buckingham Palace forty years later!

The "Duchess of Death" wrote more than eighty mystery novels — not to mention short stories and plays — and all so effortlessly that she never seemed to be busy with her writing. She died at age eighty-five, taking with her the keys to her prodigious imagination.

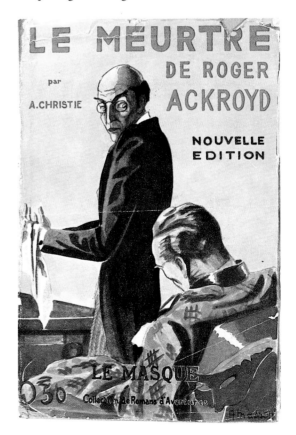

More than eighty mystery novels, with hundreds of thousands of copies sold in many languages.

ANAÏS NIN

FRANCE 1903 — UNITED STATES 1977

Anaïs Nin searched ceaselessly for love and pleasure. *Henry and June,* the tale of her intense relationship with Henry and June Miller, was not published until all of its characters were dead. The film based on the book starred Maria de Medeiros as Anaïs, Fred Ward as Henry, and Uma Thurman as June.

Anaïs Nin patiently recorded her life, day after day, year after year. "To write is to look within, to dig, to penetrate to the core." That line from her *Diary* — considered her best work — summarizes her career as a writer and her experience as a human being.

She was born in Neuilly, near Paris. Her father was the Cuban composer and concert pianist Joaquín Nin; the family's residence was in Barcelona but they traveled widely, following his concert itineraries, even when Anaïs was a child.

At the age of nine, she experienced the first in a series of events that would result in her vocation and her literary career: her parents separated. She left for New York two years later, in 1914, accompanied by her mother and her brothers. She began her career during the long, unhappy sea voyage to a continent she hated sight unseen. Separated from the egotistical father she adored, homesick, and terrified by the unknown, she turned to writing. The *Diary* in fact began as a letter to her father. Anaïs wanted to stay in contact by telling him all the small details of her daily existence, but her mother prevented her from sending the letter, claiming that it might be lost.

Gradually, the person to whom the lines were originally addressed was forgotten. Anaïs looked within herself, and as the years passed, fragments of her imagination became novels and tales. The *Diary* also reflected the evolution of her language: she wrote in French until 1920, then in English. Moreover, the journal was a witness to her hurts and her resolution to be open to everything that could happen to her.

Anaïs Nin's true adventure was her life, her untiring search for intense human relationships. Her introspection began with an intellectual and therapeutic friendship with the psychoanalyst Otto Rank. And in her quest for love and pleasure she sought to attain the truth she never doubted would come through full exchange.

In the 1920s Anaïs married Hugo Guiler, a banker who was also an engraver and film producer under the name of Ian Hugo. He followed the demanding lead of his wife and participated in the variety of experiences she sought out in her obsessive search for personal development.

In Paris in the early 1930s, Anaïs met the audacious author Henry Miller and initiated her literary career with an essay on the life and work of D.H. Lawrence. She was in her element in the brilliant and cosmopolitan cultural world of Paris. She and her husband took a house in Louveciennes, and there she began her close relationship with Miller and his wife, June.

Anaïs had never met two people with whom she had so much in common. June — extraordinarily feminine, beautiful, capricious, untruthful — was unfaithful to everyone, even herself. She fascinated Anaïs and often humiliated her to ex-

tremes. Anaïs followed her step by step, struggling to find the truth behind June's strange, incessant lies. Henry was in the same position; his

The desire to understand June united Henry and Anaïs.

explosive erotic relationship with Anaïs was defined by their common effort to explain June, as we now know thanks to the publication of *Henry and June*, a part of the *Diary* that Anaïs refused to publish during the lifetime of the protagonists, including herself.

For Anaïs, writing was part of living. She said that when she did not write, she felt her universe become smaller. She felt imprisoned, lost her fire and her passion. She could no more stop writing than the tide could refuse to go out. To write was to breathe.

At the dawn of World War II she left Paris for New York and continued to write. She published the books herself; not until 1966, with the first

volume of the *Diary*, was her place in American literature recognized. She was still adding to the journal — there are fifteen thousand pages, and only a condensed version has been published. The *Diary* is quite frank, for not only did the scandalous Anaïs dare to shock with her erotic writing, she was not afraid of the word "I" and she had a talent for commentary and analysis.

Although the *Diary* is considered her greatest work, it is far from her only one. In addition to two collections of erotic short stories, *Delta of Venus* and *The Little Birds*, her works include *House of Incest* (1936), *A Spy in the House of Love* (1954), the five-volume *Cities of the Interior* (1959), *Seduction of the Minotaur* (1961), and *Collages* (1964).

Anaïs Nin died in Los Angeles in 1977. She

Anaïs shocked the world with her erotic writing.

left some of literature's most explicit pages, rich in teachings on eroticism. They reflect the image of a triumphant woman who would not renounce her own being in approaching areas that had always seemed reserved for men.

Virtuoso pianist, wife of a genius who sank into madness, eight times a mother — Clara's soul was claimed by music, she devoted her heart to Robert Schumann, and her children took all her courage.

Friedrich Wieck, a music teacher in Leipzig, cultivated the gifts of his precocious daughter Clara from the age of five. She could write musical notes before she knew a single letter of the alphabet. According to her diary, Clara had "lost" her mother by this time; in fact, her mother had left Wieck and obtained a divorce. Her departure was heartrending for the little girl, "the first discord" of her life. Clara spent her youth with her father, her piano, and her violin. "It was a good thing for me that he was extremely strict, criticizing me where I needed it," she later wrote. "He kept me from becoming overproud at the world's praises." At nine she gave her first public recital and by the age of eleven she had composed and published four polonaises.

In 1828 Clara made a new friend - Robert Schumann, who was Wieck's pupil and boarder. Four years later, after playing in Paris and in Weimar, Clara joined her name to that of the composer for the first time by interpreting his works. Clara was already famous, Schumann was not.

Their warm friendship started to turn into a romance. Robert had been betrothed to another Wieck pupil, but they broke their engagement by mutual agreement in January 1836, and when Clara returned home from a tour, Schumann realized that it was she he loved. The feeling was mutual.

Wieck opposed their marriage. Robert was too poor and the marriage could only hurt Clara's artistic career. The lovers were separated. Their conflict with Wieck lasted four years, during which time they exchanged clandestine correspondence and met in secret. In agony, Robert wrote his music for Clara, and she, ever more acclaimed, dreamed of making this music famous. Finally she took shelter with her mother in Berlin and initiated a court action against her father. Wieck publicly accused Schumann of drunkenness. The

CLARA SCHUMANN
GERMANY — 1819-1896

To Brahms she was "this magnificent woman."
Clara Schumann lived for music and for the family she cherished.

maneuver failed; the couple won and were at last married in a small country church on September 12, 1840.

The next day they started to keep a diary together. It began with the words "Work, economy, fidelity," qualities that indeed marked the life of this close, affectionate, happy couple. Six months after her marriage, she noted: "Love is the most beautiful thing in the world, and each day we become more one heart and one soul." Schumann's talent had reached maturity; he was composing, teaching, and conducting. For herself, she did not want to abandon her career as a pianist, which brought in much-needed money. Although she bore eight children, she continued to give concerts and go on tour.

Schumann had long been mentally unstable, and as the years went on the problem increased. The couple's last happy period was when they met the young Johannes Brahms, who became a close friend. Several months later, on February 27, 1854, Schumann attempted suicide by throwing himself in the Rhine. Clara was not told because she was expecting their eighth child. In early March, at his own request, he was institutionalized near Bonn. When it became clear that he would not be released soon, Clara took the situation in hand with the help of Brahms, who worshiped her husband. Short of money, she started to play again, accompanied by the violinist Joseph Joachim. During a tour she wrote: "How incredibly hard it is to appear before the public when one's heart is broken."

Toward the end of July 1856 she rushed to the bedside of her husband, who had grown much worse. He was able to recognize Clara before he died on July 29. She could not allow grief to overcome her, for she had to provide for their children, the eldest of whom was barely fifteen. After putting them to board in three different places, she embarked upon a round of lessons, concerts, and overwork. During a rest cure the doctors prescribed a break from music. She replied: "Impossible! Music will forever be my joy and my life!"

A virtuoso pianist, Clara loved to play the music of her husband, Robert Schumann. After his death she devoted herself to promoting his music.

Never losing her "inconsolable heartbreak," Clara became the apostle of Schumann's music and led the itinerant life of a concert artist. Between 1856 and 1891, when she gave her last performance, she toured Russia, went to Paris twice, and visited England sixteen times. She had a passionate friendship with Brahms. He never published anything without her approval, and it was with his help that Clara edited the complete works of Schumann.

She grew old. She received honors and endowments, and had the joy of seeing her husband's fame increase. Her art was a religion for her. She wrote to Brahms: "Art is the most faithful consolation, whose breath, like an ever-gentle wind, surrounds our doleful hearts, strengthens our soul." She needed that consolation, for she lived through the deaths of four of her children and had to commit one of her sons for insanity. Her daughter Elise moved to America, but her other daughters, Marie and Eugenie, both musicians, were with her when she died.

Shortly before her death, Brahms wrote to their friend Joachim: "And when she will have left us, will our faces not light with joy only in thinking of her, of this magnificent woman..."

SARAH BERNHARDT

FRANCE — 1844-1923

A woman of exceptional talent, free and fantastic, Sarah
Bernhardt lived life immoderately.

A public prodigy, born to live immoderately: her genius, her character, her luck — everything about her was extraordinary. Even at age seventy, Sarah Bernhardt was still appearing in Racine's *Athalie* onstage, despite the loss of one of her legs — as if she were immortal, invincible.

As a child, she was nicknamed "Sarah, Fleur de Lait" by her nurse, but her real name was Henriette-Rosine Bernard. The daughter of a law student and a beautiful milliner who would later become a courtesan, the little girl did not interest her parents very much. At first she was cared for by a nanny in Brittany, where she was showered with the affection every little girl needs. Then the two of them rejoined Sarah's mother at Neuilly, just in time to see her depart on a long voyage. Sarah's father decided to take charge of her education and sent her to board at the convent of Grands-Champs in Versailles. There she discovered religion and, although she was Jewish, expressed her desire to become a nun. Once she had left the convent she forgot this idea, but remained resolved never to marry. She kept this resolution despite the generous legacy she would have received from her father's estate upon taking a husband.

Sarah's mother wanted to provide her with a career that would guarantee her financial independence. One of her lovers suggested that Sarah should become an actress and arranged her admission to the Conservatoire, the national school of music and dramatic arts. She finished her studies with second place awards in both tragedy and comedy. She then received a proposal of marriage, and despite the inheritance and other advantages this would have brought her, she refused.

Her first employment, at the Comédie-Française, was short-lived: she was fired for slapping another actress. She appeared in light comedies, then signed a contract with the Odéon theater, promising to behave herself. In 1869, she had her first great stage success with the role of Zanetto in François Coppée's *Le Passant* (The Passerby). Meanwhile, Sarah had developed an independent life, taking an apartment and bearing a son, Maurice, by Henri, Prince de Ligne.

Little is known of this love affair; the actress was circumspect about her personal life, even in her autobiography. Others would later make up for her silence by spreading all sorts of tales about her.

In 1870, during the Franco-Prussian War, she organized a clinic at the Odéon to take care of the wounded. Then she set off to join her family where they had sought refuge in Germany, traveling through the thick of the war to reach them. She brought them back with her to Paris; the thought of hiding in a safe place did not occur to her. Sarah was never afraid to stare harsh reality in the face: opposed to capital punishment, she witnessed four executions, and after the publication of Emile Zola's famous *J'accuse,* she withstood the condemnation of the press to join Zola in defending the unjustly imprisoned Alfred Dreyfus.

After the war, the Odéon reopened and in January 1872, Sarah Bernhardt played Queen Maria in Victor Hugo's *Ruy Blas:* "I felt that I was destined for fame. Up until that day, I had remained the schoolchildren's little fairy: I was now the public's Chosen One." She returned with head held high to the Comédie Française, where she

"A moving image with living eyes" the writer Jules Renard said of her.

The public idol.

was acclaimed for eight years. After Hugo saw her in his *Hernani,* which triumphed in 1877, he wrote to her: "I wept. This teardrop that you caused to fall is yours and I am at your feet."

When her conquest of Europe was complete, she formed her own company and left for America with eight tons of baggage. It was in America that Sarah Bernhardt first played Marguérite in *La Dame aux camélias,* which would become her special role. She captivated audiences. In her travels to the four corners of the world she created new roles, each more successful than the last. She loved to play male parts, including the title roles in *Hamlet* and *L'Aiglon,* but was equally divine in completely feminine roles such as Phedra or Ophelia. She was praised ceaselessly; even Jules Renard, known for his scathing reviews, wrote, "When she descends the spiral staircase of her mansion, it is as if she remains motionless and the staircase revolves around her."

Her Paris mansion was part of her legend. Filled with bric-a-brac from around the world, it was an Oriental bazaar with heaps of cushions and rugs, bibelots and plants, the height of the baroque. Sarah allegedly slept there in a coffin,

leaving her bed to her ailing sister; another part of her legend. She also raised wild cats — lynx, baby lions, tigers — when she wasn't busy hunting alligators or flying in hot-air balloons. She was "a sorceress," declared a Canadian bishop.

Sarah Bernhardt was above all a free woman.

Sarah Bernhardt left her mark on her century and the annals of dramatic art.

Whimsical to the point of outright weirdness, she could also be very much a conformist in her paintings, her sculptures, and the plays she wrote. She lived surrounded by her friends, loving the company of women, despite all the talk of jealousy and discord. And she would not leave the stage even after losing a gangrenous leg in 1915.

"A strange bundle, consisting of a shock of blond hair and Oriental fabrics, with the fierce eyes of an aging lioness, a dying woman dragging herself from one piece of furniture to another, strong as a Turk, and who ends up with her arms crossed against a medieval door, this is the memory Madame Sarah Bernhardt leaves us," wrote Jean Cocteau.

ISADORA DUNCAN

UNITED STATES CA. 1878 — FRANCE 1927

The scarf that killed Isadora Duncan has achieved a fame of its own, overshadowing her life and work. She lived her life to excess, swinging between the extremes of tragedy and triumph; for her work, she is justly called the mother of modern dance.

When asked when she had begun to dance, Isadora replied that it was in the womb, no doubt inspired by her mother's diet: though very poor, she said, her mother was paradoxically able to swallow nothing but iced oysters and champagne — the foods of Aphrodite.

Isadora wrote in her memoirs, "My life and my art were born in the sea. . . . It was upon contemplating the waves when I was very small that my concept of dance came to me." She was born in San Francisco and gave her first dance lessons at the age of six, when her mother came home to find her teaching arm movements to half a dozen children. Her mother, a music teacher, sat down at the piano to accompany what Isadora introduced to her as her "school."

The little enterprise eventually became lucrative enough for the girl to ask to be allowed to devote all her time to it instead of going to the local primary school. The family needed the money: Isadora's mother and her four children lived a transient existence, being evicted time and time again when they could not pay the rent. Isadora's mother had washed her hands of the child's father shortly after Isadora's birth, and the girl grew up with no memory of him. Her aunt had told the little girl that her father was a demon who had ruined her mother's life, and Isadora envisioned him that way, with a tail and horns — until the day he appeared in the flesh. For a brief period, until another in his series of financial "setbacks," he provided the family with a nice house.

Isadora rejected traditional dance lessons and formal schooling, preferring to read at the public library and to study music and poetry in the evenings with her mother. At the age of twelve she scrutinized the condition of married women and vowed never to stoop to that state, which she considered degrading.

Isadora Duncan became famous for her tragic death — to the detriment of her reknown as a dancer.

The family moved to Chicago, then to New York, where the young Isadora enjoyed modest success, though she believed that her style of dance would be better received in Europe. A fire in their hotel provided the impetus for their departure: the Duncans found themselves penniless in the street. The resourceful Isadora made the rounds among millionaires' wives and was able to collect enough for their passage overseas. With her brother, sister, and mother, she departed for London and glory — aboard a ship transporting livestock!

After an uncertain debut in London, Isadora made a name for herself dancing in the salons of the famous and fashionable. But soon the Duncans left for Paris. When Isadora was not dancing for the elite of Parisian society, she spent her time in the Louvre, the Bibliothèque Nationale, or the Opéra library. After Paris, she went on to Berlin, Budapest, Vienna, and Munich, finally ending up in her artistic mecca: Greece.

The Duncan clan accompanied her to Greece, where Isadora was inspired by Hellenic culture and especially by the expressive power of the dances and choruses of Greek tragedy. Isadora believed in the ideals of truth and beauty, and began to express them in a combination of mime and movement far different from traditional dance.

Following her first trip to Russia in 1905, where she met Sergei Diaghilev, Isadora founded a dance school in Berlin. That same year she experienced passionate love for the first time, with theater designer Gordon Craig; she gave birth to a daughter named Deirdre. Isadora's prior opinion about marriage's effect on women was not disproven by this union: "Living with him meant giving up my art, my personality, perhaps my life, my sanity." She left to tour Russia, then the United States, without Craig. Undaunted by the difficulties in this first love affair, she soon plunged into another — with millionaire Paris Singer, whom she nicknamed Lohengrin. She had a second child, Patrick, during this stormy relationship, which she declined to legalize. During one of the happier periods of this affair, when Isadora was feeling content and confident, tragedy struck: her chil-

Isadora the teacher, with pupils.

Largely self-taught, Isadora Duncan created her own style, which was a big step toward modern dance.

dren and their nurse were drowned in a limousine that somersaulted to the bottom of the Seine.

It was 1913. In her grief, Isadora considered taking her own life. To ease her depression, her brother invited her to work with him in a refugee camp in Albania. Confronted with the misfortune of the refugees, she regained her interest in life and decided to get back to work. But first she asked a stranger on an Italian beach to father a child for her. The infant died in Paris shortly after birth.

Isadora again flung herself into dancing, teaching, and touring, but found it difficult to regain her former success. Fortune smiled on her again in 1920: she was invited to open a school in Moscow. The next year she married Sergei Esenin, a Russian poet seventeen years her junior.

As the United States recoiled in horror at the "red peril," Isadora was accused of working for

"It was while contemplating the waves . . . that my concept of dance came to me."

Lenin and Trotsky, and was widely denounced. She took refuge in Nice with Sergei, who began to drink and became increasingly unstable. In 1925, he left her and committed suicide in Leningrad. Isadora was tired and alone when the famous final tragedy of her life overcame her: she took a ride in a sports car, wearing a long, floating scarf. It caught in the rear wheel and Isadora was strangled.

FRIDA KAHLO

MEXICO — 1907-1954

Frida Kahlo married the most famous Mexican painter of the century, Diego Rivera. Her works were very personal while his were extroverted, monumental social commentaries.

Suffering was Frida's fate. She kept it at bay by devoting all her considerable force of character to portraying the story of her broken body in her painting. The French critic André Breton wrote: "Frida Kahlo's art is a ribbon around a bomb."

She was of Indian and Spanish descent by her mother and Hungarian by her father. Frida was born in 1907 but preferred to say she came into the world with the Mexican Revolution. Her first misfortune came in childhood: she was a victim of poliomyelitis. She learned about pain, intensive care, rehabilitation centers. Her friends called her "Wooden-leg Frida."

At fifteen she entered a preparatory school for university. It was an exciting time, culturally and politically. She became a member of the Cachuchas, a creative, rebellious literary group. One of its most brilliant members, Alejandro Gómez Arias, was the love of her youth. Frida was intelligent, witty, and feminine, blossoming as a young women. And then came the accident.

In Mexico City one afternoon in September 1925, Frida and Alejandro boarded a bus to return to their homes. But the bus collided with a small train at a crossing: "It was a strange shock. It wasn't violent, but muffled, and everyone was hurt," Frida recalled. She was flung toward the front and a handrail went through her body "like the sword through the bull."

The piece of metal almost killed her. She had multiple fractures and internal injuries. For nine months she wore a body cast, the first of many. Her parents were so upset that at first they could not bring themselves to visit her. Her sister took care of her during the first three months of this agony. Condemned to lie immobile, she suffered, alone with her battered body.

Frida wrote regularly to Alejandro but received no reply. Her friends did not come to see her because she was too far from the town center. Gradually she began to go out, but in the summer of 1926 she again had to be immobilized, in a four-poster bed decorated for her by her mother. She had fixed a mirror on the ceiling and Frida, lying there, would look on her own face. Her

Shortly before her death, Frida posed for this picture with her doctor.
Her life had been torn by illness.

father brought her tubes of paint. Frida wrote: "Without paying much attention to it, I began to paint." She painted self-portraits, obsessively.

By 1928, Frida had recovered her interest in life and begun frequenting artistic circles. She joined the Communist Party, and it was at a party organized by the militants that she met Diego Rivera, who would prove to be the most famous Mexican painter of the century. He was colossal, outrageous, and adored by women in spite of his ugliness. Not long after this, she showed him her work. They became friends, collaborators, lovers, then husband and wife. Frida was in her early twenties, he some twenty years older. her mother and father saw it as the union of an elephant and a dove, but this did not prevent Frida and Diego from moving in with them.

Frida threw away her tomboy clothes and took up the long, colorful skirts and the laces and jewelry of the Mexican women. Only one thing was missing in this beautiful young woman's life: the ability to bear children. She became pregnant but had to have an abortion because she was physically incapable of carrying the child to term. The desire for a baby haunted her.

In 1930, Frida followed Diego to the United States, where he was to do a series of murals. It was Frida's first contact with a country of which she had dreamed, but, close up, it disappointed her. She did not particularly like the Americans and had no friends, so she painted. After a brief trip back to Mexico, the couple left for Detroit, where Frida had a miscarriage. To add to her despair, her mother died. Frida painted incessantly. Her art

became more assured. It was diametrically opposed to Diego's monumental social commentaries: it was a mirror on her life, reflecting the pains that regularly darkened her existence.

Returning to Mexico, the Riveras took up residence in San Angel, where they received stars of the intelligentsia. Frida had a liaison with the exiled Bolshevik Leon Trotsky, for whom Diego had obtained political asylum, and then an intense relationship with the photographer Nickolas Muray. She attracted and charmed men and women alike, hiding her affairs because of Diego's jealousy; he, meanwhile, had begun philandering long before.

Frida went to Paris in the late 1930s to exhibit her work. Though the exposition was not a commercial success, fellow-artists such as Paul Eluard, Yves Tanguy, Max Ernst, and Pablo Picasso recognized her talent. The fashion designer Elsa Schiaparelli was so enthusiastic about Frida's clothes that she created the "Madame Rivera" dress. At the same time, Frida continued her political activities, arranging for four hundred refugees from the Spanish Civil War to find homes in Mexico.

Diego and Frida were divorced, by mutual consent, but remarried not long after. Yet by then she had stopped hoping for anything from life. Her health deteriorated, she had to undergo surgery, she drank more and more, she took drugs. Her right leg had to be amputated. When death put an end to her suffering, the last words in her diary were: "I hope the outcome will be happy, and I hope I never come back."

Frida recorded her suffering in self-portraits.

COCO CHANEL

FRANCE — CA. 1883-1971

"I don't like people to talk about 'Chanel fashion,'" said Coco Chanel. "It is first and foremost a style. Fashion goes out of date, but style, never."

Gabrielle Chanel invented the style of her life. Certain episodes that did not suit her were tailored out, camouflaged, or draped in a mysterious haze. But what is the function of good clothes if not to conceal one's flaws and accentuate one's assets? Her father, whom she would describe as a gentleman-farmer, was more likely a day-laborer of unstable character, a roamer. When his wife died, he did not hesitate to abandon his four children and run off to America. Gabrielle found herself effectively an orphan at age six. She would later claim that she had been entrusted to the care of two aunts in the southern province of Auvergne, but the truth was that she grew up in an orphanage and at age seventeen was sent to a religious institution in Moulins, in central France. Here she found a friend, Adrienne, the same age as herself. Three years later the two were placed as dressmaker's apprentices in a shop specializing in trousseaus and layettes.

Gabrielle tried her hand at entertainment, at the cabaret La Rotonde de Moulins. One of the two songs she sang began with "Cocorico!" This number was a great hit with the audience, who would ask for it again by chanting "Coco! Coco!" Hence her new name. Later she would claim the nickname was given her by her father.

At about twenty, she left to try her luck in Vichy, thirty-five miles south of Moulins, but, unable to find work as a singer, she resorted to waiting on tables. It was her good fortune to meet Etienne Balsan, a rich, fashionable gentleman, a hunter and horseman, who became attached to her. He later introduced her to Arthur Copel, an

"The Grand Mademoiselle," here photographed by Cecil Beaton, revolutionized fashion by creating a sober, chic style, widely imitated ever since.

Chanel in 1962 in her fashion house, presenting a collection.

Chanel's famous suit made her a legend
in the fashion world. Portrait by Peter Blake.

Englishman, nicknamed Boy. It was the start of a legendary partnership. Copel, a successful and creative businessman, was impressed by Coco's intelligence; he took her to Paris and rented a first-floor shop in the Rue Cambon, where she could make and sell hats. Boy introduced her into the world, to the dancer Isadora Duncan, the comedienne Gabrielle Dorziat — and the hats sold so well that Coco branched out into dresses.

In 1913, still a protégée of Boy Copel, Coco was able to obtain financing to open a boutique in the fashionable resort town of Deauville. Her principles: comfort and strong lines. The war proved the validity of her vision. High-society women no longer had to parade in oriental veils to remain fashionable, but could now dress simply and discreetly. Coco made this sort of style available and began to build her empire. She introduced jersey fabric and made black fashionable. "It is possible that by observing nature," remarked the photographer Cecil Beaton, "she rediscovered and reaffirmed that in the animal race, the females are generally dull compared to the males. Her knack and genius were to transform this dullness into a fashion of brilliant simplicity. . . . Only when women looked like waiters in restaurants, only when they were reduced to a chic poverty,

only then would she cover them with jewels, large emeralds and rubies, and cascades of big pearls." This "chic poverty" the couturier Paul Poiret would disdainfully label "luxurious squalor."

Very much in love with Coco, Boy nonetheless made a conventional marriage to a high-society Englishwoman. This cut Coco to the quick. All her life she felt herself to be the mistress, the lover, never the bride. This was the price of her liberty. Moving freely now among the aristocracy, she became friends with Misia Sert, a patroness of the arts. When Boy died in a car accident in 1919, Coco was overwhelmed with pain, and in her grief had her room painted black. Misia persuaded her to redo it in pink. Coco and Misia maintained a close friendship for thirty years, until Misia's death. She was the only woman Coco was able to love.

In 1920, Coco launched her first perfume: Chanel No. 5. She and a chemist, Ernest Beaux, had deviated from the floral scents in current use and ended up with a strange alchemy, original and new. In 1928 she introduced trousers for women, but it was several years before women would follow the lead of Marlene Dietrich and adopt them. During this period, her lovers reputedly included the composer Igor Stravinski,

whom she broke off with because he would not leave his wife for her; the Russian Grand Duke Dimitri; and the Duke of Westminster.

A very maternalistic employer, Coco was irritated by the strikes that affected her workshop in 1936. This perhaps explains why she closed up shop and dismissed her staff without compensa-

tion in the late 1930s as war loomed. The fifteen or so years that followed were a particularly cloudy period in her life; it may have included a liaison with a German officer, which would help explain her retreat to Switzerland after the war.

Coco returned to the fashion world in 1954. Competition was tough and her prejudices against trends set by other designers made it tougher. But she launched her famous suit, and women began to wear it; by the mid-1960s it was omnipresent.

Chanel became a phenomenon outside fashion. "Couture creates beautiful things that become ugly, whereas art creates ugly things that become beautiful," she said once. No one knows in which category she placed herself.

MARIA CALLAS

UNITED STATES 1923 — FRANCE 1977

The young Maria Kalogeropoulos was anything but attractive: clumsy, ugly, and fat, she consoled herself with food; she had a long, homely nose, and was horribly nearsighted and painfully shy. Everything about her promised a mediocre future. But neither Maria nor her mother was willing to accept this fate.

Maria's talent became evident when she was ten. One day she began singing "La Paloma" with the windows wide open. People on the street below stopped to listen, and her mother foresaw a great career for Maria, with the money and glory that came naturally to a prima donna. And she was right: Maria would become La Callas, "la Prima Donna Assoluta," the empress of bel canto. But not without hard work.

Maria's mother left her husband in America and returned to Greece, their homeland, with her two daughters in 1937. Maria studied voice in Athens, working relentlessly, eight to ten hours each day, showing her fierce will to succeed. She is said to have trained by keeping time with canaries and an anecdote that has become part of her legend says a canary named Elmina passed out during one session, unable to hold its own against Maria's endless practice.

At the conservatory young Maria became a student of the great Spanish prima donna Elvira de Hidalgo, who would be part of her life for a long time as mentor, mother figure, and friend. Maria won first place at the Athens Conservatory and soon had her first stage engagement, but the opera company did not renew her contract. In 1945 the family returned to New York to Maria's father.

For two years, she went from one audition to the next, her humiliation and desperation increasing with each rejection. The tenor Giovanni Zenatello rescued her from this downward spiral

"La Prima Donna Assoluta" in *La Traviata*.

in 1947 by hiring her in Verona to sing the title role in Almicare Ponchielli's *La Gioconda*. She was not an earth-shattering success, but she did make a conquest that turned her life upside down. "I was born again that evening," she said of her meeting with the rich industrialist Battista

This Cecil Beaton portrait only hints at the eternal quality that enabled her to play more than forty roles.

Meneghini. Thirty years older than Maria, "Titta" would become her husband, father figure, manager and friend, her Pygmalion.

Maria's career gained momentum in 1948. She took on every challenge, even playing two roles nearly simultaneously — singing Bellini's Elvira at a matinee and Wagner's Valkyrie the same evening. When a few cutting remarks about her weight crept in among the showered praises after her debut at Milan's La Scala in 1950, Maria went about dieting with her usual determination. She dropped from two hundred and seven pounds to about one hundred and thirty — and then her detractors said she had lost her voice with the weight. Her new physical attractiveness increased her confidence on

stage. Giving free rein to her intense personality, she began to revolutionize opera. Partly because of her performances, the film and theater producers Luchino Visconti and Franco Zeffirelli began to work in opera. With them she achieved a perfect fusion of music, singing, and drama.

Now able to choose her roles according to her emotions, Maria Callas achieved worldwide fame. In all, she played more than forty roles and interpreted her favorite, Norma, some ninety times. She was a perfectionist, insisting on giving nothing less than her best. Those who criticized her said she was egotistical and negligent of professional obligations, but often it was her fragile health that made her miss performances. She endured the "superstar" image her husband and the press had created, but behind this facade she was still timid and oversensitive, at times nearly fainting from stage fright.

At the peak of her career, in her mid-thirties, she met Aristotle Onassis at a reception. The ship-

Maria lost eighty pounds so she would never again have to hear people criticize her figure. Above, as Medea.

Her relationship with Ari Onassis made the front pages of the scandal sheets.

ping magnate fell in love with her at first sight. She left her husband, and he his wife, so that they could live together among the "beautiful people" and their story became the talk of the world. In love for the first time, Maria began to work less and devote more time to Ari. For nine years she dreamed of marrying him, but her lover hesitated. When he finally did make a decision, in 1968, it was to marry not Maria but Jackie Kennedy. Maria was shattered when she learned this through the press.

Maria tried to drown her grief through work, starring in Pier Paolo Pasolini's film version of Luigi Cherubini's *Medea*. But she was heartbroken. "Now, I am afraid," she declared. "The public has given me a splendid situation, unique in the world. But that leaves you very much alone. Because the fall can be so hard! Glory itself is frightening. Because you understand that it is not natural."

The death of Onassis' son Alexander brought them closer again, despite his wife's jealousy, and Maria began to neglect her career once more. When Ari died in 1975, life seemed to lose meaning for her. She died two years later, on September 16, 1977, in her apartment in Paris.

Maria Callas' life was both fairy tale and tragedy. Visconti described her as "Something beautiful. Intensity, expression, everything. She was an incredible phenomenon. Almost an anomaly, the type of actress who has disappeared forever."

GEORGIA O'KEEFFE

UNITED STATES — 1887-1986

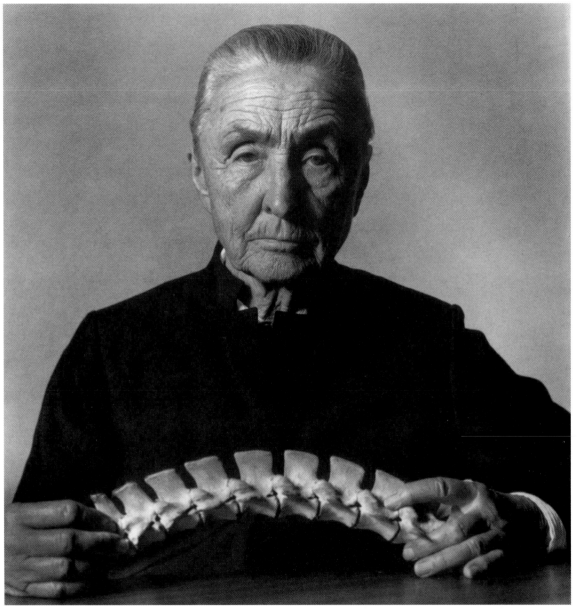

At age eighty, the face of this formidable artist seemed chiseled by time, like the mountains she so loved.

Georgia O'Keeffe was born November 15, 1887, in Sun Prairie, Wisconsin, to a family of Irish, Dutch, and Hungarian ancestry. She was the second of seven children. Young Georgia's first artistic impulses led her to music, a passion she would maintain throughout her life. But by the age of ten, her choice was made: she would be a painter, and she would use colors as music uses pure, clean sounds — to portray pure emotion.

In 1901, she entered a Catholic school in Madison, where she began her formal art training by copying plaster models. Four years later she studied anatomical drawing with John Vanderpoel at the Art Institute of Chicago. She left Chicago in 1907 to study at the Art Students League in New York, where she learned to focus on the use of rich pigments. Eventually she was attracted to abstract design, whose principles she studied with a disciple of Arthur Wesley Dow and later with Dow himself: his form combined the structure of Oriental composition with the use of natural forms, the goal being to express emotions rather than imitate them.

In 1912 Georgia started teaching, and for four years instructed pupils in Virginia, South Carolina, and Texas in her vision of art. During this time she experienced her first artistic crisis: all the work she had done so far suddenly seemed hollow and artificial to her. She destroyed it, determined to start over, and vowed to paint nothing except what she felt. Henceforth her own environment and personal experience would constitute her only sources of inspiration, providing her with forms and ideas. She would not allow herself to be seduced by any theory, any opinion on art contrary to her intuition.

In this frame of mind, Georgia made a series of charcoal drawings and sent them to an art school friend, Anita Pollitzer, for criticism. Anita remembered hearing Georgia say that she deeply admired the work of the photographer Alfred Stieglitz, so she took the drawings to him. He was dazzled. Stieglitz hung two of her works at an exhibition of the Society of Independent Artists.

She once told an interviewer that when she thought about death, the only thing that made her sad was that she would no longer be able to see "this beautiful Earth" — unless the Indians were right and her spirit survived. Georgia O'Keeffe had nearly a century to gaze upon the Earth that fascinated her so, and to communicate the raw emotions its substance and space inspired in her.

By early 1917, Georgia O'Keeffe was organizing her first personal exhibition at Steieglitz's gallery, known simply as 291 for its address on Fifth Avenue.

The following year she abandoned her teaching post at West Texas State Normal College to move to New York. For Stieglitz, this painter had become a model. He found a world in her. He photographed her from every conceivable angle for twenty years, creating almost five hundred compositions — the hands, the face, the body of Georgia O'Keeffe: extraordinary work from which grew the legend of Georgia as a femme fatale who wielded her sex appeal like a weapon.

This view of her affected evaluations of her art: for a long time, critics considered her paintings from an erotic point of view, even after she abandoned abstraction to move on to more figurative painting. When discussing her compositions of fruit, for example, critics contrived to find in these round or downy shapes the suggestion of the body that Alfred Stieglitz's lens had made famous.

The couple married in 1924. In 1929, Georgia made a decision that would mark a turning point in her life and art: she rented a ranch in New Mexico, where she would devote herself to painting for half the year. These months of separation seemed not to harm the love between her and Stieglitz but, on the contrary, to enhance it. Greater autonomy allowed Georgia to develop her art according to her own intuition. She and Stieglitz maintained an intense relationship, founded on mutual respect, until the photographer's death in 1946.

Her love of nature, of the colors and shapes of the New Mexico desert, her fidelity to her inner vision, her rejection of the "intellectual" and of conventional classification — all these defined the work of Georgia O'Keeffe.

She has been called an ascetic because of her preference for simple landscapes: stones, sand, great stretches that quenched her thirst for space. She had an almost childish fear of the world, yet her insatiable curiosity led her to travel all over

Early in her artistic career Georgia O'Keeffe vowed to paint nothing but what she felt; her own environment and personal experience would be her only sources of inspiration. Georgia O'Keeffe in the New Mexican surroundings in which she chose to live.

the globe, painting as she went. She lived alone, but was surrounded by friends, corresponding prolifically whenever she traveled.

At the age of ninety-six, she still had enough energy to travel along the U.S. Pacific coast and to Costa Rica. The following year she settled in Santa Fe, New Mexico, near her family and Juan Hamilton, a potter who had become her traveling companion, dealer, and manager. In 1985, a year before her death, President Ronald Reagan personally presented Georgia O'Keeffe with the National Medal of Arts.

BILLIE HOLIDAY

UNITED STATES — 1915-1959

She always figured nobody could sing the words "hunger" or "love" like she could, because she really knew what they meant. With her inimitable voice, Billie Holiday could transform any song into the blues. She was filled with the blues.

One has only to read the first lines of her autobiography to understand the environment in which she evolved. Her Pa and Ma, she writes, were a couple of kids when they married. He was eighteen, she was sixteen, and their daughter was three. Family life for little Eleonora Fagan Holiday didn't last long. Her father, Clarence Holiday, a guitar player, left their home town of Baltimore on tour with his orchestra and her mother often went off to work up north. The little tomboy whose father called her "Bill" was taken care of by her grandparents and by her cousin Ida, who always found a reason to beat her. Billie's favorite was her great-grandmother, who had been a slave in Virginia. The old woman's death was the first tragedy in Billie's life. They fell asleep side by side, and Billie awoke imprisoned by an arm around her neck. They had to break her great-grandmother's arm to free the child.

Billie wrote that she was already a little woman by the age of six. She started a cleaning business and every day, before and after school, went to wash white people's stoops and tiles. She did errands for the madam of a whorehouse, who, in exchange, let her listen to Bessie Smith and Louis Armstrong on the phonograph. In her autobiography she wrote that she probably wasn't the only person who heard good jazz for the first time in a brothel. Had she heard the same voices through the windows of a pastor's living room, she said, she would have done errands for him.

Billie made every song sound like the blues, although she had never been formally trained.

"Bill" became "Billie," after her favorite actress, Billie Dove, whose films she went to see by slipping in the exit of the cinema so she wouldn't have to pay. Her mother returned to Baltimore with a little money, bought a house, and took in a boarder. While her mother was gone one day, the man led Billie into a neighboring house and raped her. She was ten. As a result of this incident she was sentenced and placed in a religious institution with thieves and runaways. Her mother managed to get her released, and Billie returned to her grandparents. There she was raped again, at the age of twelve, by a trumpet player. As she wrote later, it wasn't surprising that she was terrified of sex.

In 1927 Billie went to join her mother in New York. Her mother sent her to the house of an elegant lady, not realizing this was one Harlem's most important madams. Billie became a call girl but was turned in by a client she had rejected. She served her sentence first at a Brooklyn hospital and then in prison. When she was released, she found her mother penniless and ill. Billie looked for a job to support them both. She made the rounds of the jazz clubs, trying to get a job as a dancer even though she didn't know how to dance. At a joint called Pod's and Jerry's, they asked her if she could sing. She replied: "Of course I can, what's so extraordinary about that?"

Billie, then about fifteen, had never taken a singing lesson in her life; her style was entirely natural. Her audience was moved to tears, and she was hired. She then appeared at other clubs in Harlem, and finally at the Apollo and the Café Society. When she started at the Café Society she was still comparatively unknown. Two years later, when she left, she was a star. She was still earning $75 a week, however.

Billie could never save money. At the end of every tour she used to say she had come back as poor as the day she was born. Benny Goodman had her make her first record. Between 1933 and 1944 she made a hundred records, and she never touched a penny in royalties from them. She recorded and toured with the best jazz musicians of the time, including the saxophonist Lester Young.

"Lady Day" with a little dog.

They were friends and lovers, and it was Young who gave her the nickname "Lady Day."

Her first husband, Jimmy Monroe, introduced Billie to heroin. She underwent treatment in an effort to overcome the addiction, but the police were waiting for her when she left the clinic —someone had informed on her. She was arrested several days later. When she was sentenced, she asked to be sent to a detoxification center. She was given a year in prison instead. Ten days after her release, Billie gave a concert at Carnegie Hall before more than three thousand people.

Because of her police record, she was refused the cabaret card she needed to perform in New York nightclubs. John Levy let her sing in his club, Ebony, without the permit. He gave her jewelry, clothing, and her first mink, but no salary. Levy sent her and her orchestra to the Deep South, where she found herself without a penny.

In 1949, Billie was arrested again on drug charges. She later asserted that at the time she had stopped using heroin, but she had difficulty proving it. Seven years later she was arrested yet again, along with her adored second husband, Louis McKay. Friends put up bail and she was soon released. She left the prison at five in the afternoon and sang that night in a packed club.

Billie made her last stage appearance at the Phoenix Theater in Manhattan in June 1959. Worn out by an unhappy life filled with misery, racism, drugs, police, and prison, she died a few days later. But as the trumpeter Bill Coleman put it, her voice will never die.

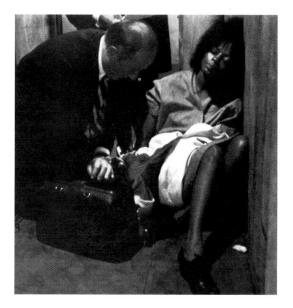

Diana Ross played Billie Holiday in *Lady Sings the Blues*, a film adapted from the singer's autobiography.

MARILYN MONROE

UNITED STATES — 1926-1962

Norma Jean, alias Marilyn Monroe, was the incarnation of feminine
attraction for thousands of moviegoers.

The movies' greatest myth was born on June 1, 1926, at Los Angeles General Hospital, father unknown. But Norma Jean Mortenson was not yet Marilyn, and her childhood was more like a Charles Dickens novel than the Hollywood comedies that made her famous.

Her mother, Gladys, had been married twice and had two children who had been placed in the care of her first husband's family. The unstable, far from motherly Gladys proved incapable of raising her new baby too. Norma Jean was put in a succession of foster homes, spent two years in an orphanage, went to another foster family, and finally was entrusted to a guardian.

This troubled childhood could not help but influence the star's personality. Her mother, depressive and subject to terrible temper tantrums, was institutionalized for the first time when Norma Jean was seven. Since there had been other cases of madness in her family, Marilyn Monroe's greatest fear and anguish was always the thought of going mad.

The girl known as Norma Jean Baker, like the star Marilyn Monroe, had a hard time telling truth from falsehood. It is difficult to verify anything she said about her childhood. She claimed to have been raped at the age of nine. She also said her father lived in the same building as her mother, whom he left when Norma Jean was born. When Gladys showed the little girl a picture of her father, she thought he was Clark Gable, and she came to believe this fantasy.

In 1942, Norma's legal guardian decided to marry her off; the woman wanted to move east and didn't want to be burdened with her. The happy man was a neighbor boy, Jim Dougherty, a nice guy who played football and was a hard worker. The wedding took place on June 16, shortly after Norma's sixteenth birthday. Jim, who was around twenty, soon left for the war and Norma found work in a defense plant. There she met a photographer who said he wanted to do a feature about American women's contribution to the war effort. He asked her to pose as a model at $5 an hour. These photos quickly attracted the notice of a model agency. Norma Jean's career had begun.

With the emphasis on her thirty-six-inch bust, success as a pin-up and magazine cover girl rapidly followed. But this was not enough for Norma: she wanted to be a movie actress. Propelled by her dreams, she was offered a contract with 20th Century-Fox and was renamed Marilyn Monroe. On her twentieth birthday she told this good news to Jim, whom she was in the process of divorcing.

Marilyn at the beginning of her career — dark-haired, simple, unsophisticated.

At first her career was unpromising; she was given only small roles in forgettable films. But in 1948, having been dropped by Fox after bit parts in two movies, she danced and sang in *Ladies of the Chorus* for Columbia and had her first reviews in the papers. The next year she had a brief scene with Groucho Marx in *Love Happy*. She met Johnny Hyde, one of the most influential agents in the business, who boosted her career. Although

The star hid despair behind her boundless energy.

he was ill, he promised to make her a star before he died. Sure enough, she won a role in John Huston's *The Asphalt Jungle* and a new contract with Fox, which paid $500 a week instead of the original $125.

Gentlemen Prefer Blondes went still further toward making her a star. She was getting five thousand fan letters a week and was moved into the luxurious dressing room that had belonged to Marlene Dietrich. In the summer of 1953 Marilyn was consecrated a movie queen when her hand and foot prints were recorded in fresh cement on Hollywood Boulevard.

Stardom took its toll. Marilyn started to arrive late on the set and develop a dependency on pills. Already a prisoner of her image as a sex symbol, she wanted to prove that she wasn't a dumb blond, that she was a good actress. She went a long way toward succeeding in *How to Marry a Millionaire* and *The River of No Return*. She almost drowned during the filming of the latter.

Marilyn desperately sought emotional stability. She wed the well-known baseball player Joe Di Maggio in 1954 but the marriage ended in divorce nine months later. In her next marriage, to the playwright Arthur Miller, she seemed to

have found happiness. She was nearly thirty and wanted to have a baby. They couldn't. She announced their divorce following the filming of *The Misfits*, which Miller wrote. Once again, Marilyn found herself alone. During the filming she had taken a drug overdose and was hospitalized; later she was committed to a psychiatric hospital. Marilyn was falling apart.

Although she appeared in more than twenty films in the first seven years of her movie career, she finished only six films between 1955 and 1962.

Marilyn Monroe worked hard at educating herself. She read serious novels, biographies, historical works. She was interested in politics without really wanting to participate. She moved on the fringes of political circles, and had relationships with John and especially Robert Kennedy. The circumstances of her death, officially suicide from an overdose of barbituates, were later seen as mysterious. It was rumored that she was killed because she knew too much about the Kennedys, or because scandal had to be avoided, or because enemies of the Kennedys wanted to use her to cause a scandal. Twenty years after her death, the inquest into it was reopened. Nothing conclusive ever came of the inquiry.

To the photographer Henri Cartier-Bresson, she was the "incarnation of the myth that in France we call *l'éternal féminin*." Child, seductress, sex symbol, desperate actress . . . Marilyn will never cease to intrigue us.

Andy Warhol's view of Marilyn Monroe, *The Twenty Marilyns* (detail).

EDITH PIAF

FRANCE — 1915-1963

"My conservatory was the street. My intelligence was my instinct," the singer used to say.

Alone in the middle of a darkened stage, as though at the center of the universe. Always wearing a black dress, from which her translucent hands and delicate face emerged. This was Edith Piaf, whose voice made crowds weep.

"It was under a lamppost, in front of 72 rue de Belleville, on a policeman's coat, that my daughter was born," her father, Louis Gassion, recounted. He was an acrobat and little Giovanna's mother was an Italian café singer. The girl was brought up first by her maternal grandmother, who made her drink wine to avoid the illnesses she thought water caused, and then by her father's mother, who ran a brothel in Normandy.

Edith spent nearly three years of her childhood blind as a complication from illness. "I have always thought that this time I spent in the dark gave me a sensitivity others lack," she said. "Many years later, when I wanted to really hear, really 'see' a song, I would close my eyes." One day, her grandmother took her to Lisieux, city of Saint Theresa, where she regained her vision. "For Edith, this was a true miracle. She always believed in it. After that time, she was truly devoted to Saint Theresa," her half-sister Simone recounted.

"My conservatory was the street. My intelligence was my instinct," Edith used to say. At age nine she started singing in the streets and bistros of Paris while her father passed the hat for donations. Soon Edith "hired" Simone to take over the collector's role, and the sisters became inseparable. They rented a one-bedroom apartment together, and shared the bed; when Edith took a lover, he joined the two of them in that bed, and eventually Edith's baby daughter made four. They were simply too poor to rent a larger apartment. Edith's daughter was not an occupant of the bed for very long, for she died at age two. Nineteen-year-old Edith had to prostitute herself to obtain enough money to pay for the burial.

Edith still sang on the streets and, at night, in the unreknowned cabaret Juan-les-Pins in the Rue Pigalle. She was able to move on with the help of Louis Leplée, owner of the fashionable Gerny's, who nicknamed her *la Môme Piaf*, which in argot means, roughly, "the sparrow kid." Edith knit a dress to wear for her debut but did not have time to finish the second sleeve. Someone gave her a scarf to use at the last minute, and the singer appeared on stage wearing a wool dress with one violet silk sleeve! She was a sorry sight, but the sound of her voice conquered the audience. She sang happily at Gerny's for seven months, until "Papa Leplée" was murdered on April 6, 1936.

Edith found herself penniless and accepted any engagement that came along until Raymond Asso began to manage her affairs. He found songs and created an image for her, and got her a contract at ABC, the most famous music hall of the time. She appeared there as a special guest star in Charles Trenet's show and her career took off. The singer left the streets to conquer the world.

It has often been said that Edith was not pretty. But she had beautiful violet eyes, a disarming childlike smile, and much charm. Men succumbed to her and, naively sentimental, she fell in love every time. She could not live without a man, and her partner had to pay constant attention to her. One of her lovers was temperamentally unable to meet such demands: she called the deadpan actor Paul Meurisse "an iceberg." She confided the inadequacy of Paul's affection to "her" poet, Jean Cocteau. He wrote a play about their relationship: *Le bel indifferent*. Edith and Paul played the starring roles.

"*Non, je ne regrette rien*," I regret nothing . . . the line from one of her best-known songs could have been her motto. Henri Cartier-Bresson photograph.

She had other well-known lovers: the singer-actor Yves Montand, whom she helped make famous, and the boxer Marcel Cerdan, the "Moroccan Bomber." He was the greatest love of her life. On September 21, 1948, having just won the world championship in New York, Marcel made a beeline to Versailles, where Edith was performing. This frail little woman with the astonishing voice was more important to him than any title. When he lost the championship the following year, the singer was accused of ruining his career. She could not do without him by her side, and he did anything she asked. In October 1949, he was scheduled to join her in New York via ship. Edith, impatient, asked him to take a plane so as to reach her sooner. The plane crashed in the Azores. Desperate and guilt-stricken, Edith resorted to drugs to help her perform that evening before her American audience.

In memory of the boxer, Edith sang one of her most haunting songs, *"L'Hymne à l'amour"*. Its words were composed especially for her — her love, her despair, her life. And her public was sympathetic: they forgave her memory lapses, her drunken escapades, her mood swings. She was worn out with life. She married; it didn't work out. She had several disappointing love affairs. Edith had come to expect nothing more from men when she met a handsome twenty-seven-year-old Greek named Théo. He brought her happiness again. He wanted to sing, so she gave him a name, "Sarapo," based on the Greek for "I love you," and had him join her in performances. They were married in October 1962.

But her downward spiral continued, barely interrupted. For twenty years she had contended with accidents, depression, drug and alcohol abuse, and illness. Finally came a case of pulmonary edema. "I can die now," she said, "I have lived twice!"

For her funeral, more than two million Parisians formed an honor guard to accompany her casket from her apartment to the Père Lachaise cemetery.

UM KALTHUM

EGYPT — CA. 1900-1975

For the Egyptians, and throughout the Arab world, Um Kalthum was much more than a singer. She was their voice, their best ambassador, "the Star of Egypt," "the Lady," "the Fourth Pyramid."

She was nicknamed "the Nightingale of the Nile" when she was still in her teens and sang verses from the Koran at religious festivals, dressed as a boy. Her father, Ibrahim, was the imam of the mosque in a village in the Nile delta. Her mother, worn out from working at home and in the cotton fields, wanted Um Kalthum to receive the same instruction in the Koran as her elder brother. Although the girl was not enthusiastic at first, she acquired a liking for words as she grew up.

One evening during Ramadan, the holy month of fasting, the Nightingale and her troupe played before Sheik Abul Ala Mohammed, the greatest singer of the time, and the lute player Zakaria Ahmed. At the end of the show, the man she already thought of as her mentor proposed to sponsor her and find her work in Cairo, the city the Egyptians call "the Victorious," "Mother of Civilization." She had to wait a year before undertaking this great adventure but finally it was arranged for her to sing before a rich merchant. The experience was a disappointment. Her host treated her like a peasant and the money she earned was stolen. She went home. Not until two years had passed, in 1923, did her sponsors convince her to sing in a theater and to let them take over her training.

The old master introduced Um Kalthum to secular songs and poetry, despite the worries of her father, who was so concerned about her respectability that he once placed a notice on the stage: "Do not touch." Ultimately the doors of success opened for "Mrs. Um Kalthum," as her

"The Star of the Orient" during a 1967 performance at the Olympia music hall in Paris.

Um Kalthum, an ardent defender of Arab culture, was nicknamed "Nasser's Bomb."

father insisted she be called. She was no longer afraid of Cairo, which at the time was stirring to the nationalist ideas of Saad Zaglul, the new prime minister, and his Wafd party.

She met the young romantic poet Ahmed Rami, who made her the inspiration of his poetry. Only her death, many years later, would separate them. She sang his poems and she sang of absolute love that continually hovers between the sacred and the profane, the spirit and the flesh. The word habid, or "beloved," which occurs often in her songs, is also one of the many names of Allah.

In her early twenties, Um Kalthum was a star. She decided to assert her femininity as well. For her first concert with an orchestra, she exchanged her masculine clothing for a dress and unbound her hair, clutching a handkerchief to hide her stage fright. The handkerchief became her trademark.

By the time her mentor Sheik Abul died, the young woman had matured and was chosing her own texts and having them set to music. In 1927, on the death of Prime Minister Saad Zaghlul, Um Kalthum stopped performing for a time. When she reappeared on the stage it was to sing "Saad has gone away from Egypt."

She became her country's voice, embodying the revival of Arab music. In 1932 she went on tour for the first time, to Libya, Lebanon, Syria, and Paris. She performed on the radio and launched the station "Voice of Cairo" with one of her songs. Then came her monthly radio programs, which became a ritual. The first Thursday of every month, everyone listened to hear her latest songs. She also made a number of movies.

A very private person, she never revealed anything about her personal life. One day she told her friend Mustafa Amin, a journalist, "I am married to my art." She avoided most other reporters. This didn't prevent speculation about her private life, but it remained a mystery up to and including her marriage at the age of forty-nine to her doctor, Hassan Hanafi.

When the state of Israel was created, Um Kalthum went to great effort to sing for and encourage her people, though she was exhausted and ill because of eye trouble that had plagued her since childhood. Soon she had to go to the United States for a goiter operation. After Colonel Gamal Abdel Nasser led the officers' revolt that toppled the monarchy in 1952, she was criticized for having sung for the deposed King Farouk and was censured on the radio. Nasser himself intervened to restore her reputation. She opened her first concert for the revolution with a song called "The Voice of the Country" before returning for further treatment in America.

Following his election as president, Nasser announced the nationalization of the Suez Canal. His radio speech was preceded by one of Um Kalthum's songs. And it was Nasser who brought about her partnership with the composer Abdel Wahab, Egypt's greatest male singer, who from then on wrote many of her songs.

"The Lady" was already very tired when Egypt was defeated by Israel in 1967. She nonetheless undertook a tour in the West. In Paris, she sang for five hours two evenings in a row and raised hundreds of thousands of francs for her country. She was called "Nasser's Bomb" and the "Nun of Islam." She returned to Egypt and then undertook a further tour, through the Arab nations.

In 1975, Um Kalthum gave a last concert, and died one month later. Yet, as the Egyptian-born actor Omar Sharif has written, she is reborn each morning in the hearts of one hundred and twenty million Arabs.

Three hundred thousand people went to her funeral to say good-bye to "the Lady."

GRACE KELLY

UNITED STATES 1929 — MONACO 1982

The woman who attained the dreams of little girls the world over,
the beautiful Grace Kelly shone as a Hollywood star before
becoming a jewel in the crown of Monaco.

The queen of film and her prince . . . Grace Kelly's life was a fairy tale: granddaughter of a blue-collar laborer, she achieved stardom on the silver screen and then became the Princess of Monaco. But this tale would end tragically.

Grace's grandfather, John Henry Kelly, was an Irish immigrant to the United States who worked in a textile factory. Of his ten children, five were successful: among them was Jack, Grace's father, who made a fortune at brick manufacturing and settled in Philadelphia. His wealth brought him ample comforts but could not buy him entry into Philadelphia's high society.

Jack had four children; he favored the other three over Grace. Of fragile health, shy, and inhibited, she preferred reading and the theater to sports and lacked the competitive spirit of the other Kellys. Throughout her life she would try to win her father's love and approval, but never felt she had succeeded. When she won an Oscar as best actress for 1954's *The Country Girl*, her father told the press he had always believed his daughter Peggy would outshine Grace.

Grace Kelly attended a Catholic school, where, at a very young age, she demonstrated her theatrical talent. Her only disadvantage was a nasal voice, which she later worked hard to correct. Upon finishing high school, she left for New York in 1947 to study at the Academy of Dramatic Art. Her parents installed her in a boarding house for young girls, whose strict rules forbade the admission of men. But despite her very proper white gloves and hat and her demure demeanor, Grace rebelled against the rules and the moral code behind them, and entertained lovers in her room. She entered into liaisons with those who could introduce her into society or help further her career. She didn't need to: her talent was sufficient to take her where she wanted to go.

After appearing in a Broadway play in 1949, she began to work in television, becoming a pioneer in that medium. Then it was the cinema, a return to the theater, and eventually films again: Fred Zimmerman asked her to star in *High Noon* with Gary Cooper (1952). Naturally she fell in

The assured Princess Grace welcomed nervous Lady Diana Spencer to a 1981 charity benefit that Prince Charles chose as his fiancée's first royal engagement.

under control. The ever-hungry press delighted in whatever excesses the royal family committed, increasing Grace's feelings of oppression. She involved herself in artistic endeavors — drawing, poetry recitals, narrating a documentary film — to express herself and to escape from the palace and her royal obligations. Meanwhile, the seventeen-year-old Stephanie was turning out to be as big a handful as her older sister.

It was a tired, drained Grace who lost control of her car one September day in 1982 as she was driving down from her country house with Stephanie. The teenager survived with a few fractures, but Grace was dead. The image we cherish of her is not that of her final years, but of the proper young woman in white gloves — close and yet coolly remote.

love with the actor, more than twenty years her senior, to the delight of the tabloid press — and the fury of her mother, who went to California to chaperone Grace during the shooting. Then came John Ford's *Mogambo*, with Clark Gable. This springboard role won her an Oscar for best supporting actress of 1953.

Her work with Alfred Hitchcock in the lead role of his film *Dial M for Murder* was a turning point in her career. Hitchcock, understanding the complexity of her personality, was able to mine fully the depths of Grace's talent. Their collaboration was a personal and financial success.

After winning the Oscar for her performance in *The Country Girl*, Grace was invited to represent the United States at the Cannes Film Festival. By now an established actress, she led an austere life, very different from her previous style. She lived quietly, hoping stability and marriage would find her. But her father rebuffed all her suitors, none of whom was serious enough in his eyes. In Cannes, the magazine *Paris Match* arranged a meeting between Grace and Prince

Rainier of Monaco, and the match of the century was made. Jack Kelly not only welcomed this suitor, he even paid a dowry of $2 million. Finally Grace had won his approval.

The wedding took place amid unimaginable chaos. With seven thousand guests to entertain and fifteen hundred journalists past all restraint, Grace lost eleven pounds in less than two weeks.

High Society, in 1956, had been her last film. As a princess she could no longer think of being a movie star. At first it was hard for her to get used to royal life, but she soon dedicated herself to family matters, bearing and raising three children: Caroline, Albert, and Stephanie. She also threw herself into community work. Thanks to her influence, a new constitution granted women the right to vote in Monaco. Grace remade herself in the image of a princess, solemn and remote. But the loneliness that had plagued her since childhood continued to weigh upon her.

In Paris, an almost-grown Caroline did a little too much as she pleased. Just as her own mother had done, Grace joined her daughter to keep her

For her role in *The Country Girl*, Hollywood voted Grace the best actress of 1954.

GRETA GARBO

SWEDEN 1905 — UNITED STATES 1990

When she left the movies, the divine Greta wrapped herself in a veil of silence. The mystery surrounding her — which some thought hid infinite sadness, or obsessive shyness, or excessive reserve — remained complete. Her face, forever hidden, remains fixed in immortality.

Greta Gustafsson came from a humble background in Stockholm. She started to work at the age of fourteen or fifteen, first as a hairdresser's assistant, then as a salesgirl in a department store. After appearing in several advertising shorts she decided to try the movies. Erik Petschler, a director, gave her her first role in *Luffar-Petter* (Peter the Tramp). When the film was finished, he sent the seventeen-year-old Greta to the Royal Dramatic Theater school.

There she met the man who was to become her Pygmalion: the director Mauritz Stiller. She did a screen test but was considered too stiff, awkward, and fat. However, Stiller had confidence in his protégée, saying, "Have you examined her face? There will be no equal in this century." He gave her the name Greta Garbo and a large part in *Gösta Berlings Saga* (The Legend of Gösta Berling). As a result, G.W. Pabst brought her to Berlin for a part in *The Joyless Street*, which she accepted despite Stiller's jealousy. He must have forgiven her because when Louis B. Mayer invited him to work in Hollywood, Stiller insisted that Garbo accompany him.

They landed in New York at the beginning of July 1925. She soon wanted to leave, since the welcome she received was cold and indifferent. According to one story, an MGM public relations agent, realizing she was incapable of facing journalists, told her to answer, "I want to be alone." The line became a Garbo trademark, although

"Have you examined her face? There will be no equal in this century." The director Mauritz Stiller predicted her future correctly. His protégée, Greta Gustafsson, became the divine Greta Garbo.

190

At thirty, she was called
the most beautiful woman in the world.

she later insisted, "I never said that I wanted to be alone, but that I wanted to be left alone."

The New York photographer Arnold Genthe was the first to take an interest in her intriguing face. When talent scouts saw the photographs, they immediately sent Greta to Hollywood. She settled there, but didn't join the mad Hollywood social scene. The "Swedish sphinx" remained aloof. Garbo worked as she would always work: she was punctual, disciplined, and professional. Her first two films in Hollywood, *The Torrent* and *The Temptress*, sealed her image as an enigmatic seductress, a divine beauty. She inspired the dress designer Gilbert Adrian to creat the Garbo look, including the famous soft felt hat, which became all the rage. Publicity campaigns made her into an acknowledged movie queen.

Seeking a salary worthy of her star status, Garbo rebelled against the authority of the studio. MGM refused to give her an increase and she went on strike. The studio finally gave in and she starred in *Love*, in which she played Anna Karenina; *The Divine Woman*, portraying Sarah Bernhardt; and *Mata Hari*. She moved to talking pictures with *Anna Christie*, a film she detested.

She never indulged in tantrums on the set but she did have idiosyncracies. For example, the moment her feet were hidden from the camera, she insisted on wearing slippers. She especially could not bear curious glances. When she sensed an intruder, she stopped everything and ran to her dressing room. Alone. She fled from people.

One day a director, seeing that she was tired, advised her to go home and rest, saying: "You must be dead." She sighed and answered: "I've been dead for years." Had she died when Stiller did? His death in 1928 had greatly upset her.

Garbo made a few friends and had a few affairs, which she tried to hide from the insistent journalists. The woman who at thirty was called the world's most beautiful woman was also considered profoundly detached and solitary.

She won the New York Critics Award for the 1935 sound version of *Anna Karenina* and for *Camille* the next year. Garbo incarnated a kind of spiritualized eroticism, unlike Marlene Dietrich — or Mae West, who said she should let a man know what she was thinking once in a while. The fleshly West wasn't in the same league as Garbo. West provoked fantasies, Garbo inspired dreams.

The conductor Leopold Stokowski met Garbo and loved her. They had an affair, but she refused to marry him and they separated. Her box office rating was declining. She accepted a different kind of role: *Ninotchka*, for Ernst Lubitsch. The public adored her in this comic role; she found the film vulgar, and years later gave a tongue-lashing to the studio publicity man who came up with the line "Garbo Laughs!" Her next film, *Two-Faced Woman*, was a flop. During the filming she said, "They're trying to kill me." They were trying to make her into an all-American pin-up girl. The film was judged immoral, was watered down and cut. The result, released in 1941, was disastrous.

At thirty-six, with more than twenty American films to her credit, Greta Garbo decided to quit, at least temporarily. Time went by, and no script tempted her back to the screen. The photographer Cecil Beaton later wrote that she lost interest in everything and everybody, that she

became as difficult to live with as a invalid, and as self-centered. Perhaps, he continued, her magic was merely a quirk of nature that made the public imagination turn her into an ideal to which she could never match up.

Garbo spent the next half century as a recluse, always avoiding the journalists whom she considered the lowest form of life. She relieved her solitude with liquor and with forty cigarettes a day. Her death in a New York hospital was as hidden as her life. Her funeral was limited strictly to relatives and close friends. The sphinx became a shadow, and her mystery was never solved.

MGM created the Garbo look and a myth
around this mysterious, solitary woman.

Amalia Rodrigues, a young girl from Lisbon, started out singing in the streets of her working-class neighborhood.

AMALIA RODRIGUES
PORTUGAL — 1920-

Amalia is the voice and soul of Portugal. She sings of despair, the mystery of life, inevitable death. Yet, as she well knows, the poignant and nostalgic music called fado has the power to bring happiness to people, to her public.

It was thanks to her singing that Amalia Rodrigues was able to escape from the working-class district of Lisbon where she lived with her family. Her mother, too poor to raise her, placed her in the care of her grandmother, an embroideress. Amalia stayed with her until she was fourteen. Following a brief period of schooling, she started work at age twelve as a dressmaker's apprentice. She already had a large repertoire of fados and tangos, which she sang at festivities to families in her district. Amelia wasn't made to spend the day in a hot workshop; she preferred to sell oranges in the street, in the open air. She always sang there, and her voice attracted passersby. The neighborhood women, often moved to tears, would give her sardines, cakes. But her brothers did not appreciate their sister making a spectacle of herself. They forbade her to continue and forced her to work in a cannery.

The spirit of fado already lived in Amelia. "I wanted to kill myself every day," she recalled later. "The least thing upset me. Of course, I only wanted revenge — I didn't know what death was. But it was me, my temperament, always."

"Fado" is derived from the Latin *fatum*, fate. The music is slow and repetitive, the words are often melancholy. Fado is a moan sung in a deep and solemn tone, a voice of "torn velvet," as one critic put it. Amalia has said: "Five centuries ago, many Portuguese sailors roamed the world's seas. . . . This is how the fado began. They were far from home and their loved ones, facing unknown worlds; they lived under difficult conditions and truly suffered, submitting to the uncertainties of fate. For us, the Portuguese, the fado is a kind of atavism."

At sixteen, Amalia was singing for her district at the festivities for the people's saints called "the March of Lisbon." People starting talking about her. In 1939 one of her neighbors introduced her to the guitarist of the best-known fado cabaret in Lisbon, the Retiro da Severa. She sang for him and he was impressed, but she explained that her parents would never allow her to become a nightclub singer. The managers of the club visited her parents and persuaded them that she had a promising career ahead of her. Amalia remembers: "Five months later, I already had top billing in a theater. I didn't have to struggle — it was very easy."

She soon became the breadwinner of the family. They nonetheless continued to tell her what to do, chiefly by preventing her marriage to the guitarist Francisco Cruz. She overcame their objections, only to divorce after a year of marriage. The path to fame and glory opened before her throughout the country and in every social class. Antonio de Oliveira Salazar, the prime minister, called her "the soul of Portugal," and Don Juan of Spain, father of the future King Juan Carlos, came onto the stage once to kiss her hand. Solicited by filmmakers, she played the heroine in a dozen movies. And she set off to conquer the world with fado. She sang in Brazil, the United States, Germany, France, Italy, Japan. She was received with the same enthusiasm, and the same tears, in North and South America, in Europe, in Africa, in the Near and Far East.

Amalia Rodrigues still performs all over the world and then returns to Portugal, where women cross themselves when she passes. For her compatriots, she is not only the sole Portuguese popular artist who is internationally known, not only one of the country's richest women, but also a kind of madonna.

Twenty years after her family tried to prevent her marriage to Francisco Cruz, her public tried to stop her from remarrying. Once again she ig-

With what a poet called her "strangled Portuguese voice," Amalia is the uncontested queen of fado.

nored the objections, she wed an engineer, Cesar Seabra, in 1961, then left to live in Brazil. The following year, however, she returned to Lisbon by popular demand.

In 1964 she recorded an album in English, which included such well-known songs as "Summertime" and "Blue Moon." When she decided to release the record in Portugal, some twenty years later, she explained that, at the time of the recording, her people would not have forgiven her for singing in English. But in the 1980s the Portuguese were proud of her hit.

Fado, which had been highly criticized at the beginning of Salazar's dictatorship, had gained fame only to be censured again after the revolution of 1974, whose ideologues considered it reactionary, backward-looking, too fatalistic to sing

in a new and promising era. Amalia paid no attention to them, and the future proved her right. A new generation discovered fado and came to love it. Just as Carlos Gardel's tango will always symbolize Argentina, so will Amalia's fado be inseparable from the image of Portugal.

The queen of fado, who almost always wears magnificent black dresses, has changed little over the years. "I've gone through life like a cat, lightly," she says. "Cats are cats, and their instincts tell them to go forward. I've always acted like that, without ever finding a real reason to live." In spite of the admiration of the crowds, and the tabloid headlines spreading rumors about her life, Amalia has remained the same: sincere and despairing. When asked why she prefers to record in the dark, she answered: "Oh, I don't like light very much."

Had Cleopatra's nose been shorter, the whole history of the world would have been different.
Blaise Pascal

CLEOPATRA

EGYPT — 69-30 BC

At his death, Ptolemy XII Auletes of the Macedonian dynasty in Egypt left his throne to his two eldest children, Cleopatra and Ptolemy Dionysus, who, according to Egyptian custom, married and should have governed together. However, Cleopatra, seventh of the name, didn't like to share. The young king's guardian knew this and had her expelled from Alexandria. In the meantime, Julius Caesar had come to Egypt in pursuit of his arch-rival, Pompey, not realizing that his enemy had already been killed by Ptolemy's men for having allied himself with Cleopatra in the struggle over the Egyptian throne.

This proof of Ptolemy's friendship did not satisfy Caesar. He decided to settle the question of the Egyptian succession and set himself up as an arbiter. Cleopatra, seeking to plead her cause personally with Caesar, discreetly slipped into his palace (hidden in a carpet, tradition has it) and was brought to him as a gift. She emerged from the package and presented herself before Caesar. She was about twenty years old and already accomplished in the art of seduction.

Despite coins and bas-reliefs, it is difficult to tell what Cleopatra really looked like; in all likelihood she was less beautiful than is generally thought. Yet her cultivation and her gift with words, testified to by Plutarch, were considerable, and she spoke almost all the languages of the Mediterranean basin. Caesar was captivated. He rallied to the cause of his new mistress, declaring that she would sit on the throne at her brother's side.

Ptolemy objected; he besieged Caesar. But the Romans succeeded in getting the upper hand. Ptolemy fled and was drowned in the Nile. Cleopatra married her youngest brother, Ptolemy XIV, and was crowned queen of Egypt.

Caesar returned home without Cleopatra but he brought her to Rome later with the boy Caesarion, who, she announced, was Caesar's son. Cleopatra was highly unpopular there, and when Ceasar was assassinated she returned to Egypt.

The queen of Egypt cherished dreams of power and glory, but Rome was stronger.

Octavian — Caesar's great-nephew and official heir — and Mark Antony divided the empire between them, Octavian taking the West and Antony the East, including Egypt. Cleopatra set out to seduce this newcomer. She joined Antony at Tarsus, where he was preparing a campaign against the Parthians, and appeared before him like Venus, on a gilded barge with purple sails. She invited him on board and feasted him. Antony quickly succumbed to her charms. He forgot about the Parthians and followed her to Egypt, where a life of feasts and orgies awaited them. Cleopatra had three children by Antony.

Back in Rome, meanwhile, Antony's wife, Fulvia, quarreled with Octavian, and Antony had to return to Italy. Fulvia's death put an end to a disagreement that could have resulted in civil war. The two men reconciled, sealing their pact with Antony's marriage to Octavia, Octavian's sister.

Antony lived with her for three years in Athens while Cleopatra, jealous, schemed to win him back. The opportunity arose when Antony undertook a new campaign against the Parthians. Cleopatra joined him in Syria, diverted him from war, took him back to Egypt with her, and married him.

Antony plunged back into the delights of life with Cleopatra, exchanged his toga for Oriental clothing, and with a crown on his head and a gold sceptre in his hand proclaimed himself "King of Kings." They reigned over the great eastern empire and distributed provinces to Cleopatra's children. Fury in Rome reached its height when Antony included these in his will, since they were Roman provinces.

Octavian declared war on Cleopatra. She took advantage of the situation to make Antony formally repudiate Octavia. Then she pushed him into a naval battle, even though his strength lay in his land forces. Antony's ships attacked the Roman fleet. The battle was fully engaged, with no clear advantage yet to either side, when Cleopatra — for reasons never discovered — suddenly turned and left, followed by her sixty galleys. When he saw the queen leave, Antony abandoned his ships

At the death of Caesar, Cleopatra turned to Mark Antony,
who, like his predecessor, succumbed to her charms.

and had himself transported to her flagship. Plutarch says that Antony stayed near the helm for three days, head in hands, without saying a word. Back in Alexandria the two lovers tried to forget the tragic incident in feasting.

Octavian prepared himself to attack Egypt. Cleopatra prepared herself to die. She had a huge

One of the few true portraits of Cleopatra,
a tetradrachma from Antioch, coined in 36 BC
on the occasion of her marriage to Antony.

mausoleum built, in which she hid with all her treasure as soon as Octavian arrived. She ordered that Antony be told she was dead; grief-stricken, he immediately stabbed himself. Cleopatra asked that the dying Antony be brought to her, and he expired in her arms. But if Cleopatra thought to soften Octavian's heart with this touching tableau, she was wrong. He remained immovable as marble. Refusing to appear at his triumphal entry into Rome, the queen decided to kill herself.

After pouring final libations on Antony's tomb, Cleopatra bathed, dressed in her royal garments, and ate a last meal. She then had a basket of figs brought to her in which was hidden an asp, a snake whose bite does not distort the features. The next day they found her unblemished body in her bed of gold. Octavian, the future Caesar Augustus, commanded that she be royally buried beside Antony.

THEODORA

BYZANTIUM — CA. 500-548

Theodora, at center in this 6th century mosaic, was often derided by historians,
who criticized her unsavory past and her despotism.

"I could not exist stripped of royalty, nor live a single day without being hailed as 'empress' by those who have so recognized me," Theodora, a former prostitute, declared several years after becoming Empress of Byzantium.

Theodora was born in Constantinople, the city whose influence spread quickly as Rome's dominance waned. Her father was Akakios, a guardian of circus bears. He died while Theodora and her two sisters were still very young, and left them and their mother destitute. So that the family would have enough to eat, the little girls first went begging in the street, then tried performing on stage. Theodora made her dramatic debut with her elder sister, Comito, then created her own success performing comic pantomimes. She did not know how to sing or play the flute, but had a gift for making people laugh. By the time she was fifteen, her ivory complexion, lively dark eyes, and supple body had begun to turn heads.

Theodora's early history is known only because the historian Procopius recorded a colorful version of the scandals of the empress' youth in his posthumously published *Anecdota*. His work shows a malevolent fascination with Theodora — who was certainly no saint, but was not as flawed as he claims. He notes, for example, that her reputation was so bad that people turned away to avoid her in the street, and he dwells at length on her debauched nights and her prowess as a nude dancer.

Theodora left Constantinople for a time, following Hecebolas, a Syrian ambassador to Northern Africa, in hopes that he would marry her and rescue her from the perils of prostitution. But they had a falling out and she found herself with no means of support. She traveled along the African coast to Egypt, where she made friends with several members of the Monophysite sect of Christianity, who believed that Christ was entirely divine. She eventually returned to Constantinople, where she again used her physical charms to earn a living.

It is not clearly known how the prostitute met Justinian, nephew and heir of the Emperor Justin. Some said she attracted his attention with magic. Forty-five years old to her twenty-five, Justinian showered Theodora with gifts and went everywhere with her. He even spoke of marriage, despite the opposition of his aunt, the Empress Euphemia, a former slave who was well acquainted with Theodora's sort of ambition. The empress died a timely death, however, and the emperor revoked the law banning marriage between nobles and actresses. The wedding took place.

Four months before he died, Justin had Justinian proclaimed co-emperor with the rank of augustus, and Theodora became augusta. Proud, austere, and ever proper, Theodora must have behaved impeccably throughout her reign, since Procopius found nothing to say about it. Other than the fact that Justinian noted in the preamble to each law that he had consulted "his most reverend spouse," Theodora exercised power very discreetly. Much of the time she lived tranquilly in her villas on the Sea of Marmara, or in the Heraion, her palace on the Bosporus.

In January 532, a revolt broke out, spreading throughout Constantinople and threatening to endanger the crown. Justinian, by nature not particularly brave, was preparing for their departure when his wife declared that she would rather die than flee: "I pray the heavens that I will never be seen, not a single day, without my diadem and my purple robes," she said. "If you wish to flee, Caesar, you have the treasures, you have the sea,

Theodora had great influence during the reign of her husband, Justinian. Detail from an 11th century Byzantine crown.

you have the vessels — as for me, I shall abide by the ancient maxim, that the throne makes a glorious tomb." Her steadfastness inspired the emperor and his men to new courage, and they were victorious.

From that day on, the empress expressed her authority more openly, exerting immense influence on the empire's public affairs and foreign policy. She devoted attention to the Byzantine provinces in Asia and Egypt, where she tried to promote religious tolerance and peace. She retained a fondness for the Monophysites even when Justinian was combating the heretical sect, and she had several of them named bishops. For this and other reasons Theodora incurred the church's lasting condemnation; as much as ten centuries later a cardinal called her "a despicable creature; a second Eve too docile with the serpent; a citizen of hell stung by the devil's fly."

Her enemies said she was a magician and referred to her as Demonodora. They affirmed that

she kept a network of spies and that she did not hesitate to get rid of anyone who stood in her way. Some historians also saw her in a harsh light, accusing her of having promoted incompetent officials and of inspiring the worst policies of Justinian's reign.

It should be noted to her credit, however, that 6th century Byzantium saw great progress toward equality between the sexes, thanks to Theodora's influence over Justinian, who promulgated a series of laws protecting women. It was Theodora who was responsible for laws that

Sarah Bernhardt as Theodora in a drawing by René Lalique.

prohibited traffic in girls and altered divorce regulations to benefit women. And on her own authority she created a refuge for prostitutes and single mothers, and was involved in improving the lot of actresses.

Statues were raised in Theodora's honor and her name was joined to her husband's in prayers. In spite of her flaws, in spite of her reported avidity and cruelty, she gave the reign an expansive dimension it would never have had without her. At her death, Justinian, who had always loved her, mourned her greatly.

ISABELLA THE CATHOLIC

SPAIN — 1451-1504

The woman who would be queen . . . By having herself crowned as sovereign of Castile, Isabella changed the course of history in Spain and the world, and laid the foundations of a great empire.

Isabella was barely three at the death of her father, King Juan II of Castile. She lived at Arévalo with her insane mother until the age of thirteen, when her older brother, King Henry IV, summoned her to the Castilian court to be able to watch over her more closely. There Isabella received excellent schooling, as well as valuable experience of public life and power struggles.

Henry IV's opponents had gathered around her younger brother, Alfonso, and proclaimed him king of Castile at Avila. When Alfonso died three years later, his supporters solicited Isabella to take his place and claim the Castilian throne. She was wise enough to refuse, and this display of stability and maturity paid off: on September 19, 1468, the two cliques and signed an agreement recognizing Isabella as heiress to the Castilian throne.

Yet Isabella violated this pact and the oaths she had sworn when she married Prince Ferdinand of Aragon without her brother's consent. This act defied not only the king but also canonical law, since it was made possible by a forged papal bull, a letter signed by the pope permitting blood relatives to marry. It was a diplomatic scandal, for Aragon was suspected of having designs on the riches of the kingdoms of Leon and Castile.

Pope Sixtus IV granted a pardon to Isabella and gave her the requested dispensation, but he ordered that a new wedding be celebrated, since the first was considered unlawful. Henry did not interfere, believing that this marriage would harm his sister's popularity and be her downfall. Should this occur, the throne of Castile could pass to his

Isabella and Ferdinand receiving Christopher Columbus. The queen financed his voyages to what he thought would be the Indies.

daughter Juana instead of Isabella. The controversy over the succession was solved in a quite unexpected manner when Henry died. Isabella was in Segovia when she heard the news. She went to a church and had a Mass said for her brother. The next day, on December 14, 1474, she had herself crowned, as if this were the natural thing to do.

When her opponents arrived, she was seated on the throne and giving audience to members of the court. Those who did not immediately recog-

"The Catholic kings" brought Spain into the Renaissance.

nize her were relieved of their functions. She sent messengers everywhere to announce her accession to the throne and was so busy organizing her triumph that she didn't think about her husband until three days after her coronation.

Ferdinand was on his way to Castile. When he reached the border, he took the title of king, even though all the messages had announced that the leadership of Castile belonged solely to the queen. Isabella remained unshakable before all the arguments put forth by her husband, who felt that as a man he was the only possible heir. Not knowing where to turn, he sought to go back to Aragon. At this, Isabella gave in and agreed to call in arbitrators to end this domestic quarrel. The cardinal of Spain and the bishop of Toledo ar-

La Reconquista: Ferdinand and Isabella entering Málaga in 1492.

ranged for the sovereigns to share power and defined the specific duties of each.

The sovereigns defended their legal position by destroying documents referring to Henry IV and by overseeing the drafting of histories that would assure their place for posterity. The only blight on their happiness was that Henry's daughter Juana also bore the title of queen of Castile. There was little problem contesting this title, however, since many believed that Juana was actually the daughter of a nobleman named Beltrán de la Cueva; she was even nicknamed la Beltraneja. Isabella got rid of her rival by sending her to Portugal.

The Portuguese, allied with Isabella's opponents, invaded Castile in 1475 and were defeated four years later. This victory by Isabella and Ferdinand marked an end to violence and local disputes in their realm. At about the same time, the death of Ferdinand's father, King Juan II of Aragon, permitted the couple to extend their authoritarian and centralized rule over Castile and Aragon, thus laying the base for modern Spain.

Isabella personified the absolute monarch. Her sense of duty and personal honor sometimes led her to be intolerant. She would not permit any discussion about her supreme authority and fiercely defended Castile's autonomy. But she was also hard-working and reflective, and could be generous. Ferdinand was an excellent policymaker. The two knew how to combine their different characters for the betterment of Spain.

Isabella undertook the reform of the clergy, and she and her husband played a decisive part in the Reconquista, the reconquest, which after nine years of battle ended in the expulsion of the Moors from their last Spanish bastian, Granada. Isabella also financed Christopher Columbus' explorations and later took an interest in the fate and rights of the Indians. Yet her reign was also marked by the abuses of the Spanish Inquisition.

The Borgia pope, Alexander VI, proclaimed Isabella and Ferdinand to be the "Catholic kings" of Spain. Isabella died triumphant. Under her reign, Spain had become a great power and entered the Renaissance.

MARY STUART

SCOTLAND 1542 — ENGLAND 1587

Mary Stuart, Queen of Scots, spent eighteen years as the prisoner of Queen Elizabeth I of England.
At first Mary had a luxurious captivity, with hunting, sport, and visitors allowed.
But over the years she was moved continuously, her living conditions
and health deteriorating with each move.

"A splendid genius, if she had been less capricious," was how a historian of her time described Mary Queen of Scots. This reckless and impulsive woman largely brought about her own execution.

If Mary sobbed at her coronation, it had more to do with her age than her emotions: she was only nine months old at the time. Her father, King James V of Scotland, had died shortly after her birth and her mother, Marie de Lorraine, hoped to safeguard the crown despite the English invasion of southern Scotland. The war dragged on for several years, so in 1548, at age five, Mary was sent to join her fiancé, the young Dauphin of France.

As a royal child of the Renaissance, Mary received an excellent education: she learned Latin, Greek, and music, and studied poetry. At age ten, she debuted at court with her fiancé, nine-year-old François II. They were married six years later at Notre Dame Cathedral in Paris.

Before the wedding, the adolescent Scots queen was persuaded to sign a secret treaty stipulating that if she died childless, the Kingdom of Scotland would pass to the King of France. A fifteen-year-old, now more French than Scots, she could hardly be blamed for this technically treacherous act. And the action that would prove her undoing was probably committed just as impetuously, with as little consideration of the consequences.

When her cousin Mary Tudor, the Catholic Queen of England, died, Mary Stuart joined the English coat of arms to her own, in effect declaring herself its new ruler. By this act she made herself the focal point for continual Catholic rebellion against England's Queen Elizabeth, Mary Tudor's Protestant half-sister. For the Catholics had never recognized Henry VIII's divorce from Mary Tudor's mother, his creation of the Church of England, nor his subsequent marriage to Elizabeth's mother. To them, Elizabeth was the bastard usurper of a throne that should have belonged to Mary Stuart. The Catholic faction plagued Elizabeth throughout her reign, and she never forgave Mary Stuart for adding fuel to their fire.

Mary's father-in-law died in 1559, leaving the throne of France to the weak, sickly François. Mary Stuart had been Queen of France for only seven months when her husband succumbed to illness on December 5, 1560. The eighteen-year-old widow was pretty enough to turn heads, but had up to then shown little political savvy. Catherine de Médicis took over as regent of France, and Mary returned to Scotland, a country she barely remembered.

Her mother had died a year before, and Mary's illegitimate half-brother, James Stuart, had essentially been ruling Scotland. A Protestant, he had convinced the Scottish Parliament to abolish the Catholic Church and had conspired with England's Elizabeth to bring the preacher John Knox and his Calvinist reform to Scotland. Mary had great difficulty even obtaining permission to attend Mass in her private chapel.

The Queen of Scots had hardly settled into Holyrood Palace when she took several more steps toward her downfall. Mary refused to ratify the Treaty of Edinburgh, made with the English in 1560, demanding that it be modified to name her as Elizabeth's successor. And instead of marrying a favorite of the English queen, which would have thawed the relationship between them, she fell in love with her cousin Henry Stuart, a Catholic and a potential claimant to Elizabeth's throne. Mary wed him in July 1565, thus strengthening her claim on the English crown.

Darnley, though ambitious, proved to be a drunken cad, and the queen sought the political counsel of David Rizzio, an Italian musician who had become her secretary. In revenge, Darnley had Rizzio violently murdered before Mary's eyes, when she was six months pregnant with the son who would eventually inherit Elizabeth's throne as James I of England. Darnley was soon murdered in his turn, probably by the man who was Mary's new lover: James Hepburn, Earl of Bothwell. Mary married him in May 1567. This proved another fatal error in judgment. The Scottish nobles ousted Bothwell and forced Mary to abdicate in favor of her son. She was imprisoned by her brother James

MARIE STUART S'ÉCHAPPANT DU CHATEAU DE LOCH-LOWEN

Imprisoned first in Scotland, Mary managed to escape to England, where a sad fate awaited her.

— who had himself named regent for his nephew — but escaped on May 2, 1568.

At this point Mary Stuart made her biggest mistake: instead of seeking refuge in France, she threw herself into a lion's den in England, naively believing that Elizabeth would help her regain her crown. Elizabeth had her locked up instead, on the pretext of trying her for Darnley's murder. Mary was at first held captive in luxurious surroundings. She maintained regular communication with the pope, Catherine de Médicis, her mother's family, and Philip II of Spain. But this convinced Elizabeth that Mary was plotting against her, so the captive queen began to be moved from castle to castle, with living conditions and privileges worsening at each change. For as long as

Mary Stuart lived, she represented hope for a return to Catholicism in England.

During her eighteen years as a prisoner, Mary never met Elizabeth. Abandoned by her brother, her ministers, her friends, and her son, she lived in isolation, her health deteriorating in the damp cold of the castles where she lived. Eventually she made a final, fatal error: Mary allowed herself to be involved in a plot against the crown in 1586. She was judged guilty of treason and Elizabeth signed the death sentence, although she would have preferred to get rid of her rival in secret.

Mary Stuart met her death calmly and with dignity. She was beheaded with an axe, rather than a sword. The executioner had to try three times before finishing the deed.

ELIZABETH I

ENGLAND — 1533-1603

When King Henry VIII gave in to his passion and married Anne Boleyn, he could not know this union would produce one of history's most famous and most fascinating figures: Queen Elizabeth I. Though her reign was marked by conflict and scandal, "Queen Bess" was one of the best-loved monarchs of England.

Henry was married to Catherine of Aragon when he became enchanted with Anne. To divorce his wife and marry his new love, the king renounced his country's allegiance to the pope and the Roman Catholic Church — which forbade divorce — and created the Church of England with himself at its head. But after giving birth to Elizabeth, Anne fell from favor and Henry had her beheaded.

Treated as illegitimate after her mother's death, Elizabeth was raised in Hertfordshire, far from court, facing an uncertain future: her best prospects were a mediocre marriage and a lifetime in a remote province; her worst, the risk of assassination. Nevertheless she received a superb education. Elizabeth learned to speak French, Italian, and Spanish, was fascinated by ancient history, played several musical instruments, and danced and rode excellently. The dangers and hardships she experienced in her youth taught her the skills she would need as a queen: lying, deceit, negotiation, self-interest, and especially patience.

Elizabeth had to endure four of Henry's marriages, the execution of her stepmother Katherine Howard as well as that of her own mother, and the reigns of her younger brother Edward and older sister Mary, before acceding to the throne herself at the age of twenty-five.

The Catholic Mary Tudor's five-year reign of religious intolerance — during which Elizabeth was briefly imprisoned in the Tower of London — had earned her the sobriquet "Bloody Mary." The strife continued when Elizabeth took the crown: the Calvinists tried to convince her to

One of England's most popular monarchs, Elizabeth I always sought advice on her subjects' feelings, but held the reins of government firmly in her own hands. Elizabeth visiting Blackfriars in 1600.

support the Reformation and eliminate the Church of England. But she preferred an Anglican hierarchy, with the throne as its head, to the independent power of Roman Catholicism or Calvinism. Working with good advisors, including Secretary of State William Cecil, she reestablished the authority of the Anglican church.

The Roman Catholics did not give up easily. In their eyes, Henry's divorce from Catherine of Aragon was not legal, so Elizabeth was illegitimate. The Catholics rallied repeatedly behind her

During Elizabeth's reign England took its place as a world leader. Elizabeth knighting the explorer Francis Drake aboard The Golden Hind after his round-the-world voyage.

The "Virgin Queen" inspected dozens of suitors, but kept them — and everyone else — guessing about her private life.

cousin, Henry's great-niece Mary Stuart of Scotland, whom they considered the rightful claimant to the English throne. Elizabeth's forces took Mary prisoner, but even in custody she remained a threat. Elizabeth's refusal to marry and produce an heir aggravated the situation. Finally, Elizabeth had Mary beheaded for treason.

Religious conflict was not the only difficult issue Elizabeth faced upon becoming queen. The war against Spain, economic difficulties, and a society in upheaval beset her. But although vain and temperamental, Elizabeth let neither praise nor passion interfere with her wise and effective direction of the affairs of state.

Elizabeth had her favorites — notably Hatton, Raleigh, Dudley, and Essex — but would not take a husband. She inspected dozens of hopeful suitors, and listened to ambassadors from potential bridegrooms at length, making vague promises. A master of the art of procrastination, she led them all on.

Her private life, the subject of intense speculation, became legendary; she nurtured the legend. She was called the Virgin Queen, and never denied the label. Elizabeth was very emotional, and with those close to her she was familiar and outgoing. But lack of respect for the throne was never permitted: with merely a change in her tone of voice she quickly subdued any hint of insubordination. Cultivated and sensitive, she surrounded herself with poets and writers. The bright lights of the English Renaissance flourished during her reign: William Shakespeare, Edmund Spenser, Christopher Marlowe, Francis Bacon.

Elizabeth's great strength was her popularity. She had an instinct for adopting policies approved of by her subjects. A pragmatic monarch, she made no move before her advisers had studied the issue exhaustively, but she held the reins of government firmly in her own hands, exercising an almost absolute authority over Parliament.

During her reign England took its place as one of the premier powers in the world. Elizabeth was the first sovereign to pay heed to the cultural legacy her country would leave. The empire she began would continue to grow and dominate the world for centuries.

CHRISTINA OF SWEDEN

SWEDEN 1626 — ITALY 1689

Queen Christina, the "Nordic Pallas" who transformed her court into a "New Athens" by attracting the finest intellectuals of her time to Stockholm, could have been a great king. But in one of history's famous puzzles, she abdicated and went wandering through Europe.

Christina wrote in her memoirs: "I was born covered with hair from head to knee; only my face, arms, and calves were hairless. I was all fuzzy. I had a deep and strong voice. All this made the women who received me think that I was a boy." Her father, Gustavus II Aldolphus, realized that the ladies were mistaken and said: "I hope that this girl will be worth a boy to me. . . . She will be clever, since she has fooled us all."

And clever she was. She was given a boy's education, like that of her giant of a father, whom she far preferred to her dainty and sweet mother. He died when she was six, and Christina became queen, though under a regent. "I was so small that I knew neither my unhappiness nor my good fortune, but I do however remember that I was delighted to see those people at my feet kissing my hand." From that time on Christina expressed herself as a monarch, speaking of "my crown," "my armies," "my ministers."

She was an enthusiastic and gifted student who devoted six hours each morning to her studies and spent the afternoon learning foreign languages. Saturdays were given over to sports: riding, fencing, target shooting. She was not only driven by an intense desire to learn everything but was also exceedingly ambitious. At twelve she began to occupy herself with affairs of state, at fifteen she started to receive ambassadors, the following year she participated in the Regency Council, and at eighteen she took over the reins of power, which she had no intention of sharing. For this reason

Christina of Sweden: a "virile" queen who ruled her country with an iron hand . . . until her abdication.

and because, as she later wrote, she did not want to be used as a peasant uses his field, she refused to consider marriage and rejected all suitors. She did have amorous adventures with both men and women; generally she found women antipathetic and uninteresting, but certain refined and cultivated women, such as the beautiful Emma Sparra, her lady-in-waiting who also waited on her in bed, were able to overcome her adversion.

Compared with the members of the refined and ceremonious courts of Europe, Christina acted like a peasant. She was indifferent to her appearance and took to wearing masculine — and often dirty — clothing. Her movements were uncoordinated, her hair disheveled, and she straddled chairs. Her speech was no more refined than her manner. She was rude and vulgar and took her vocabulary from the gutter. She was fond of practical jokes and amused herself by reciting obscene passages from the Roman poet Catullus and the *Satyricon* of Petronius. Yet Christina was a true intellectual. She gathered around her the greatest minds of the 17th century — such as the French philosophers René Descartes and Claude Saumaise, and the Dutch jurist Hugo Grotius. She also participated in the revival of the classics in Sweden and reformed the country's educational system.

Sweden was already powerful when Christina inherited the throne. But she made her country into a real empire that dominated the Baltics and included parts of Germany. The burden of these wars on the treasury was heavy. Lands were sold to nobles and taxes were levied on the discontented middle class. After ten years in power, citing public complaints and the burden of ruling, Christina abdicated on May 21, 1654, in favor of her cousin, who became Charles X Gustavus. She left Sweden to travel through Europe.

The following year she publicly converted to Catholicism at the cathedral in Innsbruck, Austria. She had secretly converted earlier, but Catholicism was proscribed in Sweden and this was undoubtedly behind her abdication and departure. She had herself confirmed by Pope Alexander VII

Highly educated, Christina was a patroness of the arts and letters. She is pictured here with Descartes at her right.

as soon as she arrived in Rome. The pope called her "a woman born a barbarian, barbarically raised, and living with barbaric ideas."

She took up residence in Rome at the Farnese Palace and gave splendid receptions, but society was disconcerted by this woman who claimed the

A public festival given in honor of Christina.

same honors and protocol as the pope. Christina made enemies. Two years after her abdication, she left Rome in search of a crown.

In Paris she concluded an agreement with the statesman-cardinal Jules Mazarin, who promised her Naples. Instead, however, this crown went to the Duc d'Anjou. At the death of her cousin, King Charles X Gustavus, Christina returned to Sweden hoping to regain the throne. Forced to renounce this attempt, she focused her designs on Poland — and failed there, too. Nor did she succeed in her efforts to have her protector, Cardinal Decio Azzolino, elected pope.

Between the cardinal and the former queen was a great love, which lasted a quarter of a century. Azzolino was one of the last to remain with this corpulent little woman, whose character did not improve with age. At the end, Christina renounced the world. In 1688 she wrote: "Leave me in oblivion and obscurity. Do not try to draw me out." She died the following year.

CATHERINE THE GREAT

GERMANY 1729 — RUSSIA 1796

Even before the assassination of her husband, Catherine acted as a spokeswoman of Russian
nationalism, and after his death she was proclaimed empress of all the Russias.
Portrait by Catherine's court painter, Virgilius Erichsen.

The empress of all the Russias has inspired countless volumes. Was she virtuous and great, or depraved and despotic, even bloodthirsty? Self-taught, she herself determined the path that took her from Germany to Russia and placed her on the throne of the czars.

Catherine, born Sophie of Anhalt-Zerbst, was a princess without a dowry. But when she was quite young she ambitiously planned to marry her cousin, Karl Ulrich of Holstein, grandson of Peter the Great and heir to the Russian throne. She confided in her *Memoirs:* "The title of queen, even when I was a child, flattered my ears."

Their marriage, the first step in her ascent, was celebrated on August 21, 1745. She was fifteen. Upon her arrival in Russia the ambitious and intelligent young bride immediately sought to please her mother-in-law, the Empress Elisabeth — and neglected her husband. Catherine became a Russian enthusiast. She learned the language and practiced the Russian Orthodox faith in order to gain the people's support.

Catherine endured eighteen years of silent humiliation under the Empress Elisabeth's firm rule. The empress, noting Catherine's barren condition, procured a noble young lover for her, Sergei Salykov. Catherine's first two pregnancies resulted in miscarriages through her own carelessness. During her third pregnancy, Elisabeth kept a strict watch over her. The child, Paul, was taken from Catherine at birth and raised by Elisabeth. Soon afterward, disappointed by Salykov, who was a Don Juan, Catherine embarked on a tumultuous love life.

Upon Elisabeth's death, Catherine's husband acceded to the throne as Peter III. Catherine considered his political and religious opinions dangerous, however. He despised all things Russian, his policies were pro-German, and he took steps against the Orthodox clergy. Hence the friendship he had shared for many years with Catherine deteriorated. She became the spokeswoman of Russian nationalism.

A coup d'état, prepared by the army and led by Catherine's lover, Grigory Orlov, and his two brothers, overthrew Peter. He was imprisoned and later assassinated, without his wife's consent. On June 28, 1762, Catherine entered Saint Petersburg at the head of the Russian troops and was proclaimed empress. She was thirty-three. She would reign for the next thirty-four years, surrounded by luxury and splendor. The dream of the dowerless princess had become reality.

Nourished by the encyclopedists of the French Enlightenment and histories of empires and great rulers, influenced by the political philosophy of Voltaire and Montesquieu, Catherine sought to accomplish the impossible task of reconciling liberty and serfdom. But she knew nothing about the harsh realities of the lives endured by 90 percent of her people, most of whom were serfs living in misery. She who could state, "I am an aristocrat — that is my job," saw her subjects only from behind the curtains of her carriage. The hopes for justice expressed in the Nakaz code, her legal reforms, were only theoretical.

Social injustice led to a popular uprising in Russia from 1773 to 1775 under a former Cossack officer, Yemelyan Pugachov. Yet his movement did not succeed in convincing Catherine that social reform was needed. What she took for a Cossack revolt was the first flicker of the fire that would consume all Russia and culminate, ultimately, in the Bolshevik revolution.

Grigory Potemkin, a young officer ten years Catherine's junior, now took his place in the czarina's life and his country's history. He is considered by many to have been her greatest love. Though their affair lasted only two years, he remained her friend and counselor to her death, and is said to have helped her procure the young lovers who became something of an obsession in her last years. Catherine's grandson Alexander, whom she had raised and loved dearly, despised her for this. Alexander refused to bypass his father to become heir to the throne, though later he participated in a plot that resulted in Paul's abdication and his own accession as Alexander I.

Catherine the Great completed the work begun by her husband's grandfather, Peter the Great.

She centralized power, unified and expanded territorial Russia, and brought Russian culture to its height. By the time of her death, she had forged an immense empire. With her *Memoirs* she helped establish the personality cult in Russia, which became a tradition, and propagated her own legend. "If I were to live two hundred years," she wrote, "then, without doubt, all of Europe would be subject to Russia's scepter."

Catherine built an immense empire, finishing the work begun by Peter the Great.

Marlene Dietrich was a beautiful Catherine in Joseph von Sternberg's film *The Scarlet Empress*.

QUEEN VICTORIA

ENGLAND — 1819-1901

Her very name evokes a certain image of Britain. During Queen Victoria's reign, the British monarchy regained its prestige and entered the modern era, even as other European royal families felt their power crumbling.

It took unusual circumstances to bring Victoria to the throne at the age of eighteen, for this granddaughter of George III was at birth only fifth in the line of succession. Her father, the Duke of Kent, had married the German Princess Mary Louisa Victoria, but died only a few months after the birth of Victoria. At the death of George IV, Victoria's uncle became King William IV, but his children all died in infancy.

Victoria did not consider her childhood a happy one. She felt unmitigated affection only for her Uncle Leopold — her mother's brother, later the first King of the Belgians. His frequent letters comforted her. She was educated as befitted a future queen, learning German, Italian, and French, and showed a great aptitude for music. Though her mother hoped to become regent for Victoria, William IV did not oblige; he clung to life until just after Victoria's eighteenth birthday.

The young queen applied herself to her new role very seriously, instilling hope in the British people, who were weary of the succession of odd, incompetent monarchs they had been recently subjected to. Victoria lacked confidence at first and was sensitive about her tendency toward plumpness and her short stature. The prime minister, William Lamb, Lord Melbourne, helped her a great deal as she learned to rule, and Uncle Leopold completed her political education. Soon she developed an authoritative manner and an intuitive understanding of her country.

In 1840, Queen Victoria married a cousin, Prince Albert of Saxe-Cobourg-Gotha. But she intended to wear the pants in the family and at

Her Majesty the Queen in her robes of state.

first allowed Albert only a ceremonial role, which soon began to suffocate him. The couple had nine children, and Albert paid more attention to them than she did. Yet as head of the family he found ways to assert himself with Victoria, and soon he worked his way into public affairs; the queen made him her adviser upon Lord Melbourne's departure. She came to admire her husband's gifts for business and politics as the charms of these subjects wore thin for her, leading her to declare that women were not made to govern.

The adult Victoria had achieved a contentment far beyond that of her childhood. She guarded her happiness and her intimate moments

More "Victorian" than ever in 1897, here sits the "grandmother of Europe."

A silhouette familiar to all British people,
a queen who embodied the values of the country.

with Albert carefully, unwilling to share him even with their children. Victoria had grown homelier with age, but felt young and fit, while her husband aged far less gracefully. He died of typhoid fever in 1861, only forty-two years old.

Grief stricken, Victoria adopted severe mourning and withdrew from the world, becoming known as the "widow of Windsor." She worshiped the memory of her husband and preferred the company of his ghost to anyone else for

nearly thirty years. It wasn't until she was about seventy that she regained her taste for living. None of her noble peers could end her self-imposed isolation, for Victoria did not feel at home among them; it was a Scottish servant, John Brown, who finally succeeded in arousing her affection.

In London, their relationship caused much speculation, most of it exaggerated; people began to circulate caricatures of "Mr. and Mrs. Brown." Victoria's good friend and confidant, Prime Minister Benjamin Disraeli, urged the queen to reassert her authority, and passed a law proclaiming her Empress of India to regild her image.

Very interested in international politics, Victoria cultivated her influence over the royal families of Europe. She understood, however, that her strength came first and foremost from the

confidence her own people showed in her. She loved the bourgeois values of the middle class, and indeed embodied them perfectly; the aristocracy she found frivolous and selfish. Victoria was an Everywoman whose frank and naive opinions people appreciated, and, at the same time, "The Great White Queen," a living symbol of Britain's greatness. Her moral authority, austere and matriarchal, became a model for the style of rule that British sovereigns follow to this day.

Queen Victoria's popularity continued to grow until the end of her life. Her sixty-four year reign was the longest and most glorious in Britain's history. By the time she died at the age of eighty-one, Victoria's numerous grandchildren had married into other royal families, earning her the name "grandmother of Europe."

TZ'U-HSI

CHINA — 1835-1908

Tz'u-hsi, the last dowager empress of China, loved power more than anything. She knew how to intrigue at court effectively and how to obtain and keep power, but she did not see that the danger to her rule would come from outside the walls of Beijing's Forbidden City. She lost the struggle between the old and the new, and thus was a key figure in the decadence and downfall of the empire over which she was the last to truly reign.

In the 17th century, the Manchu leaders of Manchuria established their supremacy in China. The dynasty of the Ch'ing replaced the Ming dynasty in the Forbidden City. The Chinese people were forced to exchange their chignons for long Manchu pigtails, but in all else the Ch'ing assimilated into Chinese culture rather than impose their ways upon their immense new empire. They soon achieved stability throughout the country, and China's prosperity, based on agriculture and commerce, reached its zenith in the following century.

But it was a country on the decline, overextended and overpopulated, and affected by the presence of profit-seeking foreign powers, when Tz'u-hsi was born in Beijing on November 29, 1835. She is variously reported to have been the daughter of an officer, of a government clerk, of a nobleman; whatever her background it included education, for she knew how to read and write and had studied the Chinese classics. At seventeen she was chosen to participate in a great competition: it was time for the new emperor, Hsien-feng, to choose his consorts. Twenty-eight maidens were submitted to the appraisal of the dowager empress and imperial eunuchs. The number was not unreasonable, for the Son of the Sky could take as many as seventy concubines.

Having been chosen to enter the Forbidden City, the young girl started to make allies in order to approach her imperial spouse. The dowager empress did not like her, but the girl found supporters among the powerful eunuchs, who would always remain faithful to her. After biding her time for three years, she was at last brought to the emperor. Hsien-feng found her charming, culti-

Tz'u-Hsi knew how and when to be patient,
and became one of the most powerful women in the world.

210

vated, and subtle. He began to confide in her and soon promoted her to the rank of second concubine. His senior consort, who was under the protection of the dowager empress, was barren. Thus it was Tz'u-hsi who presented the emperor with his only son, the future T'ung-chih, in 1856.

By this time the nationalist and progressive Taipang Rebellion had begun. The emperor, suffering from paralysis, handed over the reins of power to his half-brother, Prince Kung. Tz'u-hsi allied herself with the prince and Tz'u-an, the senior consort. Tz'u-hsi's role as regent became official when she had her son declared crown prince in August 1861. The move was curiously well-timed; the emperor died twenty-four hours later. Rumors began to circulate; had Tz'u-hsi had a hand in this sudden death?

The Taiping Rebellion was put down in 1864 with the help of the Western powers, the "foreign devils" who were gradually gaining the upper hand in many Chinese territories and who had negotiated what were widely seen as unfair treaties. In 1860, during the so-called Arrow War, they had even sacked the emperors' summer palace. It was in this political context that Tz'u-hsi and her two fellow-regents, Prince Kung and Tz'u-an, ruled until her son attained his majority in 1873. The young emperor was much more tolerant of the Western powers than his mother was. Like Prince Kung, T'ung-chih realized that China had to enter the 19th century. Tz'u-hsi disagreed, but the emperor did not always listen to her advice.

Two years after taking the throne, the emperor died. Distraught, his pregnant young wife committed suicide shortly afterward. Tz'u-hsi once again held the reins of power. She adopted her nephew and had him proclaimed Emperor Kuang-hsü with herself and Tz'u-an as co-regents. When Tz'u-an died suddenly and inexplicably in 1881, Tz'u-hsi was at last the undisputed dowager empress of China.

In 1889 she surrendered her power to Kuang-hsü and took up residence in the summer palace. But these were troubled times for the empire. China lost a war with the more modernized and better-armed Japan. When Kuang-hsü, seconded by astute advisers, attempted in 1898 to reform an outmoded system, Tz'u-hsi overthrew him and resumed her position as regent. She was aided by General Yüan-shih-k'ai, a future president of the Republic of China. Kuang-hsü's efforts at reform had lasted barely a hundred days.

Faced with the ever-increasing presence of the Western powers, the dowager empress supported traditionalists and secret societies such as the group known in the West as the Boxers. In 1900, the Boxers set fire to foreign legations in Beijing and massacred missionaries throughout China. The empress declared war against foreigners, and the result was bloody. In the face of the Western powers' retaliation the imperial court was forced to flee the capital.

In September 1901 China signed a protocol obliging it to pay huge reparations, which bankrupted the state and humiliated the Ch'ing dynasty. Following this defeat, Tz'u-hsi undertook educational, administrative, and military reforms. But they came too late. Inertia, the upset in the balance of power, and an inability to adapt to the changing configuration of the immense nation would soon bring about the dynasty's downfall.

The woman known as "the Old Buddha" had been capable of everything and anything to retain personal power, but she failed to ensure the future of her unstable empire. She was no longer the most powerful woman in the world — more powerful, as she had loved to reflect, than her contemporary, Queen Victoria.

Shortly before her death in 1908, Tz'u-hsi chose as Kuang-hsü's successor the child who would briefly reign as Hsüan-t'ung — the "Last Emperor." Four years later, the Republic of China was proclaimed.

Authoritarian, reactionary, cruel, temperamental, uncompromising, and quick-tempered, Tz'u-Hsi is branded on China's memory.

EVA PERON

ARGENTINA — 1919-1952

The former actress who became much more than the
wife of a head of state, Eva Péron smiles at her mirror reflection.

"Yes, I admit that I have one personal ambition: I want the name Evita to figure somewhere in the history of my country." Eva Perón succeeded in her ambition. This social-climbing, power-thirsty, luxury-loving woman died at the height of her glory, adored by the Argentine people, who took her for a saint. Her country is still haunted by her memory.

Maria Eva Duarte, the illegitimate daughter of a humble farmer, was born at Los Toldos in the pampas some 170 miles from Buenes Aires. Her mother, Juana, taught her daughters that the only way for a woman on her own to get ahead was to find a protector. The lesson bore fruit. Eva wrote in her autobiography that until the age of eleven she thought the poor grew like grass and the rich like trees. One day a worker told her that the reason there were so many poor people was because the rich were too rich. As soon as she had understood the mechanism of social injustice, she had only one idea: to become rich.

At fourteen she met a second-rate tango singer, José Armani, who dazzled her with the idea of success in the capital. Six days later she set off for Buenes Aires. Eva wanted to be an actress. She was tall, slender, and pretty, but had meager talent and a strong provincial accent. She was nonetheless determined to succeed. Since Armani could not be of much help, she seduced more influential men. Eva gradually made progress, receiving minor roles in the movies and on the radio. In 1943 she won the leading female role in a popular weekly serial on Radio Belgrano. Eva started a new life, the life of a star.

That same year, a group of pro-fascist officers overthrew the civilian government to prevent a U.S.-backed coalition of liberal and conservative groups from gaining power. Some of these officers were Eva's friends. In her radio commentaries she spoke a great deal about one man: Juan Perón, the labor minister of the new government. He was implementing Mussolini's theories concerning state control of the unions, and promoting bills favorable to the working classes. Perón recognized in the unorganized masses a source of support.

"The immortal Eva Péron": after her death, the myth of Evita grew even greater.

Evita the "saint" brings luck to the faithful.

When Eva met Juan Perón in October 1943 she was twenty-four, he was a widower of forty-eight. Their liaison might have lasted only a few months had not each understood that the other could be useful. Eva began to help Perón at political rallies. She unionized the radio actors and had herself named the union's president, a perfect position from which to punish those who had previously stood in her way. She continued to rise and so did her power and income. *Time* magazine mentioned this young actress who had burst forth from obscurity and was considered a close friend of Juan Perón — who by 1945 had become minister of war and vice president.

Perón was clearly aiming to become president, but repressive measures he had ordered were brought to light and he was dismissed and imprisoned on October 9, 1945. Eva met with leaders of the workers, rallied the unions, and persuaded them to demand Perón's release. After a general strike, Perón was freed on October 17. He expressed himself as overcome with gratitude for the woman who had suffered, he said, as much as his own mother during his imprisonment. Peronism and the Evita myth were born. Juan Perón married Eva Duarte soon thereafter, and on February 24, 1946, Perón received 56 percent of the vote in the presidential election.

Eva presented herself as a role model for the poor, promising them a social ascent like her own. She became the mother of the *descamisados*, the "shirtless" ones, the very poor. She created the Eva Perón Foundation, a kind of state within the state that controlled enormous sums of money — part of which went into a Swiss bank account, but much of which went to build hospitals, schools, and other institutions. Having won the workers' hearts, she gained the support of women by fighting for their right to vote. The first lady, who listened to the pleas of her "subjects" three times a week, was invested with the halo of a saint. But she was a saint fond of hats, jewelry, furs, and other luxuries, and these desires of hers had to be satisfied before one could obtain a post or win a contract.

As a star of international politics, Evita toured Europe in the summer of 1947. She met the Spanish dictator, Francisco Franco, and Pope Pius XII, but canceled a visit to England because Buckingham Palace, citing protocol, refused to receive her. She was insulted in Italy and stones were thrown at her in Switzerland. Yet she returned to her country in triumph. People who opposed Eva ran into trouble, since she controlled the Argentine media. Nonetheless, the army vetoed her candidacy for the vice presidency in 1952. By that time Evita was very ill with cancer. She died in July after successfully begging her *descamisados* to support Perón again.

The day of her death, the flower shops were sold out in Buenos Aires. Her body was embalmed and the cult of Saint Evita began, though the pope refused to recognize it. When Juan Perón fell from power in 1955, Eva's casket disappeared and began a journey through Europe, where Evita was finally buried under a false name. In the 1960s, in their effort to regain popular support, the Peronistas brandished Evita's name as a symbol. Perón regained power. He was elected to the presidency in 1973; at his side was his third wife, Isabel, who copied the irreplaceable Evita. Two years earlier Perón had recovered Evita's casket from Italy, thanks to mediation by the Vatican. As Evita says in the Tim Rice-Andrew Lloyd Webber musical inspired by her life, "Don't cry for me, Argentina. The truth is, I never left you."

INDIRA GANDHI

INDIA — 1917-1984

Motilal Nehru rightly prophesied at the birth of his granddaughter Indira that she could prove more worthy than a thousand sons. Indira Gandhi became prime minister of the world's largest democracy, a respected and venerated figure, though sometimes feared and often controversial.

Indira was born in 1917 into a Kashmiri Brahmin family, and thus belonged to India's highest caste. She had an exciting childhood, daily witnessing the struggle for independence led by her grandfather, her father, and Mahatma Gandhi. Her first political act, as a child, was to respond to appeals to consume only Indian products: she burned her clothes and even her doll, which had been made abroad.

With a sickly mother and a father often in prison, she developed a taste for independence and action at an early age. When Indira was still too young to participate directly in the independence movement she created her own organization, the "army of monkeys." It was entirely made up of children, who took charge of administrative details, manufactured flags, saw to provisions during demonstrations, and, most importantly, gathered information — a considerable asset.

Following an irregular early education, Indira left for England to study modern history and anthropology at Oxford University from 1935 to 1941. After her return to India she married Feroze Ghandi (no relation to the Mahatma). They both took up the struggle against the British as members of the Indian National Congress Party.

Jawaharlal Nehru, Indira's father, became India's first prime minister when the country gained its independence in 1947. Indira served as his hostess and traveling companion. Her filial devotion could not but harm her already shaky relationship with her husband. She abandoned

She had been prime minister of the world's largest democracy. A year after this 1979 photo was taken, Indira Gandhi was returned to power.

him for the political and diplomatic career she began to build in Nehru's shadow. Accompanying her father on his trips, she met the great leaders of the period and formed some deep friendships.

In 1959, Indira started an independent career, becoming president of the Congress Party, which dominated politics in India. Two years after the death of Nehru, the party designated her to succeed the late Prime Minister Lal Bahadur Shastri; she took office on January 19, 1966. In choosing Nehru's daughter in subsequent elections, the Indian people expressed their wish to continue following the ideals of their first leader.

But she had inherited a country in crisis. She faced serious economic problems and a difficult political situation. Following her election in 1967

The daughter of Jawaharlal Nehru, Indira grew up under his influence and that of Mahatma Gandhi.

and re-election in 1971, she gradually took over absolute power and began to rule India like a despot. In 1975, after being charged with violating election laws, she declared a state of emergency. Though she always defended her actions as necessary to preserve democracy, she used and, according to many, abused her power.

The country rejected Indira's leadership in

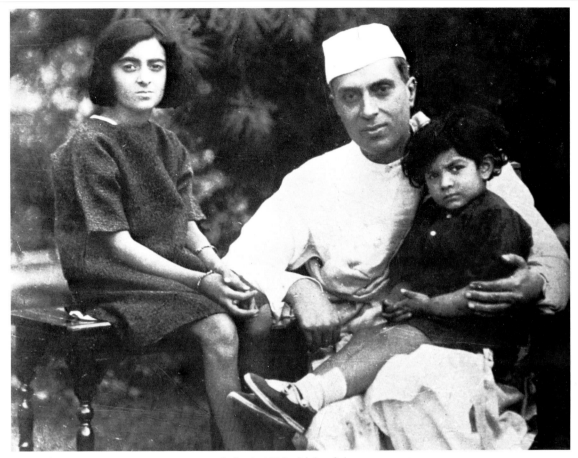

Indira in 1920 with her father

the elections of 1977 and she resigned on March 22. She did not, however, disappear from the political scene. In spite of accusations, she continued to travel throughout India and proved herself indispensable in many problem areas. With this nationwide campaigning, Indira recovered the hearts and trust of the people of India. She returned to power triumphantly in 1980.

Although she was a fervent believer in democracy, Indira Gandhi underestimated the complexity of the religious and ethnic problems that plagued her country. Her leadership had not improved the situation; in particular her actions against extremists of the Sikh faith proved fatal. Two Sikh members of her personal guard assassinated her in October 1984.

That evening, her son Rajiv, who succeeded her, made a television speech to the nation in which he urged his people to keep calm and in which he tried, in vain, to prevent reprisals against the Sikh community. He began his speech by announcing that Indira Gandhi, the prime minister, had been assassinated. She was not only his mother, he continued, but the mother of the entire nation. No one could contradict him.

Through her political achievements, Indira Gandhi generated cohesion in an incredibly diverse country with more than eight hundred million inhabitants. Steadfastly maintaining neutrality toward the Soviet Union as well as the United States, she affirmed the policy of non-alignment proclaimed by her father and ensured India's position as a leader in the Third World. To the Indian people, Indira Gandhi stands as a member of their first ruling dynasty, a link with the myths of her father and Mahatma Gandhi.

MARGARET THATCHER

ENGLAND — 1925-

Margaret Thatcher never shirks from taking the lead. Political power seems
to fit her even better than her Tory-blue tailored suits.

The Iron Lady, Margaret Thatcher commands fierce devotion and loyalty — or intense hatred. During her eleven years at the helm of Britain's government, her strident style and righteous conviction cowed those who opposed her. Both at home and abroad, Europe's first woman prime minister used an iron hand, rarely softened by the velvet glove. Yet can this woman really be as monolithic as she leads the world to believe?

Margaret Hilda Roberts was born on October 13, 1925, in the heart of England, in the Lincolnshire town of Grantham, where her father, Alfred Roberts, owned and ran a grocery. Margaret grew up with a boundless admiration

for her thrifty, taciturn father, an inflexible, conservative Methodist who ruled his middle-class family firmly but fairly and devoted much time to local politics.

In 1943, a scholarship enabled Margaret to study chemistry at Oxford University's Somerville College. She joined the University Conservative Association soon after arriving and eventually became its first woman president. After obtaining her degree, she took two posts as a research chemist and then left this field; it had been a useful experience, but her calling was elsewhere.

Everyone in Britain expected the ruling Labour Party to trounce the Conservatives, or

"Tories," in the general elections of 1950, but this did not deter Margaret from running for the parliamentary seat from Dartford. Aged 24, she was the youngest Tory candidate. Britain's debutante politicians sharpen their teeth on their first few contests and are expected to lose unless they have a famous name or fantastic luck. Margaret was no exception; she lost. But she'd had the chance to catch the attention of the media and her party.

By this time she had met Denis Thatcher, a fellow campaigner for the Conservatives and the director of his family's firm. Denis, who had been divorced for some time, courted Margaret for two years and in December 1951 married her in a Methodist church in London. He continued with his business career, becoming increasingly successful, yet even before his retirement in 1975 Denis managed also to support Margaret in her endeavors. As he said, he was the loyal co-worker who was always "half a step behind her."

Two years after their marriage, she gave birth to twins, a boy and a girl. Motherhood did not detour Mrs. Thatcher from her chosen path for long. Her husband's position enabled her to delegate the domestic chores and to study law. In 1953 she was admitted to the Bar and began her practice, specializing in taxation. Politics still beckoned, but when she sought to run again for Parliament, the Conservative Party selection committee hinted that she would be better off minding her home.

Undeterred, she let the twins get a little older. Then in 1959 Margaret got the break she was waiting for: she was selected to run for Parliament for Finchley, a traditionally Conservative constituency in the north of London. She won that election and has held the seat ever since.

Once in the House of Commons, few obstacles hindered her. She stood out in an era when women were beginning to forge ahead in public life. In 1970, when Edward Heath led the Conservatives to victory, Margaret was named Secretary of State for Education and Science.

The politicians might have expected her to relate well to other women but she soon became

Tenacity became one of Mrs. Thatcher's trademarks.

a bête noire of the feminists. They couldn't persuade her to increase pre-primary facilities or childcare centers for working mothers. Margaret even cut free milk at schools. Her fellow Tories would breakfast over front-page newspaper photos of mobs of angry mothers waving placards and shouting "Thatcher, Thatcher, Milk Snatcher."

After nationwide labor strife and economic problems brought about the fall of the Heath government in 1974, a struggle began for leadership of the Conservative Party. The right wing of the party supported Keith Joseph. An unwise public speech forced him to resign from the race and Margaret took his place, but no one expected her to win. When the vote was held in February 1975, she triumphed in the second round. Heath was out and Thatcher was in! Britain, so long dominated by the male establishment, was stunned.

Margaret Thatcher was now Leader of Her Majesty's Opposition. She and Keith Joseph

worked to build a policy package, something to hand the voters the next time the nation went to the polls. What they created was Thatcherism: a combination of hard-line, right-wing policies favoring anti-inflationary economic measures, decentralization, entrepreneurship, "privatization," and strong support for capitalist democracies. "Labour isn't working," proclaimed Thatcher's Tory party campaign in the 1979 elections. The British people evidently agreed. They swept the Conservatives to victory and Margaret Thatcher became Europe's first woman prime minister. Under her leadership the Conservative Party remained in continual control of the British government for more than a decade — the best record for 150 years.

After Margaret became prime minister, the Soviet news agency Tass nicknamed her the "Iron Lady" and the label stuck. She hectored other European Community leaders mercilessly; she refused to budge on Commonwealth demands for sanctions against South Africa; under her draconian economic measures the unemployment figures soared higher than ever before. "The lady's not for turning," she would insist, sticking with her unpopular policies until they brought the results she was waiting for. Even her cabinet — to which only one woman was ever appointed — was said to suffer under her bulldozing style.

Always ready for battle, Margaret Thatcher is the self-proclaimed champion of the British middle class. In 1982 she fought a war against

Margaret is the champion of Britain's middle class.

Argentina over the Falkland Islands; that victory won her a second term by a landslide. When Iraq invaded Kuwait in August 1990, she was the first to join the United States in sending troops to the Middle East. But British public opinion polls were already showing Labour consistently ahead. The Tories began discussing alternative leaders.

In November 1990 Mrs. Thatcher's lead-

With husband Denis behind her, Margaret was the first woman to reach 10 Downing Street as Prime Minister.

ership of the Conservative Party was challenged. She won a big majority on the first ballot, yet was still four votes short by the party's complex rules. She announced immediately that she'd fight on. For the next thirty-six hours a stream of Tory friends pressed her to step down. On November 22 Margaret announced her resignation. The Thatcher era was over. But no one doubted that Europe's first female prime minister had left her mark on her country and the continent.

BENAZIR BHUTTO

PAKISTAN — 1953-

To many Pakistanis, Benazir Bhutto symbolized their own suffering. When martial law ended, chanting crowds welcomed her home from political exile and voted her the first woman to govern a Muslim nation since the 13th century.

Before her fortieth birthday, Benazir Bhutto witnessed her father's execution, suffered imprisonment and exile, returned triumphantly to her homeland to become the first woman to govern a Muslim nation since the 13th century and was ousted after less than two years in office. Poised between tradition and progress, Benazir Bhutto has walked on the frontiers of history.

A descendant of a noble clan, Benazir was born into a powerful family of Pakistani landowners whose feudal way of life had been abandoned by her progressive grandfather. Her father,

Zulfikar Ali Bhutto, studied at the University of California at Berkeley and Oxford University. He first entered public life in 1957 as a member of Pakistan's delegation to the United Nations.

Bhutto always took part in the education of his children. Benazir's mother, Begum Nusrat, herself an educated woman, also contributed to her children's upbringing, and taught them the fundamentals of Islam. A Shiite Muslim of Iranian origin, she did not wear the black veil normally imposed on women of the Bhutto family. Benazir's father insisted that his two daughters, too, be

exempt from this tradition, freeing them from "a life spent in perpetual twilight."

Benazir was the first Bhutto woman to study abroad. At fifteen she entered Radcliffe College at Harvard University. Before her departure, her father gave her a Koran and much advice, fearing that her initiation into the world of democracy would involve a great cultural shock. In fact she adapted quite well, but her studies in comparative politics were to influence her more than the new freedom in her personal life. Her father's letters, sharing his progressive vision of world events, also played a part in the formation of Benazir's world view.

In 1971, war broke out between India and Bhutto's West Pakistan over the struggle for independence by East Pakistan, now Bangladesh. Bhutto was to appear before the United Nations Security Council and asked his daughter to join him in New York, where she received her first real lesson in politics: Bhutto, refusing to be "a party to surrender," walked out of the council chamber to protest what he deemed an unfair peace proposal. Not many days later, he became leader of Pakistan. Benazir was at his side when he signed a peace treaty with Indira Gandhi of India. From then on, Benazir accompanied him on his travels.

Benazir entered Oxford in 1973 to complete her studies. As a fledgling orator at the prestigious Oxford Union, she followed in the footsteps of many great political leaders. In the spring of 1977 she became the first non-British citizen to be elected the union's president.

She returned to Pakistan early that summer to witness her country's accelerating political drama. On July 5, 1977, Bhutto was overthrown and imprisoned by General Zia Ul-Haq. Three weeks later, popular pressure brought about his release, for despite occasional corruption and demagoguery, Bhutto's efforts at reform were much appreciated by his countrymen.

But Zia soon had Bhutto arrested again. For Benazir and for Begum Nusrat, who had assumed the leadership of Bhutto's political party, the drama became a nightmare; they were placed

Despite the rise of Islamic fundamentalism, Benazir managed to become not only the first modern woman to head a Muslim country, but the first to give birth to a child while prime minister.

under house arrest, which was to last seven years. And during this ordeal, when Benazir was twenty-five years old, her father was condemned to death. She had half an hour, as she later recalled, to say goodbye to the person she had loved most in her life, and she forbade herself to cry, to break down, to make her father's ordeal more difficult. The next morning, on April 4, 1979, Zulfikar Ali Bhutto was hanged. Benazir resolved to take over his struggle for Pakistan's future.

International pressure won her permission to leave the country in 1984. She went to London, where she denounced Zia's regime and became the leader of the Pakistani opposition in exile. After Zia was finally forced to end martial law and allow opposing political parties again, Benazir returned triumphantly to Pakistan in May 1986. A massive crowd welcomed her with garlands of flowers. "Zia out!" she promised them.

Benazir organized. She campaigned throughout the country, weakening Zia's power. Meanwhile, to be a "whole" woman in the eyes of her society, she had to marry — their way. Yielding to family pressure, she accepted the proposal of Asif Ali Zardari, a successful businessman she had never met. It was a politically advantageous match. The wedding, which Benazir intended to be simple and dignified, became a media event, a grand spectacle projected onto a video screen for the public, confined behind barricades.

The birth of her first child fell in the middle of her campaign for the general elections called after Zia's sudden and mysterious death in an airplane crash. On November 17, 1988, her party won 39 percent of the vote and the next month she was sworn in as prime minister of Pakistan.

Promoting national unity and reconciliation in a country scarred by ethnic confrontation, Benazir attempted to handle the army and the aristocracy with kid gloves. Her great enemy remained the radical Islamic faction. The army became increasingly critical of her government. Rumors began circulating that she would be dismissed and new elections called. In the summer of 1990 it came to pass, and Benazir Bhutto's political future was cast into uncertainty.

It is tempting to liken her to Corazon Aquino or Indira Gandhi. Benazir herself prefers comparison with John F. Kennedy: both young, both idealists, both firm believers in the greatness of their respective lands. Though she has many battles yet to win, her story has already made Benazir Bhutto a legend.

Benazir's beloved father, Zulfikar Ali Bhutto, with his wife (left) and children nine months before he was hanged.

HYPATIA

EGYPT — CA. 365-416

Mathematician and philosopher, Hypatia was the recognized head of the Neoplatonist school of philosophy in Alexandria, whose great library is depicted in this 1880 Hungarian engraving.

She was called "the beloved of the gods." The intelligence of Hypatia, mathematician and philosopher, enlightened Alexandria and her beauty adorned the city. She was a wise, modest, tolerant woman . . . who was murdered by fanatics.

Hypatia was the daughter of Theon, also a mathematician, who taught at the renowned Mouseion, the great research institute and center of learning at Alexandria. He had revised Euclid's *Elements* and *Optics* and had written a commentary on Ptolemy's *Almagest*. Theon quickly realized that his daughter was exceptionally intelligent. He made sure she received the finest education available at a period when most women were barely literate. She was instructed in mathematics, drawing, plane geometry and trigonometry, astronomy, and philosophy. Hypatia soon surpassed both her father and her teacher, Philostorgius, in the breadth of her knowledge and the depth of her wisdom.

She preferred geometry of all the branches of mathematics, but also pursued other subjects. Carrying on the work begun by her father, she wrote commentaries on mathematical and scientific treatises. Sadly, these have been lost, with the exception of several fragments on Ptolemy's astronomical canon. Hypatia was highly interested in astronomy and employed her great technical knowledge to assist in the construction of the apparatus that her pupil Synesius would call the astrolabe. Her father arranged for her to enter the Mouseion, where she taught mathematics and philosophy for many years.

Although she gained fame for her scientific teachings, her philosophy courses made her "the divine Hypatia." She was respected and admired for her eloquence and intelligence. Her commentaries on Aristotle and Plato were given full consideration. She became the recognized head of the Neoplatonist school at Alexandria. Neoplatonism, which also had schools in Athens, Rome, and Syria, was not really new but based upon a selective choice and synthesis of the epoch's philosophical theories; it included elements from the Pythagoreans, Plato, Aristotle, the Stoics, and

Hypatia as imagined in a comic strip by Hugo Pratt.

possibly Oriental mysticism. The goal of Neoplatonism was to elevate the soul through steps called hypostases, leading to a state of luminous self-consciousness permitting fusion with the divine. Hypatia, "the brilliant star of divine wisdom," attracted to her courses and to her home many students from all over the world, including politicians, orators, and sages.

She founded her own school where she taught rhetoric, mathematics, geometry, and astronomy in addition to philosophy and utilized both ancient Greek and Oriental music. One of her students was Synesius of Cyrene, who became bishop of Ptolemais in about 410. He wrote of Hypatia, "She possesses exceptional powers of rhetoric, great flexibility in expression, and a unique methodology." She was also said to be versed in white magic and was reputed to have healed the psychosomatic illnesses and heartbreaks of many of her students.

We know almost nothing about Hypatia's private life. She was devoted to her work and never married. This does not mean she did not have lovers. Her famous beauty must have conquered more than one man, among them doubtless some of the greatest men of her time, who numbered themselves among her students.

The tensions between Christians and non-Christians that racked Alexandria in Hypatia's time had a profound effect on her. The early Christians' fanaticism identified learning and science with paganism, which they were determined to eliminate. Fearing for her safety, Hypatia left Alexandria and took refuge in Athens. The philosophers' schools were still active there at the beginning of the fifth century and Hypatia received a warm welcome. Although we do not know the length of her stay in Athens, history does record Hypatia's residence in the city, the fact that she gathered pupils around her in the Acropolis, and her friendships with Themistius and Plutarch, leaders of the Athenian Neoplatonist school.

Hypatia was no longer young when she returned to Alexandria, where she was toasted by the city's intelligentsia as a scholar at the summit of her arts. But hostility toward all things Hellenic gained momentum, reaching a height in 412 with the ascension of Cyril to the patriarchate of Alexandria. Although he was an educated man, Cyril hated everything non-Christian. He wanted to purge the Mouseion, that bastion of Greek philosophy. And he wanted more than religious power. Cyril was soon in conflict with the city's

pagan Roman prefect, Orestes, Hypatia's student and friend. In spite of Orestes' petitions to Byzantium, the Emperor Theodosius II and his sister and co-ruler Pulcharia supported Cyril.

The patriarch passed Hypatia's house one day and saw important public figures among her students. Since Orestes' position made him inaccessible, Cyril decided that Hypatia would be his scapegoat, that he would attack her instead. Taking advantage of the local monks' ignorance, he slandered his victim and the monks spread the rumors — in the name of Christian peace and love. The monks claimed that this female mathematician, philosopher, and astronomer was a witch who should be burned or thrown to the lions.

One morning when she was on her way to visit Orestes, Hypatia was attacked by a crowd of Christians. They dragged her through the streets, beat her to death, tore her body into pieces, then burned the remains. This crime, denounced to Byzantium, went unpunished and signaled Alexandria's decline as an intellectual center. The irony is that, according to Synesius, Hypatia had intended to convert to Christianity, a religion that, like her philosophy, extoled high moral standards and purity of the soul.

SISTER JUANA INES DE LA CRUZ

MEXICO — 1648-1695

Although her only teacher was the silent company of books, Sister Juana Inés de la Cruz — called "The Phoenix of Mexico" and "The Tenth Muse" — left her mark on poetry written in Spanish. She devoted her life to study and to writing, and she dared to transgress the law of silence imposed on women, who were supposed to be ignorant. She was the first woman in Spanish-language literature to speak in her own name and that of her sex.

Juana Inés de Asbaje was born in a hacienda some forty-five miles from Mexico City. She was illegitimate and never met her father; her mother, though from a good Creole family, was illiterate, as was not uncommon at the time. A lonely and inquisitive child, Juana was passionately interested in learning. At six or seven, she knew how to read and write. When she heard of the universities where the sciences were taught, she begged her mother to send her, dressed as a boy. Her mother refused and she had to be content studying alone in her grandfather's library.

Juana set strict rules for herself. Hearing that cheese dulled the mind, she deprived herself of her favorite food. She gave herself a time limit in which to assimilate each new subject. The time was counted by the length of her hair. She willingly sacrificed her hair at the beginning of each subject. If she had not finished when her hair grew back to the same length, she cut it again. For Juana, knowledge was "the most desirable ornament" a head could wish.

When she was still quite young her grandfather died and her mother, who could not afford to keep her, sent her to Mexico City to stay with relatives. In her mid-teens she met the Marquesa de Mancera, wife of the new viceroy. The marquesa was moved not only by Juana's situation but also by her intelligence and the breadth of her knowl-

The thirst for knowledge was considered unacceptable in a woman, but Juana defended her sex: "Frivolity is not exclusively feminine, intelligence is not men's privilege." Portrait in Museo de América, Madrid.

edge. She took the girl as a lady-in-waiting and the two became fast friends, as Juana's poems reveal.

The young woman lived for four years at the palace and attended many public festivals and ceremonies. She may have been courted — in the New Spain of the 17th century, married men were permitted to call on the young girls of the court, as long as these affairs did not bear fruit. It is said that during her time at the palace Juana had a great love, but there is no documentation except her passionate verses.

When Juana was not yet twenty she decided to become a nun. She considered marriage a "total negation" and wished to live with the silence of her books. According to the 20th century Mexican writer Octavio Paz, she had no religious vocation and took this step because she was illegitimate, poor, and inclined to a scholarly life. She tried a Carmelite convent but disliked the strict rules. About two years later she entered the Convent of San Jeronimo.

There her lonely calling was frustrated by the obligations of community life, though she found no fellow students with whom she could talk. Juana accepted her duties in order to be able to devote herself later to study. For several years she was in charge of the convent's accounts and archives, but she refused to take on administrative duties.

A new viceroy was appointed to the colony in 1680. His wife, Maria Luisa de Gonzago, Condessa de Paredes, became intimate with Juana. The ardent verses dedicated to her, considered Juana's best poems, indicate that they were more than friends. Juana lived under the protection of the viceroy and his wife until 1690. By then she had built up some savings, a library of four thousand volumes (said to be the largest in South America), and a collection of musical and scientific instruments as well as jewelry and rare objects. She was commissioned to write eulogies, poems, plays. Her fame spread.

The parlor of Sister Juana Inés de la Cruz became a literary salon where theology was dis-

cussed and poems were read. She devoted herself to the arts and sciences, neglecting the scriptures in order to avoid conflict with the church. She was reproached for her love of secular writing, but what was actually held against her was her thirst for knowledge, considered unacceptable in a woman. For Juana defended her sex: "Frivolity is not exclusively feminine, intelligence is not men's privilege." The censure grew with Juana's fame, which soon reached Europe. Thanks to the friendship of the viceroy and his wife, however, the critics could not touch her.

Juana's most audacious act eventually caused her downfall: she wrote a letter criticizing a sermon by Father Antonio de Vieyra, a celebrated Brazilian Jesuit who was confessor to the King of Portugal and Christina of Sweden. The bishop of Puebla published this letter, prefacing it with an epistle of his own, written under the pseudonym Sister Filotea de la Cruz. He praised Juana but at the same time reproached her for not devoting herself to "sacred matters" and affirmed that a mere woman should not discuss certain topics with such assurance and daring. His intention was to force Juana to retract her letter.

The exchange created a stir. Juana soon responded by publishing her "Repuesta a Sor Filotea" (Reply to Sister Filotea), in which she told of her studies and claimed her right and the right of all women to knowledge. This was going too far. Her confessor begged her to stop writing. She refused. The bishop of Puebla withdrew all support of her and the archbishop of Mexico, who despised her, seized his opportunity.

By that time the viceroy had lost much of his influence because of famine, epidemics, popular uprisings, and repressive measures, and the church had gained in strength. Juana was on her own, no longer protected. After two years of fighting back, fear brought her to humble herself and seek refuge with her confessor. She was reconciled with the ecclesiastical hierarchy, renounced her studies, disposed of her library and her collections, and began a life of repentance. She died nursing her sister nuns during an epidemic.

MARIE CURIE

POLAND 1867 — FRANCE 1934

"Marie Curie is, among all famous individuals, the only one whom glory has not corrupted," said her friend Albert Einstein. Twice awarded the Nobel Prize for her research on radioactivity, she always remained natural, generous, ingenuous, and diligent in her work.

She was born Manya Sklodowska in an old quarter of Warsaw, the last of five children. The family was not rich, but they were close. Manya's father taught physics and mathematics, while her mother kept a boarding house for young girls.

Manya was eleven years old when her mother died of tuberculosis; one of her sisters had already succumbed to the disease. Bronia, the eldest sister, kept house, while their father tried to keep the family from despair. His long conversations with his children about his work impassioned Manya, as did her studies in physics.

Brilliant at elementary school, she went on to a Russian high school, where her sense of patriotism ripened. At sixteen she was finished with high school and could speak and read Polish, Russian, German, and French. The university was closed to girls, but this did not stop Manya. She secretly attended the nationalist "free university," where volunteer professors taught — and risked prison by doing so. In turn, she gave lessons to workers. This was a happy, carefree time for her.

But she soon had to find paid work, to help finance Bronia's medical studies in Paris. Manya became a governess, and was a favorite with the second family she worked for — until the day the eldest son announced his wish to marry her. When Bronia finished her studies and married, she invited her sister to join her in Paris. In 1891, the newly arrived young Polish girl enrolled at the Sorbonne under the name Marie Sklodowska. She could scarcely believe her good fortune.

Two years later, she had earned her degree in physics, placing first in her class; a year after that she had a degree in mathematics as well, placing second. In the meantime, she had met Pierre Curie, already a well-known physicist; soon he asked her to marry him. In July 1895 she wed the man she would later describe in these words: "He was as

A gentle, unassuming woman, and a genius: Marie Curie twice received the Nobel Prize.

much as, and more than, I could have dreamed of when we were first married." They lived, loved, and worked together.

In 1896, Marie received top marks in the the rigorous entrance examination for teaching posts in the French secondary schools. After giving birth to a daughter, Irène, she continued her research and worked toward her doctorate. Following up on Henri Becquerel's recent discovery of what Marie later called "radioactivity," working in barely adequate facilities, and eventually joined in the effort by Pierre, she discovered radium and presented her findings to the Academy of Sciences in Paris on December 26, 1898.

After publishing a number of articles on radium, firmly establishing their professional reputations, the Curies could at last live more comfortably. Pierre obtained a post as a lecturer at the Sorbonne, while Marie received a similar appointment in Sèvres, a Paris suburb, at the Ecole Normale (teacher training college) for girls in 1900. She continued working with radium, seeking a chemically pure metal or salt that would enable her to measure the atomic mass of the newfound element. She recorded her results in her doctoral thesis in 1903. Later that year, at the age of thirty-six, she received the Nobel Prize for physics along with her husband and Becquerel. She was the first woman so honored.

The Curies' glory and fame did not go to their heads; they preferred familial tranquility to public adulation. Pierre was awarded a chair at the Sorbonne, and Marie meanwhile gave birth to their second daughter, Eve.

Tragedy struck on April 19, 1906: Pierre Curie was run over by a truck. His inconsolable widow began writing to him in a private journal: "My Pierre, I think of you endlessly, my head is bursting with it and I am losing my mind. I cannot comprehend that I have to live without you, without smiling at the sweet companion of my life."

Marie refused the government's offered pension, but agreed to take over her husband's post; she was the first woman to teach at the Sorbonne. Without discussion, she took up where Pierre had

Marie Curie in 1923, in her laboratory, where she welcomed scientists from all over the world.

UNE NOUVELLE DÉCOUVERTE. — LE RADIUM
M. ET Mme CURIE DANS LEUR LABORATOIRE

The Curies' research on radioactivity won them fame.

left off in his courses. While her daughters grew up, Marie continued her research.

In 1910 she published a treatise on radioactivity. She went on to isolate pure radium, and deposited 21 milligrams of it with the Office of Weights and Measures. There it would serve as the standard for measuring radioactivity. In December 1911, her work earned her a second Nobel Prize, this time in chemistry.

Marie founded Radium Institutes in Warsaw and in Paris. She also founded a hospital, now the Curie Institute, in Paris. During World War I, she abandoned her research to devote herself to the wounded by equipping military hospitals and ambulances with radiology equipment.

In the remaining years of her life, Marie traveled extensively and welcomed researchers from all over the world to her Paris laboratories. There her daughter and son-in-law, Irène and Frédéric Joliot-Curie, discovered artificial radioactivity in 1934. For this they, too, were awarded a Nobel Prize. The year of their discovery, Marie Curie died of leukemia, caused by her prolonged exposure to radiation.

LOU ANDREAS-SALOME

RUSSIA 1861 — GERMANY 1937

The exceptionally intelligent Lou Andreas-Salomé frequented intellectual and artistic circles.
She was considered a seductress, and doubtless was — in spite of herself.

Lou Andreas-Salomé lived in perfect harmony with her motto: "Dare everything . . . Need nothing." With her strong personality, her intelligence, and her desire to live her own life, she was much more than a muse to some of the great men of her day.

Gustav von Salomé, a general in the Russian army, was nearly sixty when his wife became pregnant for the sixth time. He already had five sons and was delighted to have a daughter at last. Protected by her father's love, Louise grew up in a masculine world. Although a member of high society, she didn't care about such things but lived in another world, her own, where God held a prominent place. She was not interested in the views of her own circle, either, but did follow the political events and agitation sweeping Russia.

At seventeen, in full rebellion against the Orthodox Church, she met Hendrik Gillot, minister to the Dutch embassy at Saint Petersburg. The encounter changed her life. He introduced her to Western social sciences, literature, and culture. These influences profoundly affected the young girl, who worshiped her teacher like a god and devoured the books he gave her.

The inevitable occurred: Gillot fell in love with his student. She was outraged by his advances and refused to have anything to do with a man of forty-three who had a wife and two children. Louise decided to leave Saint Petersburg and study at the University of Zurich, where women were admitted. Her father had recently died, so her mother agreed to accompany her. The day before she left, Gillot proposed to her, calling her "Lou." Though she refused him, she kept the nickname for the rest of her life, a souvenir of her first disillusionment. Gillot, victim of his love for a girl who was a femme fatale in spite of herself, was the first in a long list.

One of her professors in Zurich declared to Lou's mother: "Your daughter is really an exceptional woman. . . . She is a diamond." Lou took courses in philosophy, theology, and art history and excelled in her studies. She was admired and held in awe for her intelligence and independence.

Reconstruction of a well-known photograph of Lou, Friedrich Nietzsche and Paul Rée for a film.

poet Rainer Maria Rilke, some fourteen years her junior, and became his mistress, mother, sister, and idol. He wrote to her: "You alone are real. We are brother and sister, but as in the far past, before marriage between brother and sister became sacrilege."

Accompanied by Lou's "unofficial" husband, they visited Russia, where Lou met the novelist Leo Tolstoy. She and Rilke later took another trip to Russia but by then Lou was becoming tired of him. She wrote: "I am eternally faithful to memories. I shall never be faithful to men." Their love affair ended after three years but they remained good friends. Rilke declared to his doctors on his death bed: "Lou, who knows everything, doubtless knows a remedy for my pain."

Lou Andreas-Salomé was one of the first

The original photo, a souvenir of the triangular friendship that ended when Nietzsche wanted to marry Lou.

When Lou drove herself to a state of mental exhaustion, the doctors counseled her mother to take her south.

The two women arrived in Rome in January 1882. Three months later Lou met Paul Rée, a philosopher, who introduced her to Friedrich Nietzsche. The German philosopher impressed Lou, who found him alternately attractive and repulsive. She dreamed of sharing an apartment with her two philosopher friends while her mother dreamed solely of taking her back to Russia.

Lou Salomé, Friedrich Nietzsche, and Paul Rée became an inseparable "Trinity" in spite of a temporary disagreement between Lou and Nietzsche over her friendship with the composer Richard Wagner, who had no use for philosophy. Lou's anticonformist character delighted in this triangular friendship based on intellectual understanding, but she refused to enter into the game of passion when both men declared their love for her. She declined Nietzsche's offer of marriage and, although he later declared otherwise, did not have relations with him. In the end Nietzsche left his two friends, and he never forgave Lou.

Lou cohabited fraternally with Paul Rée in Berlin, surrounded by friends and work. At twenty-three, she wrote *Im Kampf um Gott* (A Struggle for God). Three years later, in 1887, she left Rée to marry a noted Orientalist, Friedrich Andreas, who taught Persian and Turkish. She found a father figure in this man who was fifteen years her senior, but she refused to find in him a lover. She never shared his bed and remained totally independent.

At the age of thirty-one, Lou began to write seriously. In ten years she published ten books and nearly fifty articles, which ensured her literary fame. She traveled and visited with European artists, and her reputation as a seductress grew. Yet she had not taken her first lover — in all likelihood Doctor Friedrich Pineles — until she was over thirty. Younger than she, Pineles played the role of her "unofficial" husband for twelve years in Vienna. During this period, Lou met the

women to practice psychotherapy. She met Sigmund Freud at Weimar in 1911 at an international gathering of psychoanalysts and asked to study with him. She attended his courses in Vienna and Freud grew attached to this intelligent woman, who became his confidante.

Lou wrote and studied to the end, when she found herself alone and widowed in her house at Hainberg, Germany. She confided in her memoirs: "If I let my thoughts wander, I don't find anyone. The best, after all, is death."

RACHEL CARSON
UNITED STATES — 1907-1964

Rachel Carson's *Silent Spring* helped form the foundation of the environmental movement. Thanks to this gifted marine biologist, the world came to realize that nature could die, leaving behind nothing but devastation and silence.

Rachel Louise Carson was born on May 27, 1907, in Springfield, Pennsylvania, the daughter of Robert Warden Carson and Maria Frazier McLean. From earliest childhood, her mother fostered in Rachel a profound love of nature. In 1929 she received her bachelor's degree from the Pennsylvania College for Women (now Chatham College), and three years later earned her master's from Johns Hopkins University.

Rachel's postgraduate research at the Woods Hole Marine Biology Laboratory in Massachusetts was the beginning of a long association with that institution. And as editor-in-chief for the U.S. Fish and Wildlife service she focused her energy on bringing science to the public. In 1951 she published *The Sea Around Us*, which received the National Book Award for that year and was eventually translated into more than thirty languages. The book marked the beginning of the most intense period of Rachel's career. It eventually took its place in a trilogy with *Under the Sea Wind*, which had been published in 1941, and *The Edge of the Sea*, in 1955.

This was the postwar period, when no one worried much about the consequences of the spectacular expansion of modern technology. On the contrary, the general mood was optimistic and confident: technological progress had provided solutions to natural catastrophes and had increased personal comfort, production, and profits. Humankind was perceived as having truly achieved dominion over nature. During the 1940s

A lover of nature and a gifted scientist, Rachel Carson also devoted herself to bringing science to the public and thereby helped to found the environmental movement.

Silent Spring awoke the world to the devastation being caused by modern "progress."

spraying intended to kill only mosquitoes, Rachel decided to write again — not an article this time, but a book on the theme of toxic chemicals, their dangers, and the need for regulation. *Silent Spring*, published in 1962, was a best seller.

The book tells a somber tale about Earth's environmental situation and the potential for future devastation, giving detailed examples. *Silent Spring* awakened America's collective consciousness, which had been numbed by prosperity and progress. President John F. Kennedy announced the formation of a committee to study the effects of chemicals on the environment.

Silent Spring's success and the government's reaction encouraged the biologist to begin another book. However, it remained unfinished when Rachel Carson died of cancer in 1964 in Silver Spring, Maryland.

Today, when the debate on the environment is one of the dominant public and political issues, it seems strange to think it was a mere curiosity when first considered less than thirty years ago. Whatever the Earth's future holds, it owes a debt of gratitude to Rachel Carson, whose dogged de-

fense of nature in the face of public indifference and scepticism put the human race on the road to environmental responsibility.

Rachel used her microscope and pen to explode the complacency of international industry.

and '50s, industrial expansion, pollution, an increasing amount of waste — some of it toxic — and the possible atmospheric impact of nuclear weapons were irrelevant details in the daily life of the average person.

Only a biologist's sensitive perception could begin to detect the destruction that "progress" was wreaking on the environment. Rachel Carson would play a critical role in alerting the public to such danger, but it would take time. In the 1940s the introduction of DDT had greatly alarmed her. But in those days, the articles she published in the national press pointing out the chemical's hazards were considered unacceptable criticism of what was looked upon as a panacea.

When a bird reserve belonging to one of her friends was destroyed within hours by a DDT

Rachel Carson's legacy was an environmentally aware public that would pressure politicians to deal with the consequences of industrial pollution.

ALEXANDRA DAVID-NEEL

FRANCE — 1868-1969

In 1924 a foreign woman entered the forbidden city of Lhassa for the first time.
She was Alexandra David-Neel, who had undertaken
the long journey on foot, disguised as a beggar.

"Choose and follow a star," Alexandra David-Neel once said. This superwoman's star led her to the summit of the Earth, where she became known as "the Lamp of Wisdom."

Born in Saint-Mandé, France, she came from the middle class. She adored her free-thinking father as much as she detested her narrow-minded mother. At the age of five, she started to run away from home; by adolescence this had become a passion that would last all her life. Her love for travel began when her father gave his little daughter an atlas. He said at the time: "My daughter has a white skin, but her soul is yellow." She became a Protestant, like her father, and soon felt a mystical calling that made her dream of becoming a missionary.

At the age of eighteen, Alexandra was absorbed in studying philosophy and music. At twenty she wrote her first essay, *Pour la vie* (For Life), which was published ten years later, in 1898. In this work, Alexandra viewed herself as "a free soul, scornful of joy and sorrow, impervious to worldly desires." It is not surprising, then, that her introduction to the Theosophical Society during a visit to London changed the course of her life. She immersed herself in the treatises of Raja Yoga, the Vedic philosophical writings called the Upanishads, and that other great Hindu devotional work, the Bhagavad Gita. She learned Sanskrit, haunted the Guimet collection of Asian art in Paris, and studied Buddhism.

With a legacy from her godmother Alexandra took her first trip to Asia. She was shocked by the "wretched yellow figures" in Sri Lanka but was enthusiastic about India, "the country of many marvels." She traveled for eighteen months, during which she wrote many articles, before running out of money and returning to Europe.

For a time she tried a career as an opera singer, under the stage name Alexandra Myriel. This took her as far as Hanoi and Athens, but she could not find work in Paris. In July 1900, in Tunisia, she met a beguiling man named Philippe Neel. Four years later this intellectual woman and her sensualist lover were married. It was a stormy, almost unnatural union, for their characters were diametrically opposed and they could truly love only from afar.

Philippe became the "best of husbands" when, in 1911, he encouraged his wife to travel. Alexandra had embarked upon a busy career of writing, teaching, and lecturing. She was being criticized for intellectual snobbery even as she decided to renounce everything to broaden her knowledge of Asia's religions and philosophies, thanks to the financial support of her husband. Philippe would not see her again for fourteen years.

She first returned to Sri Lanka, then went to Calcutta, where she studied the tenets of Hindu-

Alexandra at her home in Digne, France, where she lived in later life when not traveling.

ism. She resisted the call of Siva, however, preferring Buddhism with its ocher robe and orange stole that protect the believer from the agitation to which all human flesh is prey. She left Calcutta for Darjeeling, where she began work on *L'Inde mystique* (Mystical India), then went to the small Himalayan state of Sikkim. There she became friends with the crown prince, Sidkéong, and met the Dalai Lama and other Himalayan religious leaders. Throughout this period of travel and spiritual evolution, Alexandra faithfully wrote to Philippe and sent articles to French newspapers. By 1913 Alexandra's Buddhist pilgrimage had led

her to Banaras, in northern India, when Crown Prince Sidkéong, whose father was dying, sent for her. She returned to Sikkim and received a royal welcome. On this visit she met a fourteen-year-old boy, Yongden, who would abandon his family and inheritance to follow her for the next forty years as her adopted son.

After an unsuccessful attempt to explore Tibet, Alexandra and Yongden traveled to Japan, Korea, and China. However, she had not abandoned her plan to visit Lhassa, the holy city and capital of Tibet. Following many months of hardship and danger, traveling on foot disguised as a beggar, she finally passed through the doors of the forbidden city. "During a period of two months, I moved about the Tibetan Rome, visited the temples and walked upon the highest terraces of the Potala Palace without anyone suspecting that a foreign woman had gazed on the forbidden city for the first time since the world was created," she wrote in her best-known work, *Voyage d'une Parisienne à Lhassa.*

When she returned to Europe, Alexandra received an enthusiastic welcome. She took up residence in Digne, France, but at the age of sixty-eight once again set out for China, accompanied by the faithful Yongden, and did not return for some ten years. Following the death of her adoptive son, Alexandra continued to write, tirelessly, remaining in her chair even for the four or five hours a night when she slept.

The explorer died peacefully at the age of one hundred and one. An associate, Madeleine Peyronnet, whom Alexandra called "the Tortoise," wrote frankly of the good and bad sides of Alexandra's personality: "I will say that you were extraordinarily intelligent, because that is true. And I will add that you had an outlook as vast as all the galaxies combined. . . . And I will also say that Alexandra David-Neel was an ocean of egotism and a Himalaya of despotism."

On February 28, 1973, "the Tortoise" scattered the ashes of Alexandra and her adopted son, Yongden, in the Ganges River at Banaras.

At the time of her visit, Tibet was a world unknown.
Festival in a Tibetan monastery, engraving by L. Sabatier, ca. 1990.

SIMONE DE BEAUVOIR

FRANCE — 1908-1986

Simone de Beauvoir helped give birth to modern feminism, and withstood violent criticism for encouraging women to take control of their own lives and end the slavery of traditional family roles.

"One is not born, but rather becomes, a woman," Simone de Beauvoir wrote in *The Second Sex*, the book considered the foundation of the modern feminist movement. As a writer and philosopher, de Beauvoir made freedom a way of thought and a way of life. And with Jean-Paul Sartre, freedom became a new way of love.

Simone de Beauvoir grew up in the Montparnasse district of Paris. Her eccentric, perpetually broke father had a law degree but never practiced because he considered work demeaning. Her mother played the piano while Simone's father recited poetry or read dramatically from his favorite plays. The family's unorthodox lifestyle was the source of neighborhood gossip.

At the age of five, Simone, who could already read, write, and recite poetry, was enrolled at the first of a succession of private schools. At home, her mother supervised her studies and taught her English, while her father instilled in her a love for literature and the idea that to be a writer was the most desirable of ambitions. During World War I the family was forced to economize, and it became a habit. Ever afterward, Simone remained convinced that the waste of anything, including one's self, was to be avoided.

The de Beauvoir family had property in the Limousin region, and there, during the summers, Simone walked for hours on end and read in secret the works of Honoré de Balzac, Colette, and Pierre Loti. She became insolent and rebellious, realized that she was an atheist, and began to write. At fifteen she decided she wanted to become "a famous writer."

At the Sorbonne, Simone worked on degrees in literature and philosophy; to finance her studies she taught — a career that would last until her first novel was published during World War II. A brilliant student, she devoured works by avant-garde writers, awed her friends, and frequented Montparnasse cafés with members of the young intelligentsia, such as Simone Weil and Jean-Paul Sartre. With her philosophy degree completed, she began studying for the *agrégation*, the highest-level competitive examination for teachers. At age twenty-one, Simone de Beauvoir was the youngest in her graduating class. Rigorous, precise, demanding, and technical, the budding philosopher was nicknamed "the Beaver." She won second place in the *agrégation*; Sartre took first. In him, Simone knew she had found the soul mate she had long imagined.

De Beauvoir and Sartre shared each other's private lives without living together; this was essential to their relationship: in every aspect it was intended to be transparently honest, stripped of all constraints. Within it, each would gain the experience necessary to grow as a writer. But each perceived, and satisfied, the need for other lovers.

Olga Kosakiewicz, a student of Simone's, entered their life to become the third corner of a triangle. The story of this relationship would later provide the framework for *She Came to Stay*, Simone's first novel, with its existential theme of the Other. In 1939 de Beauvoir relinquished her individualism to be caught up in solidarity. She published novels, narratives, and essays, as well as articles for *Combat*, the Resistance newspaper that Albert Camus edited.

In the latter half of the 1940s, the existentialist philosophy — based on human freedom and responsibility — reached its peak and became a way of life for the young intellectuals who haunted the subterranean bars of the Saint Germain quarter on Paris' Left Bank. Sartre and de Beauvoir initiated the movement and, with Camus, were its most widely read authors. In 1947, "the Beaver" left for the United States to do a series of tours. There she met a new love, the writer Nelson Algren. She included an account of their relationship in *The Mandarins*, which won the prestigious Goncourt literary prize in 1954.

In 1949 Simone published *The Second Sex*, the two-volume landmark work in which she exhorted women to take control of their lives and their freedom, to end the slavery of the traditional

Symbols of the intellectual's commitment to society, de Beauvoir and Jean-Paul Sartre, side-by-side, tell the world of their support for the French student rebellion of May 1968.

family. The book was violently criticized and the international stir caused by the book made her famous.

Sartre was also producing prolifically. The two traveled widely together, taking stands on political issues, campaigning for Algeria's independence from France, supporting Maoism and Soviet Communism, participating in the student upheavals of May 1968 in Paris. They represented the idea of "committed literature" and a new form of couple, ignoring conventional limits. In her letters to Sartre, de Beauvoir, who always addressed him with the formal *vous*, detailed everything, including her affairs with men and women.

Her last work, *La Cérémonie des adieux*, recounts Sartre's death in 1980 with deeply moving sincerity. Six years later, almost to the day, Simone herself died. The posthumous publication of her letters to Sartre and her war journal disclosed ambiguities in her private life and raised debate about her. Nevertheless, the image of Simone de Beauvoir's face, framed in a headband, will remain a symbol of women's freedom.

By 1947 Simone had proven herself as a novelist, political essayist, and leader of the existentialist movement.

BIBILIOGRAPHY

The First Woman

Lucy:
Johanson, Donald: *Lucy, une jeune femme de 3,500,000 ans*, Laffont, Paris, 1983.

The Myths of Creation

Gaia:
Campbell, Joseph: *Occidental mythology: The Masks of God*, Penguin Books, New York, 1976.
Graves, Robert: *The Greek Myths*, Penguin Books, London, 1979.
Hesiod: *La Teogonia*, Editorial Iberia, Barcelona, 1964.
Rose, H.J.: *Mitologia griega*, Labor, Barcelona, 1973.

Ishtar:
Contenau, G.: *Le Déluge babylonien*, Payot, Paris, 1952.
Poema de Gilgamesh, Editora Nacional, Madrid, 1980.

Lilith:
Bril, Jacques: *Lilith*, Payot, Paris, 1984.
Markale, Jean: *La Femme celte*, Payot, Paris, 1982.

Eve:
Philips, John: *Eve, The History of an Idea*, Harper and Row, San Francisco, 1984.

Hine-Nui-Te-Po:
Grimal, Pierre, ed.: *Mythologie des peuples lointains ou barbares*, Larousse, Paris, 1963.
Johansen, J. Prytz: *The Maori and His Religion and Its Nonritualistic Aspects*, Copenhagen, 1954.

Amaterasu:
Herbert, Jean: *La Cosmogonie japonaise*, Dervy, Paris, 1977.
Piggot, J. : *Japanese Mythology*, P. Hamlyn, Toronto, 1969.

Ixquic:
El libro de los libros de Chilam Balam, Fondo de Cultura Economica, Mexico City, 1979.
Girard, R.: *Esotérisme du Popol Vuh*, Maisonneuve, Paris, 1960.
Girard, Raphaël: *Le Popol Vuh*, Payot, Paris, 1972.
Popul Vuh, antiguas leyendas del Quiché, Ediciones Oasis, Mexico City, 1977.

Sedna:
Savard, Rémi: *Mythologie esquimaude*, Université Laval, Quebec, 1966.
Grimal, Pierre, ed.: *Mythologies des peuples lointains ou barbares*, Larousse, Paris, 1963.

Dewa Sri:
Porée-Maspero, Eveline: *Etudes sur les rites agraires au Cambodge*, Mouton et Cie, Paris, The Hague, 1962.
Sukanda, Vivianne: *Le triomphe de Sri en pays soundanais*, Ecole française d'Extrême-Orient, Paris, 1977.

Pandora:
Panofsky, Dora and Erwin: *Pandora's Box*, Routledge and Kegan Paul Ltd., London, 1956.
Panofsky, D. and E.: *The Changing Aspects of a Mythical Symbol*, Routledge and Kegan Paul Ltd., London, 1956.

The Epic Heroines

Sita:
Bonnefoy, Yves, ed.: *Dictionnaire des Mythologies*, Flammarion, Paris, 1981.
Le Ramayana, Dervy-Livres, Paris, 1985.

Helen of Troy:
Homer: *L'Illiade*, Gallimard, La Pléiade, Paris, 1968.
Valmont, Frédéric: *La Belle Hélène*, Gallimard, Paris, 1958.

Penelope:
Homer: *L'Odyssée*, Gallimard, La Pléiade, Paris, 1968.
Peyrefitte, A. and R.: *Le Mythe de Pénélope*, Gallimard, Paris, 1949.

Medea:
Apollonios of Rhodes: *The Voyage of Argos* (Book III), Penguin Books, London, 1979.
Euripides: *Medea*, Cambridge University Press, Cambridge, 1939.
Mallinger, Léon: *Etude de littérature comparée*, Slatkine Reprints, Geneva, 1971.

Shirin:
Nizami: *Le Roman de Chosroes et Chirin*, Maisonneuve, Paris, 1970.

La Cava Florinda:
Irving, Washington: *Leyendas de la conquista de Espana*, Miguel Sanchez, Granada, 1974.
Menendez Pidal, Ramón: *Espana y su Historia*, Minotauro, Madrid, 1957.
Menendez Pidal, Ramón: *Flor nueva de romances viejos*, Espasa-Calpe, Madrid, 1973.

Isolde:
Béroul: *Le Roman de Tristan*, Ernest Muret, Paris, 1903.
De Rougemont, Denis: *L'Amour et l'Occident*, Plon, Paris, 1972.

The Founders

The Queen of Sheba:
Deribeau, Maurice and Paulette: *Au pays de la reine de Saba*, France-Empire, Paris, 1977.
Hemmert, D., and Roudène, A.: *"La reine de Saba,"* in: *Les Secrets des amours célèbres*, Rombaldi, Paris, 1973.
Perol, Huguette: *Contes et Légendes d'Ethiopie*, F. Nathan, Paris, 1966.

Semiramis:
Grimal, Pîerre, ed.: *Contes et Légendes de Babylone et de Perse*, F. Nathan, Paris, 1962.
Nuñez Alonso, Alejandro: *Sol de Babilonia*, Planeta, Madrid, 1967.

Dido:
Defrasne, Jean: *Récits de l'histoire de Carthage*, F. Nathan, Paris, 1972.
Virgil: *L'Enéide*, Flammarion, Paris, 1965.

Queen Pokou:
Delafosse, Maurice: *Essai de manuel de langue agni*, Librairie africaine et coloniale, Paris, 1901.
Loucou, Jean-Noël: *La Reine Pokou: fondatrice du royaume Baoulé*, ABC, Paris, 1977.

Marianne:
Agulhon, Maurice: *Marianne au combat*, Flammarion, Paris, 1979.
Bonheur, Gaston: *La République nous appelle*, Laffont, Paris, 1965.

The Intercessors

The Pythia:
Flacière, R.: *Devins et oracles grecs*, PUF, Paris, 1972.
Homer: *Himnos Homéricos*, Gredos, Madrid, 1978.
Roux, G.: *Delphes, son oracle et ses dieux*, Les Belles Lettres, Paris, 1976.

The Virgin Mary:
Warner, Marina: *Alone of All Her Sex*, Weidenfeld and Nicolson, London, 1976.

Maria Lionza:
Pollack-Eltz, Angelina: *Maria Lionza: Mito y Culto Venezolano*, Univ. Catolica Andrés Bello, Caracas, 1985.

Ezili:
Métraux, Alfred: *Le Vaudou haîtien*, Gallimard, Paris, 1977.

The Sirens

Mélusine:
Arras, Jean: *Melusina o la noble de lusignan*, Siruela, Madrid, 1987.
Bulteau, Michel: *Mythologie des filles des eaux*, Editions du Rocher, Paris, 1982.
Markale, Jean: *Mélusine ou l'androgyne*, Retz, Paris, 1983.

The Lorelei:
Derche, Roland: *"Lorelei,"* in : *Quatre mythes poétiques*, Société d'Edition d'Enseignement, Paris, 1962.

Fantasies and Fictions

Cinderella:
Bettelheim, Bruno: *Psychanalyse des contes de fées*, Laffont, Paris, 1976.
Grimm, J. and W.: *"Cendrillon,"* in : *Contes de l'enfance et du foyer*, Gallimard, La Pléiade, Paris, 1963.
Perrault, Charles: *"Cendrillon,"* in *Les Contes*, Michel de l'Ormeraie, Paris, 1971.
Von Franz, Marie-Louise: *La femme dans les contes de fées*, La Fontaine de la Pierre, Paris, 1984.

Sheherazade:
Dehoi, Enver: *L'Erotisme des 1001 Nuits*, Jean-Jacques Pauvert, Paris, 1960.
Lahy-Hollebecque, M.: *Le Féminisme de Shéhérazade*, Radot, Paris, 1927.
Mardrus, Charles, trans.: *Les mille et une nuits*, Laffont, Paris, 1986.

Juliet:
Shakespeare, William: *Roméo et Juliette*, Aubier, Paris, 1971.

The Little Mermaid:
Andersen, Hans Christian: *"La Petite Sirène"*, in: *Les Contes*, Michel de l'Ormeraie, Paris, 1971.

Jan, Isabelle: *Andersen et ses contes*, Aubier-Montaigne, Paris, 1977. (In cooperation with the Carlsberg Foundation, Copenhagen).

Carmen:
Mérimée, Prosper: *"Carmen,"* in: *Romans et nouvelles* (Vol. II), Garnier Fréres, Paris, 1967.

Alice:
Carroll, Lewis: *De l'autre côté du miroir, et ce qu'Alice y trouva*, Aubier-Flammarion, Paris, 1971.
Carroll, L.: *Les aventures d'Alice au pays des Merveilles*, Aubier-Flammarion, Paris, 1970.
Carroll, L.: *Lettres à ses amies-enfants*, Aubier-Flammarion, Paris, 1977.

The Royal Favorites

Roxelana:
Rossier, Edmond: *Roxelane la Rieuse*, in: *Sur les degrés du trone*, Payot, Lausanne, 1940.
Sperco, Willy: *Roxelane, épouse de Suleyman le Magnifique*, Nouvelles Editions Latines, Paris, 1972.

Madame de Pompadour:
De Goncourt, Edmond and Gilles: *Madame de Pompadour*, Olivier Orban, Paris, 1982.
Levron, Jacques: *Madame de Pompadour: l'amour et la politique*, Perrin, Paris, 1975.

Aimée Dubucq de Riverie:
Blanch, Lesley: *The Wilder Shores of Love*, Abacus, London, 1984.
Chase-Riboud, Barbara: *La Grande Sultane*, Succés du livre/Ed. de la Seine, Paris, 1990.
Prince Michael of Greece: *La Nuit du Sérail*, Paris, 1982.

Micaela Villegas:
Palma, Ricardo: *Traditions péruviennes*, Institut de coopération intellectuelle, Paris, 1938.
Sanchez, Luis Alberto: *La Perricholi*, Universitad Nacional Mayor de San Marcos, Lima, 1963.

Wallis Warfield:
Higham, Charles: *La Scandaleuse duchesse de Windsor*, J.C. Lattès, Paris, 1989.

The Inspirations

Phryne:
Hemmert, D., and Roudène, A.: *"Phryne,"* in: *Les Secrets d'amours célèbres*, Rombaldi, Paris, 1973.

Laila:
Djamy: *Medjnoun et Leîla*, trad. Chézy, Imprimerie de Valade, Paris, 1807.

Miquel, André: *Layla, ma raison*, Seuil, Paris, 1984.
Miquel, A.: *Majnûn, l'amour poème*, Sindband, Paris, 1984.
Miquel, A., and Kemp, Percy: *Une histoire d'amour fou: Majnûn et Layla*, Sindbad, Paris, 1984.

Beatrice:
Dante: *La Vita Nuova*, Les Médecins bibliophiles, Paris, 1950.
Dante: *La Divina Comedia*, Hymsa, Barcelona, 1942.
Gilson, Etienne: *Dante et Béatrice*, Librairie philosophique, Paris, 1974.

Mona Lisa:
Hours Median, M.: *Hommage à Leonardo da Vinci*, Edition des Musées nationaux, Paris, 1952.
Ottino della Chiesa, A.: *Tout l'oeuvre peint de Leonardo da Vinci*, Flammarion, Paris, 1968.

Mumtaz Mahal:
Chagtai, Muhammad: *Le Taj-Mahal d'Agra*, Ed. de la Connaissance, Bruxelles, 1938.
Nar'Ayan: *The Taj Mahal*, K.N. Menon, New Delhi, 1960.

The Devout

Aisha:
Dermenghem, Emile, ed.: *"Ibn Abd Rabbih,"* in: *Les plus beaux textes arabes*, Editions d'Aujourd'hui, Paris, 1979.
Le Coran, Maisonneuve et Larose, Paris, 1980.
Tabari: *Les Quatre Premiers Califes*, Sindbad, Paris, 1980.

Pope Joan:
Boureau, Alain: *La Papesse Jeanne*, Aubier, Paris, 1988.
Durrell, Lawrence: *La Papesse Jeanne*, Buchet-Castel, Paris, 1974.
Perrodo-Le Moyne, H.: *Un pape nommée Jeanne*, Le Tréport, 1972.

Saint Teresa of Avila:
Teresa of Avila: *Libro de la vida*, Cátedra, Madrid, 1982.
Werrie, Paul: *Thérèse d'Avila*, Mercure de France, Paris, 1971.

Femmes Fatales

Salome:
Zagona, H.G.: *The Legend of Salome*, E. Droz, Geneva, 1960.

Countess Erzsébet Báthory:
Gould-Baring, S.: *Book of Werewolves*, Smith, Elder and Co., London, 1865.
Penrose, Valentine: *La Comtesse Sanglante*, Gallimard, Paris, 1984.

Mata Hari:
Hemmert, D., and Roudène, A.: *"Mata Hari,"* in *Les Secrets d'amours célèbres*, Rombaldi, Paris, 1974.

The Outlaws

Anne Bonney and Mary Read:
Gosse, Philippe: *Histoire de la piraterie*, Payot, Paris, 1952.
Reuze, André: *Deux femmes pirates*, Editions Colbert, Paris, 1942.
Snow, Edward D. R.: *Pirates and Buccaneers of the Atlantic Coast*, Boston Yankee Publishing Co., 1944.

Bonnie Parker:
Parker, E., and Barrow-Cowan, N.: *La Véritable Histoire de Bonnie et Clyde*, Buchet-Castel, Paris, 1969.

Maria Bonita:
De Queiroz, Pereira: *Os Cangaceiros, les bandits d'honneur brésiliens*, Julliard, Paris, 1968.
Fiorani, Mario: *Cangaceiros, ballade tragique*, Cimarron, Paris, 1979.

The Fighters

Boudicca:
Tacitus: *Vie d'Agricola*, Hachette Classiques, Ed. Pierre Grimal, Paris, 1967.

Al-Kahina:
Cornevin, Robert: *"Ibn Idhari,"* in: *Mémoires de l'Afrique*, Laffont, Paris, 1972.
Khaldoun, Ibn: *"Nuwairi,"* in: *Histoire des Berbères et des dynasties musulmanes de l'Afrique septentrionale*, Paul Guethner, Paris, 1982.

Joan of Arc:
Bourassin, Emmanuel: *Jeanne d'Arc*, Perrin, Paris, 1977.
Pernoud, Régine: *Jeanne d'Arc*, Seuil, Paris, 1981.

La Malinche:
Diaz del Castillo, Bernal: *Historia verdadera de la conquista de la Nueva Espana*, Espasa-Calpe, Buenos Aires, 1955.
Long, Daniel: *Malinche*, ed. Pierre-Jean Oswald, Paris, 1970.
Todorov, Tzvetan: *La Conquéte de l'Amerique*, Seuil, Paris, 1982.

Dona Beatrice:
Baba Kake, Ibrahim: *Dona Béatrice, la Jeanne d'Arc congolaise*, ABC, Paris, 1976.
Cornevin, Robert: *Mémoires de l'Afrique*, Laffont, Paris, 1972.

Creek Mary:
Brown, Dee: *Creek Mary*, Arrow Books Ltd., London, 1981.

Flora Tristan:
Tristan, Flora: *Les Péregrinations d'une paria*, LD/La Découverte, Paris 1983.
Tristan, Flora: *Promenades dans Londres ou l'aristocratie et les prolétaires anglais*, Edition établie par Francois Bédarida, Centre d'histoire du syndicalisme, La Découverte/Maspero, Paris, 1983.

Rosa Luxemburg:
Nettle, J.P.: *La vie et l'oeuvre de Rosa Luxemburg*, Maspero, Paris, 1972.

Margaret Sanger:
Montreynaud, Florence: *Le XXème siècle des femmes*, Nathan, Paris, 1990.
Wallace, I., A., and S.; and Wallechinsky, David: *The Intimate Sex Lives of Famous People*, Dell Books, New York, 1982.

Helen Keller:
Brooks, V.W.: *Helen Keller*, Kraft, Buenos Aires, 1960.

Dolores Ibarruri:
Des femmes dans le monde, Messidor, Temps actuels, Paris, 1982.
Newspaper *El Pais*, November 13, 1989, Madrid.

Djamila:
Arnaud, G., and Vergès, J.: *Plaidoirie pour Djamila Bouhired*, Ed. de Minuit, Paris.
De Beauvoir, Simone, and Halimi, Gisèle: *Pour Djamila Boupacha*, Gallimard, Paris, 1962.

Angela Davis:
Brunel, Françoise: *"Angela Davis,"* in: *Femmes et Société*, Vol. V, Paris, 1981.
Davis, A.: *Autobiographie*, Albin Michel, Paris, 1975.

The Healers

Mother Teresa:
Montreynaud, Florence: *Le XXème siècle des femmes*, Nathan, Paris, 1990.

The Writers

Sappho:
Mora, Edith: *Sappho*, Flammarion, Paris, 1966.
Weigall, Arthur: *Safo de Lesbos*, Schapire, Buenos Aires, 1973.

Murasaki Shikibu:
Murasaki Shikibu: The Greatest Writer in Japanese Literature, UNESCO, Tokyo, 1970.
Pigeaire, Catherine, and Fukomoto, Hideko: *Les Japonaises*, Des Femmes, Paris, 1986.

Mariana Alcoforado:
Alcoforado, Mariana: *Lettres de la religieuse portugaise*, Librairie générale française, Paris, 1979.
Brion, Marcel: *Les Amants*, Albin Michel, Paris, 1941.

Emily and Charlotte Brontë:
Blondel, Jacques: *Emily Brontë: Expérience spirituelle et création poétique*, PUF, Clermont-Ferrand, 1955.
Brontë, E.: *Wuthering Heights*, introduction and biographical note, Penguin Books, London, 1985.
Gaskell, Elisabeth: *Vida de Charlotte Brontë*, Ed: Nausica, Barcelona, 1945.

George Sand:
Barry, Joseph: *George Sand ou le scandale de la liberté*, Seuil, Paris, 1982.
Sand, G.: *Histoire de ma vie*, Stock, Paris, 1968.

Virginia Woolf:
Bell, Quentin: *Virginia Woolf*, Triad/Palladin, London, 1987.
Nicolson, Nigel, ed.: *The Letters of Virginia Woolf*, The Hogarth Press, London, 1975.

Karen Blixen:
Thurman, Judith: *Karen Blixen*, Seghers, Paris, 1986.

Agatha Christie:
Christie, A.: *Autobiographie*, Librairie des Champs-Elysées, Paris, 1980.
Rivière, François: *La duchesse de la mort*, Seuil, Paris, 1981.

Anaïs Nin:
Nin, A.: *Delta de Venus*, Bruguera, Barcelona, 1979.
Nin, A.: *Diary*, Stock/Livre de poche, Paris, 1978.
Nin, A.: *Henry and June*, Harcourt Brace Jovanovich, San Diego, 1985.
Nin, A.: *Invierno de artificio and Casa del incesto*, Gelba, Barcelona, 1977.

The Artists

Clara Schumann:
Pitrou, Robert: *Clara Schumann*, Albin Michel, Paris, 1960.

Sarah Bernhardt:
Bernhardt, S.: *Mémoires et Ma double vie*, Des Femmes, Paris, 1980.
Castelot, André: *Ensorcelante Sarah Bernhardt*, Perrin, Paris, 1973.
Cocteau, Jean: *Mes monstres sacrés*, Encre, Paris, 1979.

Isadora Duncan:
Duncan, I.: *Ma vie*, Gallimard, Paris, 1928.
Salvinio, Alberto: *Isadora Duncan*, Diffusion Retz, Paris, 1979.

Frida Kahlo:
Herrera, Hayden: *Frida, A Biography of Frida Kahlo*, Harper and Row, New York, 1983.
James, Rauda: *Frida Kahlo*, Presses de la Renaissance, Paris, 1985.

Coco Chanel:
Charles-Roux, Edmonde: *L'irrégulière ou mon intinéraire Chanel*, Grasset, Paris, 1974.
Delbourg-Delphis, Marylène: *Le chic et le look*, Hachette, Paris, 1981.
Morand, Paul: *L'allure Chanel*, Hermann, Paris, 1976.

Maria Callas:
Meneghini, G.B.: *Maria Callas, ma femme*, Flammarion, Paris, 1983.
Stassinopoulos, Arianna: *Maria Callas par delà sa légende*, Fayard, Paris, 1981.

Georgia O'Keeffe:
Cowart, Jack; Hamilton, Juan; and Kristeva, Julia: *Georgia O'Keeffe*, Adam Biro, Paris, 1989.
Hartley, Marsden: *Adventures in the Art*, Hacker Art Books, New York, 1972.
Sutherland Harris, Anne, and Nochlin, Linda: *Women Artists: 1550-1950*, Knopf, New York, 1976.

The Stars

Billie Holiday:
Holiday, B. and Dufty, W.: *Lady Sings the Blues*, Parenthèses, Roquevaire, 1984.

Marilyn Monroe:
Summers, Anthony: *Les vies secrètes de Marilyn Monroe*, Presses de la Renaissance, Paris, 1986.

Edith Piaf:
Berteaut, Simone: *Piaf*, Laffont, Paris, 1969.

Um Kalthum:
Saiah, Ysabel: *Oum Kalsoum, l'étoile de l'Orient*, Denoël, Paris, 1985.

Grace Kelly:
Spada, James: *Las vidas secretas de la Princesa*, Ediciones B, Barcelona, 1987.

Greta Garbo:
Beaton, Cecil: *Les Années heureuses*, Albin Michel, Paris, 1973.
Coxhead, Nora: *Greta Garbo*, Edito-Service, Geneva, 1972.
Ducout, Françoise: *Greta Garbo, la somnambule*, Stock, Paris, 1979.

Amalia Rodrigues:
With the cooperation of Amalia Rodrigues' Paris press service.

The Politically Powerful

Cleopatra:
Cornevin, R.: *Mémoires de l'Afrique*, Laffont, Paris, 1972.
Hemmert, D., and Roudène, A.: *"Cléopatre,"* in: *Les Secrets d'amours célèbres*, Rombaldi, Paris, 1973.
Hornblow, Leonora: *Cléopàtre d'Egypte*, F. Nathan, Paris, 1964.

Theodora:
De Lanckner, Huguette: *Théodora*, Hachette, Paris, 1968.
Rossier, Edmond: *"Théodora,"* in: *Sur les degrés du trone*, Payot, Lausanne, 1940.

Isabella the Catholic:
Ferrara, Orestes: *L'Avènement d'Isabelle la Catholique*, Albin Michel, Paris, 1958.

Mary Stuart:
Fraser, Antonia: *Marie Stuart, reine de France et d'Ecosse*, Laffont, Paris, 1973.
Henry-Bordeaux, Paule: *Marie Stuart*, Perrin, Paris, 1967.

Elizabeth I:
Strachey, L.: *Isabel y Essex*, Editorial Lumen, Barcelona, 1984.
Trevelyan, G.M.: *English Social History*, Penguin Books, London, 1984.

Christina of Sweden:
De Luz, Pierre: *Christine de Suède*, Cercle du Bibliophile, Evreux, 1971.
Castelnau, Jacques: *La reine Christine*, Payot, Paris, 1981.

Catherine the Great:
Grey, Ian: *La Grande Catherine*, Arthaud, Genève, 1970.
Oldembourg, Zoé: *Catherine de Russie*, Gallimard, Paris, 1986.

Wormser-Migot, Olga: *Catherine II*, Club Français du Livre, Paris, 1969.

Queen Victoria:
Longford, Elisabeth: *Victoria: reine d'Angleterre et impératrice des Indes*, Edito-service, Geneva, 1971.
Muhlstein, Anka: *Victoria*, Gallimard, Paris, 1978.

T'zu-Hsi:
Elisseef, Danielle: *La femme au temps des empereurs de Chine*, Stock/Laurence Pernoud, Paris, 1988.
Lugnère, Marianne: *Moi, Tseu Hi*, Casterman, Paris, 1990.

Eva Perón:
Barnes, John: *Eva Perón*, Fontana Collins, London, 1978.
Duarte, Eva: *La razon de mi vida*, Ediciones Peuser, Buenos Aires, 1951.
Montgomery, Paul: *Eva, Evita: The Life and Death of Eva Perón*, Simon and Schuster, New York, 1979.

Indira Gandhi:
Cublier, Anne: *Indira Gandhi*, Gonthier, Paris, 1967.
Ortou, Emmanuelle: *Indira Gandhi ou la démocratie dynastique*, Flammarion, Paris, 1985.

Margaret Thatcher:
Young, Hugo: *One of Us*, Macmillan, London, 1989.

Benazir Bhutto:
Bhutto, Benazir: *Une Autobiographie*, Stock, Paris, 1989.

The Seekers of Wisdom

Hypatia:
"Rites et orthodoxies," in: *Dictionnaire de la franc-maçonnerie de Ligou,"* Editions Navarre, 1853.

Sister Juana Inés de la Cruz:
Paz, Octavio: *Sor Juana Inés de la Cruz o las trampas de la fé*, Seix Barral, Barcelona, 1982.

Marie Curie:
Cotton, Eugénie: *Les Curie*, Seghers, Paris, 1968.
Giroud, Françoise: *Une femme honorable*, Fayard, Paris, 1981.

Lou Andreas-Salomé:
Guéry, F.: *Lou Salomé, genie de la vie*, Calmann-Lévy, Paris, 1978.
Peters, H.F.: *Ma Soeur, mon épouse*, Gallimard, Paris, 1967.

Rachel Carson:
Cox, Donald W.: *Pioneers of Ecology*, Hammond, Maplewood, N.J., 1972.

Alexandra David-Neel:
Chalon, Jean: *Le lumineux destin d'Alexandra David-Neel*, Perrin, Paris, 1985.

Simone de Beauvoir:
de Beauvoir, Simone: *Mémoires d'une jeune fille rangée,* Gallimard, Paris, 1958.
de Beauvoir, S.: *La force de l'age*, Gallimard, Paris, 1960.
de Beauvoir, S.: *La force des choses*, Gallimard, Paris, 1963.
de Beauvoir, S.: *Tout compte fait*, Gallimard, Paris, 1972.

de Beauvoir, S.: *Lettres à Sartre*, Gallimard, Paris, 1990.
Francis, C., and Gontier, F.: *Simone de Beauvoir*, Perrin, Paris, 1985.

General

Aziza, C., Olivieri, C., and Sctrick, R.: *Dictionnaire des figures et des personnages*, Garnier, Paris, 1981.
Bonnefoy, Yves, ed.: *Dictionnaire des mythologies*, Flammarion, Paris, 1981.
Dermenghem, Emile, ed.: *Les plus beaux textes arabes*, Editions d'Aujourd'hui, Paris, 1979.
Dictionnaire de la Bible, Librairie Touzey et Ané, Paris, 1926.
Encyclopedia Judaica, Keter Publishing House Ltd., Jerusalem, 1971.
Encyclopédie de l'Islam, Maisonneuve et Larose, Paris, 1965.
Encyclopedia Universalis, Paris, 1984.
Grimal, Pierre, ed.: *Dictionnaire de la mythologie grecque et romaine*, PUF, Paris, 1982.
Jourcin, A., and Van Tieghem, P.: *Dictionnaire des femmes célèbres*, Larousse, Paris, 1969.
La Bible de Jérusalem, Cerf-Desclée de Brouwer, Paris, 1979.
Laffont, Bompiani: *Dictionnaire des auteurs*, Laffont, Paris, 1980.
Laffont, Bompiani: *Dictionnaire des oeuvres*, Laffont, Paris, 1980.
Mazenod, Lucienne: *Les Femmes célèbres*, Mazenod, Paris, 1960.
The Jewish Encyclopedia, Funk and Wagnalls, New York, 1904.

Photo Credits

p. 10:	Alain Noguès, Sygma
p. 11: l	musée de l'Homme
p. 11: r	Alain Noguès, Sygma
p. 12:	Sculpture by David Wynne
p. 13: l	Giraudon
p. 13: t	Roger-Viollet
p. 13: mb	Sculpture by David Wynne
p. 14:	Hubert Josse
p. 15: l	Edimédia
p. 15: r	Giraudon
p. 16:	J.L. Charmet, Explorer
p. 17: l	Carol Prunhuber
p. 17: r	J.L. Charmet
p. 18:	Erich Lessing, Magnum
p. 19:	Willi, TOP
p. 19: b	Lauros-Giraudon
p. 20:	J.L. Charmet
p. 21: l	J. Guillot, CDA, Edimédia
p. 21: r	J.L. Charmet
p. 22:	Lauros-Giraudon
p. 23:	Natacha Hochman, Diaf
p. 24:	Barbonic Codex
p. 25: l	P. Hinous, CDA, Edimédia
p. 25: r	Ph. Audibert, Hoa-Qui
p. 26:	J.L. Charmet
p. 27: t	J.L. Charmet

p. 27: b	Black Star, Rapho
p. 28:	Pancho Villasmil
p. 29: m	Pancho Villasmil
p. 29: b	Pancho Villasmil
p. 29: tr	Bruno Barbey, Magnum
p. 30:	Lauros-Giraudon
p. 31: r	M.E.P.L. Explorer
p. 31: m	J.L. Charmet
p. 32:	Lauros-Giraudon
p. 33:	François Le Diascorn, Rapho
p. 34:	Lauros-Giraudon
p. 35:	Edimédia
p. 36:	M.E.P.L. Explorer
p. 37: m	Lauros-Giraudon
p. 37: r	M.E.P.L. Explorer
p. 38:	M.E.P.L. Explorer
p. 39: m	Erich Lessing, Magnum
p. 39: r	J.L. Charmet
p. 40:	Roland and Sabrina Michaud, Rapho
p. 41:	Lauros-Giraudon
p. 42:	Ted H.Funk, Rapho
p. 43:	J.L. Charmet
p. 44:	Lauros-Giraudon
p. 45: l	J.L. Charmet
p. 45: r	Cinèstar
p. 46:	M.E.P.L. Explorer
p. 47: l	Giraudon
p. 47: m	M.E.P.L. Explorer
p. 47: r	Cinéstar
p. 48:	J.L. Charmet
p. 49: l	Edimédia
p. 49: r	Bulloz
p. 50:	M.E.P.L. Explorer

p. 51:	Giraudon
p. 52:	Ian Berry, Magnum
p. 53: l	Ch. Lemzaouda, musée de l'Homme
p. 53: r	J.C. Thoret, Explorer
p. 54:	J.L. Charmet
p. 55: l	Edimédia
p. 55: mt	Bulloz
p. 55: mb	J. Bénazet, Pix
p. 55: tr	J.L. Charmet
p. 55: br	J.L. Charmet
p. 56:	J.L. Charmet
p. 57: t	J.L. Charmet
p. 57: b	Erich Lessing, Magnum
p. 58:	Bulloz
p. 59: m	Hubert Josse
p. 59: r	J.L. Charmet
p. 60:	Pancho Villasmil
p. 61:	Vasco Szinetar
p. 62:	Jonathon Wenk, Rapho
p. 63: t	Jonathon Wenk, Rapho
p. 63: r	Charles Moore, Black Star, Rapho
p. 64:	Edimédia
p. 65: m	J.L. Charmet
p. 65: r	J.L. Charmet
p. 66:	J.L. Charmet
p. 67: l	J.L. Charmet
p. 67: m	J.L. Charmet
p. 67: r	J.L. Charmet
p. 68:	J.L. Charmet
p. 69: l	Edimédia
p. 69: r	M.E.P.L. Explorer
p. 70:	J.L. Charmet
p. 71: l	Explorer

p. 71: mt M.E.P.L. Explorer
p. 71: mb Kipa
p. 71: r Kipa
p. 72: Hubert Josse
p. 73: t Hubert Josse
p. 73: b Cinéstar
p. 74: J.L. Charmet, Explorer
p. 75: l J.L. Charmet, Explorer
p. 75: r Dominique Lérault, Pix
p. 76: Cinéstar
p. 77: t J.L. Charmet
p. 77: b J.L. Charmet
p. 78: Edimédia
p. 79: J.L. Charmet
p. 79: Edimédia
p. 80: Bulloz
p. 81: J.L. Charmet
p. 82: Bulloz
p. 83: l Cinéstar
p. 83: r J.L. Charmet
p. 84: Roger-Voillet
p. 85: t © Ascona Films Inc. (Producer Georges-Alain Vuille)
p. 85: b © Ascona Films Inc. (Producer Georges-Alain Vuille)
p. 86: J.L. Charmet
p. 87: Cahiers du Cinema
p. 88: Bettmann
p. 89: l Bettmann
p. 89: r Press Association
p. 90: Erich Lessing, Magnum
p. 91: Bulloz
p. 92: Roland and Sabrina Michaud, Rapho
p. 93: l Bernard Gérard, Hoa qui
p. 93: r Tor Eigeland, Black Star, Rapho
p. 94: Giraudon
p. 95: Roger-Viollet
p. 96: Agraci, Pix
p. 97: l Edimédia
p. 97: r J.L. Charmet, Explorer
p. 98: Roland and Sabrina Michaud, Rapho
p. 99: t Roland Michaud, Rapho
p. 99: b Trigalou, Pix
p. 100: Giraudon
p. 101: Roger-Viollet

p. 102: J.L. Charmet
p. 103: Edimédia
p. 104: Edimédia
p. 105: l J.L. Charmet
p. 105: r J.P. Gardin, Diaf
p. 106: Hubert Josse
p. 107: l J.L. Charmet
p. 107: m J.L. Charmet
p. 107: r J.L. Charmet
p. 108: J.L. Charmet
p. 109: t J.L. Charmet
p. 109: b comic strip by Geoges Pichard, Dominique Leroy
p. 110: J.L. Charmet
p. 111: l Explorer
p. 111: m Cinéstar
p. 111: r Edimédia
p. 112: J.L. Charmet
p. 113: Rights reserved
p. 114: Imapress
p. 115: l Edimédia
p. 115: m Imapress
p. 115: r Imapress
p. 116: Cahiers du Cinéma
p. 117: l Roger-Viollet
p. 117: r Cahiers du Cinéma
p. 118: Hulton- Deutsch
p. 119: M.E.P.L. Explorer
p. 120: R.G. Everts, Rapho
p. 121: Huet, Hoa-Qui
p. 122: J.L. Charmet
p. 123: l Edimédia
p. 123: m M.E.P.L. Explorer
p. 123: r Cinéstar
p. 124: J.L. Charmet
p. 125: tl J.L. Charmet
p. 125: bl J.L. Charmet
p. 125: r Edimédia
p. 126: J.L. Charmet
p. 127: l J.L. Charmet
p. 127: r J.L. Charmet
p. 128: J.L. Charmet
p. 129: l Roger-Viollet
p. 129: r Roger-Viollet
p. 130: Roger-Viollet

p. 131: t Roger-Viollet
p. 131: Courtesy University of Ghent
p. 132: Edimédia
p. 133: l Keystone
p. 133: r Kipa
p. 134: Bettmann
p. 135: l Bettmann
p. 135: r Bettmann
p. 136: Bettmann
p. 137: l Bettmann
p. 137: r Bettmann
p. 138: David Seymour, Magnum
p. 139: l Keystone
p. 139: r Leonard Freed, Magnum
p. 140: l Tallandier
p. 140: r Edimédia
p. 141: l Keystone
p. 141: t Marc Riboud, Magnum
p. 141: b Errath, Explorer
p. 142: Edimédia
p. 143: t Keystone
p. 143: b Imapress
p. 143: r D. Fineman, Sygma
p. 144: M.E.P.L. Explorer
p. 145: l Bettmann
p. 145: tr Hulton-Deutsch
p. 146: Bettmann
p. 147: l Mark Edwards
p. 147: r Mark Edwards
p. 148: Edimédia
p. 149: l M.E.P.L. Explorer
p. 149: m Edimédia
p. 149: r J.L. Charmet
p. 150: Bibliothèque nationale, Paris
p. 151: Bibliothèque nationale, Paris
p. 152: Edimédia
p. 153: l Daniel Thierry, Diaf
p. 153: r Rights reserved
p. 154: Hulton-Deutsch
p. 155: l Mansell Collection
p. 155: r Hulton-Deutsch
p. 156: Roger-Viollet
p. 157: l J.L. Charmet
p. 157: r Explorer
p. 158: National Portrait Gallery, London